British Cinema in the Fifties

An emphasis on the modern and the contemporary was key to the post-war 'new look'. Contemporary debates on social issues such as the role of the state, the end of empire and new gender roles within the family looked forward to a modern future. In contrast, post-war British cinema robustly offered a respite from modernity, winning large audiences with popular war films and comedies and creating stars such as Dirk Bogarde and Kay Kendall. Its stereotypes of the war hero, the boffin and the comic bureaucrat still help to define images of British national identity today.

In *British Cinema in the Fifties*, Christine Geraghty analyses how themes of modernity are handled in the most popular films of this period. Through a series of case studies of films as diverse as *It Always Rains on Sunday, Genevieve, Simba* and *The Wrong Arm of the Law*, she explores some of the key debates about cinema of the period. Taking a broadly feminist approach, Geraghty combines cultural history and film theory as she traces the curious mix of rebellion and conformity which marked British cinema in the post-war era.

Christine Geraghty is a Senior Lecturer in Media and Communications at Goldsmiths College, University of London. She is the author of *Women and Soap Opera* (1991) and co-editor of *The Television Studies Book* (1998), and she has contributed essays on British cinema to a number of important collections.

Communication and society

Edited by James Curran
Professor of Communications, Goldsmiths College, University of London

We Keep America on Top of the World
Television journalism and the public sphere
Daniel C. Hallin

A Journalism Reader
Edited by Michael Bromley and Tom O'Malley

Tabloid Television
Popular journalism and the 'other news'
John Langer

International Radio Journalism
History, theory and practice
Tim Crook

Media, Ritual and Identity
Edited by Tamar Liebes and James Curran

Ill Effects
The media violence debate
Edited by Martin Barker and Julian Petley

De-Westernizing Media Studies
Edited by James Curran and Myung-Jin Park

British Cinema in the Fifties
Gender, genre and the 'new look'
Christine Geraghty

British Cinema
in the Fifties

Gender, genre and the 'new look'

Christine Geraghty

London and New York

First published 2000
by Routledge
11 New Fetter Lane, London EC4P 4EE

Simultaneously published in the USA and Canada
by Routledge
29 West 35th Street, New York, NY 10001

Routledge is an imprint of the Taylor & Francis Group

Typeset in Galliard by Taylor & Francis Books Ltd
Printed and bound in Great Britain by Biddles Ltd,
Guildford and King's Lynn

British Library Cataloguing in Publication Data
A catalogue record for this book is available from the British Library

Library of Congress Cataloging-in-Publication Data
Geraghty, Christine.
British cinema in the fifties : gender, genre and the 'new look' / Christine
Geraghty.
    p. cm.
Includes bibliographical references and index.
1.Motion pictures–Great Britain–History. 2. Motion pictures–Social
aspects–Great Britain. I. Title.

PN1993.5.G7 G47 2000
791.43'0941'0945–dc21
                                                            00–029108

ISBN 0–415–17157–1 (hbk)
ISBN 0–415–17158–X (pbk)

For Paul Marks, also a child of the fifties,
with love and thanks

Contents

Figures

Preface

Raymond Durgnat began his study of a similar period of British cinema by declaring that 'this is not a popular history of the British film industry' (1970: 1), and I must make the same disclaimer. This is not even a survey, following the excellent example of Robert Murphy and Sarah Street, of the films of my chosen period. Many films that I would have liked to have included are missing because of pressures of space, and, more significantly, whole genres such as science fiction and horror do not feature here. Interest in the study of British cinema has increased enormously in the last ten years and it now seems legitimate to focus on particular themes or areas without feeling the necessity to cover the whole field. In this book, therefore, I unapologetically focus on two kinds of film: dramas that deal explicitly with the social issues that were of concern at the time; and examples of the two mainstream popular genres of the fifties, the comedies and the war film. Although there is still plenty of British cinema to be reclaimed, I was particularly interested in exploring the mainstream genres, both in terms of studying particular films that have received little attention and in looking again, in a different way, at those that perhaps seem over-familiar.

The focus on these films arises from the two broad themes that weave through the book. These themes, which came out of a detailed viewing of the films, focus on how British cinema related to its social context and in particular to social discourses that emphasised what was new, different and modern in post-war British society. This is the 'new look' of the title for, although the post-war period tends now to be defined, to rephrase Durgnat's title, as moving from dreary austerity to complacent affluence, the period was one of enormous social and cultural change. The first theme takes up issues of modernity and the 'new' Britain, concepts that are explored in the first two chapters which set out the context and terms for the discussion. The rest of the book examines how the changes connected with modernity are handled in films of the period in chapters that explore both public issues such as national identity, the bureaucratic state and the Commonwealth and the organisation of private relationships, particularly within the family. A second theme, which is strongly linked to the first, looks at gender more specifically and reflects on how genre, performance and star images work to create some of the key figures of the period – the post-war housewife, the European woman, the comical crook, the wartime leader. In both cases, I have given priority to textual analysis as a way of developing the arguments and have generally chosen to focus on the detail of relatively few films rather than attempt to survey, more summarily, a larger number. Unfortunately, there was no room for the consideration of authorship, although I am conscious that I have found the work of certain directors, such as Muriel Box, Philip Leacock and Wolf Rilla, particularly rewarding to study in this context. I should also add that, although I argue that British cinema, in its mainstream genres, is at odds with much of what that was considered modern in the 1950s, I do not particularly want to criticise its regressiveness in relation to the 'progressive' ideas being put forward elsewhere or praise its resistance to what were emerging as the dominant formations. I am more interested in examining the nuances and complexities of how these issues are worked through in the separate and specific spaces that cinema offered.

A word is needed about dates. This book covers a wider period than a strictly chronological reading of the term 'the fifties' might indicate. In my discussion, I refer to the period from the end of the Second World War in 1945 to the early years of the 1960s. In terms of social context, it is crucial to take into account the post-war settlement, which continued to shape ideas, understandings and attitudes well into the 1950s; in the cinema too, the impact of the stars, genres and narrative forms of the 1940s can still be felt. Similarly, by extending 'the fifties' for my purposes up to about 1963, I am seeking to pursue some of the themes and issues that arise in the early and mid-1950s even when they persist into the early 1960s. Films from the early 1960s, particularly comedies like *The Wrong Arm of the Law* and war films like *The Password is Courage*, while they clearly have a flavour of the 1960s, can be profitably studied in the context of their 1950s predecessors. But this also works in reverse, and some films made between 1945 and 1963, particularly those of the New Wave, have a different sensibility and aesthetic. I have not been able to discuss these here.

In seeking to place the films under discussion in a social context, I have drawn on sociological and educational work that was being published, often in the famous blue Pelican paperbacks, during the period. The question of dates is also relevant here. Referring to a publication date is not always helpful in telling us when this research was being done or indeed disseminated; sometimes it will appear that I am using material published in the 1960s to inform films of an earlier date. Two examples will show why this can be legitimate. The collection of D.W. Winnicott's essays that I refer to was published in 1964 but a large part of what it contains was initially published in 1957 and the 1964 edition acknowledges the use of material broadcast in talks for the BBC much earlier. Similarly, Chapter 8 in particular makes use of material from J. Klein's *Samples from English Culture*, published in 1965. However, this book is a review of sociological and psychological material that was researched and published earlier, and it can therefore legitimately be used for examples of how childcare was thought about at a time well before its own publication date.

A final point about referencing. The academic conventions of referencing break up the flow of writing with bracketed information about dates, directors, sources, etc. I have tried to avoid this as much as possible by providing a bibliography and filmography which give the relevant information in a less disruptive manner. This means that, for example, I only give the dates of a film in the text at the point when it is going to be analysed in some detail and that I do not automatically give the name of an actor unless it is especially pertinent to the character being discussed. I hope that this is an acceptable compromise and that the book reads the better because of it.

Acknowledgements

Although my academic interests in British cinema go back to classes and summer schools organised by the British Film Institute, this book has been shaped by my work in the Media and Communications Department at Goldsmiths College, and I am grateful to my colleagues there. I particularly thank the students who took my courses on British cinema, while work on this book was developing, for their enthusiasm and insights into what, for many of them, was an unknown and literally foreign period of cinema. Among my colleagues, I thank especially Bill Schwarz for his unflagging enthusiasm and encouragement; Peter Morris in the A/V library for willingly building an impressive collection of films of the period; Richard Smith, who compiled the filmography; and my non-academic colleagues, who kept me going as Head of Department while this book was being written: Colin Aggett, Jacqui Cheal, Brenda Ludlow, Sheila Sheehan, Kay Shoesmith and Jim Rowland.

Chapter 1 contains material that appears as an article in *Framework* Volume 42, Summer 2000.

Chapter 5 is a re-working, focusing on rather different issues, of an earlier essay, 'Post-war choices and feminine possibilities', in U. Sieglhor (ed.) (2000) *Heroines without Heroes: Female Identities in Post-war European Cinema 1945–51*. London: Continuum.

Chapter 6 is an extended version of an earlier article that appeared as 'The woman between: the European woman in post-war British cinema' in *European Journal of Cultural Studies* Vol. 2, No. 2, May 1999.

1 The experience of picturegoing
Cinema as a social space

This chapter looks at the experience of British cinemagoing in the period 1945–65 and the changes that took place during that time. It is not so much concerned with the industrial and economic aspects of the cinema at the time (the emerging Rank/ABPC duopoly and the statistics for declining audiences) but with how the experience of cinemagoing in Britain was described and discussed. I want to place cinemagoing within discourses that helped to define its role in cultural life and shaped the way in which people thought about and used it. This involves thinking about cinema in relation to other entertainment formats, as well as focusing on its own specific pleasures, and looking at how the practice of going to the pictures was explained through, for instance, the age and gender of its perceived audiences. In attempting to do this, I will call on some of the material provided by and about the cinema from cinemagoers at the time and from those who commented on them – the sociologists, psychologists, teachers and others concerned with the values and effects of cinema. I will set these contemporary accounts beside reminiscences about going to the pictures by those looking back to their cinemagoing past.[1] In addition, this chapter will look at how British films of the period represented mass entertainment and how they positioned cinema within the popular forms of leisure activity that were incorporated into their stories and locations. I hope that these various sources will give us a sense of the ways in which British cinema was thought about, a sense of how it was constructed, not so much in bricks, mortar and capital as through the ideas and expectations of different audiences and their commentators. Positioning the specificities of British cinema within this broad cultural context should put us in a better position to understand the overall changes in British cinemagoing during this period and thus place the later discussion of individual films in a more specific context.

Modernism and cinema

In the 1920s and 1930s, cinema became strongly identified with forms of mass entertainment that were associated with the social and cultural consequences of modern industrialisation. The urban crowds brought to the city by the factory and the office were organised by cinema into focused and intent mass audiences. Going to the pictures became a regular event, which fitted into the leisure spaces left by the organisation of the working day. The films were made possible by the new and developing technologies of photography and sound, and mechanical reproduction meant that they could be repeated and available at different times and in different spaces. While they appeared to offer novelty, they also provided the pleasures of repetition, the reassurances of star, genre and studio. But the cinema was selling a non-material good, a shared experience of seeing a film rather than the film itself, and the responses generated – the shared laughter and tears – made the audience appear to be vulnerable, over-invested in emotion and potentially irrational. This intangible product was backed up by the rapidly developing PR industry, with advertising and publicity material controlled by the studios and reinforced by gossip columns, pin-ups and fan magazines. And as Hollywood's domination of the market tightened, the association was reinforced between the cinema and the United States, the country of the masses, which, as the films themselves reiterated, understood itself to be the country of the future.

This association of cinema with the excitement and the pressures of modern industrial society was strongly made by those concerned about the impact of the new mass media on cultural and social life. In 1936, J.B. Priestley suggested that Hollywood's 'great advantage' in making films was that it could draw on the 'quicker tempo ... the whole nervous tension of American life' (*World Film News* 1, No. 8: 3). For Adorno and Horkheimer, the experience of cinemagoing was typical of the more general transformation of culture through industrialisation. As they argued, in a book originally published in 1944:

> Amusement under late capitalism is the prolongation of work. It is sought after as an escape from the mechanized work process ... but at the same time mechanization has such power over a man's leisure and happiness ... [that] what happens at work, in the factory, or in the office can only be escaped from by approximation to it in one's leisure time.
>
> (137)

The discipline of the production line was replicated in the queues that formed to see the products of the slick and streamlined machinery of the studio system. Audience reaction was also determined by the mechanism of cinema. Cinema demanded a 'semi-automatic' response, an audience 'absorbed by the world of the movie', bombarded by the 'relentless rush of facts' and so unable to reflect on what it was seeing (127).

In Britain, cinema became the most popular form of entertainment for the masses, and the 'enthusiasts were young, working-class, urban and more often female' (Richards 1984: 15). It was a modern phenomenon strongly associated with American culture in both its organisation of space and the product it presented. Its most glamorous buildings fantastically reinvented past cultures – Egyptian friezes, Spanish balconies – for mass audiences or, in the Odeon suburban circuit, offered a streamlined and contemporary space, characteristic of 'the quintessence of the Modern Movement' (21). Industry surveys and Mass Observation work consistently described cinemagoers' preference for Hollywood films over British films. The Mass Observation survey of cinemagoing in Bolton in 1938 provoked comments that American films were more 'snappy' and fast-moving, were technically more proficient, paid convincing attention to detail and generally held the audience's attention. 'American productions are far ahead of the English,' commented one 30-year-old female cinemagoer, 'there is something snappier and altogether definitely conclusive about an American film' (Richards and Sheridan: 57). British films were associated by working-class audiences with old-fashioned class attitudes and what one industry survey called 'old school tie standards', while American films seemed to offer a more democratic approach that acknowledged and embraced mass audiences. The same survey contrasted 'the English second feature [which] is practically always frenziedly upper class' with the American second feature, which 'draws on the mass man and woman to represent the issues of their stories' (*World Film News* 2, No. 2, May 1937: 13).

If a particular set of associations was established around cinemagoing in the 1930s, a further set of associations was added by the role that filmgoing played during the war, particularly in Britain. Although cinemas were initially closed at the outbreak of war in 1939 they were quickly reopened, and cinemagoing became an important leisure activity during the war. A Ministry of Information report on cinemagoing in 1943 reported that the cinema was 'an important form of recreation for one-third of the adult civilian population, who go once a week or more often' (quoted in Thumim 1996: 246). Add to that cinemagoers in their teens, in the services and those who went less regularly and the significance of cinema as a form of entertainment during the war can be seen. This commitment to cinemagoing in the war had two consequences that are important for our purposes. First, cinema was established as a relatively 'safe' social place as well as a source of entertainment. At the beginning of the war in September 1939, *Kinematograph Weekly* argued in favour of the cinemas reopening by pointing to the need for social spaces: 'if ... the people will insist upon being with a crowd of their fellows and there is nowhere else to go, then the time for reopening the kinema ... has become an urgent public necessity' (quoted in Murphy 1989: 5). Many in the audience stayed in the cinema even during air raids: 'Nobody left. Just carried on ... You might as well be in there enjoying yourself' remembers one such cinemagoer (O'Brien and Eyles: 55). Cinemagoing could be fitted into the rhythm of even the disrupted wartime domestic day. One mass observer reported in 1940 on a visit to a cinema in south London. He observed a queue of over 100 people, 'mainly working class women, old men and a few children'. The cinema seemed to be part of their domestic life: when people in the queue spoke it was not of films but 'about domestic affairs, shops, food, stories of friends and relations'; about 25 percent of the women had empty shopping baskets with them, as if they were 'going to do their shopping after they left the pictures and before going home' (Len England's report in Richards and Sheridan: 189). For others, going to the pictures was more of a communal activity. One evacuated Londoner commented on the cinema as the place where evacuees met on a Saturday evening, 'a whole lot of us there together as friends' (O'Brien and Eyles: 28), while a woman who as a child stayed in London in the war described how pictures of absent sons, husbands and boyfriends would be put up on the screen or a soldier or airman in the audience might be welcomed home on leave: 'it was a family atmosphere – especially being all local, we all knew each other' (61).

A second consequence of the war was to give the British film industry an audience and a purpose. For some, most famously Michael Balcon at Ealing, this meant allying the British film industry with the high ideals of creating a national identity and seeking to put the cinema at the service of the war effort. Others, for example Gainsborough's Maurice Ostrer, preferred to provide audiences with the means of forgetting the war through comedy and escapism (Murphy 1989: 34). Although these different approaches clearly led to different kinds of film, the different sides of the argument in the British film industry shared a common experience during the war. They had acquired a reason to make films for their audiences; they could feel themselves to be doing something important and to be at the heart of what was the most important set of events in the world, the struggle to win the war.

By the start of our period, therefore, British cinema was marked by a number of features that were carried through into the post-war period. As part of an international phenomenon, it was strongly associated with the images and values linked to Hollywood, the United States and mass entertainment. At the same time, the war had given renewed impetus to calls for a viable British cinema industry and the assumptions about the detrimental social effects of cinemagoing had been reworked so that the cinema could be thought of as a force for good that (it was hoped) provided effective propaganda and morale-boosting relaxation. British cinema therefore finished the war with a higher profile, a stronger audience base and a greater sense of its own possibilities and importance than had been possible in the pre-war period.

Cinema as a social space

The end of the war in Britain did not see the end of privations, rationing and hardship. However, Paul Addison suggests that with the coming of peace relief at being alive combined with a little extra money found an outlet in mass entertainment: 'with many commodities on the ration and others in short supply, leisure was the most powerful magnet and the leisure industry a licence to print money' (114). Addison lists the record statistics for a whole range of popular activities: crowds turned out for sports like cricket and football, went to dance halls, visited the cinema, joined cycling clubs and went to holiday camps. This explosion in popular entertainment is well described by Peter Hennessy and three characteristics are worth noting from his account. First, as he comments 'it was largely pre-war pastimes which scooped the pool in the first years of peace' (316). The delight was in returning to popular pleasures that had been made more difficult, if not impossible, by the war. Second, with the exception of radio, the engagement with different forms of entertainment continued the wartime emphasis on going out and finding a social space in which people could get together. Not everyone had the same kind of access to going out, however, and the spaces for entertainment were differently organised around age and gender; sport was largely a male affair, while dance halls and cinemas allowed women much more control. Third, the years immediately after the war saw an intense effort in some areas to upgrade people's taste, to improve their minds through a national effort just as their bodies were to benefit from the new National Health Service which began in 1948. Thus was born in 1945 the new Arts Council, which was intended, as J.M. Keynes asserted, to usher in 'a time when the theatre and the concert hall and the art gallery will be a living element in everyone's upbringing' (quoted in *ibid*: 134). The BBC's Third Programme began in 1946 and, it was hoped, would take high culture directly into the home. Thus mass entertainment of the immediate post-war period strongly emphasised popular tastes but aimed to inject an element of culture, and British cinema's somewhat didactic stance throughout the period may stem from this approach.

This explosion in popular entertainment included cinema which improved on its wartime popularity – 1946 turned out to be a boom year, with 4,500 cinemas and annual attendance of 1,635 million visits from a population of 46 million (130). Attendances remained strong, although not quite on this scale, into the early 1950s.[2] The cinema audience was predominantly youthful even at the height of this popularity, but the scale of cinemagoing made it 'the most popular form of popular entertainment in the 1940s' (129), and its domination meant that it was part of everyone's experience. This sense of a wide, heterogeneous audience and of the diverse uses to which the spaces of the cinema could be put can be found in a humorous *Picturegoer* column of 1 February 1947 in which Eric Hall describes a trip to the cinema with his wife. The couple want to watch the film but find themselves continually having to move seats as their neighbours distract and disturb them: commercial travellers snoring; women talking; a small boy eating toffee; couples, with their hands hidden, embracing in the back row. The stereotypical nature of these complaints gives it credence as an account of a range of cinemagoers – people on their own, in family groups, with friends, with lovers – engaging in a variety of social activities that would be familiar to regular picturegoers. Another columnist got into trouble with readers for complaining, rather more sourly than Hall, that women make 'bad film patrons' because they do not concentrate on watching, they talk, eat and dote on crooners (2 August 1947 and letters of 3 August and 13 September 1947). Although cinemagoing in the late 1940s was particularly associated with women, respectable middle-aged men were still there; another *Picturegoer* writer, John Y. Stapleton, commented that when he asked some business men and a 'respectable police inspector' in a Lancashire manufacturing town about their activities the night before, they were quite happy to admit that they had been to see a double-feature horror bill (7 June 1947).

Rachel Low, discussing a social survey of cinema audiences in 1948, noted that cinema audiences went for 'an institutionalised night out' (107). Regular visits set up habits that affected how the cinema space was organised informally. Recalling visits to the cinema in the 1940s, Suzanne Waite remembers how different spaces 'belonged' to different groups; she and her father 'always sat halfway back … at the back was all the courting couples, down the front was all the kids' (O'Brien and Eyles: 60). A reader's letter in *Picturegoer* in 1947 gives a sense of a regular audience that went to the cinema as a social event rather than to see a particular film; joining a correspondence about cinemagoing in the north of England, the reader complains that 'every Saturday night one can see a practically identical audience. One family … can be seen in exactly the same seats every Saturday at the second performance and they are no exception' (19 July 1947). Presumably, although the reader is critical of such behaviour, he/she was there often enough to notice it.

Such anecdotes are important not because they are statistically reliable but because they tell us that it was still important for a magazine like *Picturegoer* to conceive of a heterogeneous audience for a hugely popular medium. Going to the pictures was an ordinary and natural event for all kinds of people. At the same time, however, entering into the cinema's space could also be exciting, since a physical sense of the cinema's glamour had been retained from pre-war days. A cinema manager, writing to the letters page, pointed out that he had to wear a dress suit, 'be able to speak from the stage, mix socially with the local "big-wigs" [and] be an expert at publicity organisation' (10 May 1947). Large cinemas could dominate a town, as Roland Miller recalls, for instance, in Exeter, where the cathedral seemed much less prominent than the Odeon (Breakwell and Hammond: 59). Cinema remained a place of refuge from privations outside. As *Picturegoer* commented, during the crisis of the US film embargo and continuing post-war rationing, 'a certain austerity has come to the cinema [but] not nearly as much as in other everyday aspects of life' (3 January 1948). Stacey explores the importance of the 'material pleasures of cinemagoing' (99) for her correspondents, pleasures that involved both escape from domestic privations ('Sometimes one went to keep warm if coal were short' (94)) and the enjoyment of luxury, the deep pile carpets, plush seats and 'fancy lighting' (96). While it could be argued that such comments are suffused with the glamour of nostalgia, it is by no means inevitable, as we shall see, that memories of cinemagoing should produce such a strong sense of physical comfort.

Cinema's importance as the most popular mass entertainment medium continued into the 1950s, though audiences were declining; Corrigan argues that 'the key years are 1954–8 when some 500 million disappear from the annual attendances at cinemas' (30). Declining audiences and the reasons for this became something of an obsession in commentary and discussion about cinema in the 1950s. In the context of these debates, the experience of cinema as a social space begins to change. In the battle with television, the contrast between home and cinema (which had been comprehensively won by cinema in the 1940s) begins to take a new turn. *Picturegoer* of 1955 (the year of the arrival of commercial television in Britain) regularly featured letters contrasting the experience of watching films in the cinema and television at home. A hopeful reader points out that television could stimulate interest in film through interviews with the stars and extracts from films, but generally the tone is competitive, with readers feeling that they have to defend their loyalty to the cinema. One reader complains of the 'gloomy silence' when visiting friends who are absorbed in watching television and declares, in a determined fashion, 'I'm going to the cinema' (19 March 1955), while another comments that films at the cinema, unlike television, offered 'more varied programmes, large screens, colour' and can be watched without 'outside interference' (3 April 1955). Cinema can still operate for some readers as 'an escape from everyday things' (2 September 1955), and a woman reader claims that films are so good now that she goes to the cinema 'up to eight times a week' (9 July 1955). The wider audience is still there in the cinema – a woman of 40 writes 'I enjoy everything the cinema offers' (27 August 1955), while a reader complains of a baby crying and another praises a cinema manager for giving 'priority admittance to the elderly and infirm' (5 August 1955). But its members are perhaps beginning to feel rather uncomfortable.

Thus, alongside the determined espousal of the cinema, there are letters complaining about continuous showings, which made for interruptions as audience members entered at odd times (5 February 1955), and that tickets cannot be bought in advance (2 July 1955). The magazine's response to a reader's complaint about the lack of comfort in many cinemas is indicative; ten years after the war, the editorial comments that 'wartime restrictions and shortages delayed plans' (5 November 1955), clearly indicating that cinema was stuck with wartime facilities and was not keeping up with the publicised expansion of consumer goods and domestic improvements in the home. One reader complained about a rude commissionaire and about the picture jumping (16 April 1955), and another emphasised the importance of good stills outside and properly closing curtains in the intervals (8 October 1955), both of which were often lacking. All these may be small things but they show that the cinema was losing its battle to be more comfortable, more special than the home. And what was on view was also beginning to change. Cinema's weapons – size, colour, scope – were being put to new and more controversial subject matter. One viewer bemoans the loss of old films screened on a Sunday (30 July 1955), while Hollywood is criticised for its 'brutality packed pictures' (25 June 1955). Another reader links the change in the type of film on show with changes in audience habits; mentioning Hollywood films in particular, the letter asks 'why so many X films? They stop the family having their Saturday night out at the pictures.' *Picturegoer*, with its commitment to the mass audience, responded gamely that 'Filmdom is just as worried for there are more on the way' (5 November 1955).

Indeed there were, and increasingly the social space of the cinema became marked by a sense of threat and heightened sexuality. Hollywood came in for criticism in a *Films and Filming* editorial for responding to television's challenge

Figure 1.1 Cardiff ABC Cinema.
Courtesy of the Ronald Grant Archive.

with films that were getting more lavish and longer; the metaphor used to describe this is significantly brutal – Hollywood, the editorial warns, 'is about to pound our senses with spectacle' (February 1956). More prosaically, the threat to cinema was associated with the increasing dominance of young people in the audience. Later that year, another editorial commented on an industry survey that announced an increase in cinemagoing among 16–24-year-olds; *Films and Filming* was rather gloomy about this trend and commented on the need to educate the young in film appreciation to avoid the situation in which films will have to 'appeal [only] to the adolescent and emotionally immature' (August 1956). In the discourses about audience, the key 'mythical' figure became the working-class male and particularly the teddy boy. A reader of *Films and Filming* associated the change in films with a change in the manners of the audience; she had enjoyed an X-rated British film, *I am a Camera*, but complained about the behaviour of 'wolves' at her local cinema in Torquay, who, when X-rated films were shown, made the assumption that 'screen morality being at a premium, so also must be that of the feminine audience' (December 1955). Sociologists commented on the phenomenon. F.R. Fyvel, in *The Insecure Offender*, found that teddy boys made the contrast between television and cinema, rejected television as not 'theirs' but found in the cinema a secure social space. The cinema was for them 'an addiction' (106) that helped to fill the empty expanses of time spent hanging around. It was also 'the sanctioned space to take one's girl to, with sex on the screen and a good deal of it in the auditorium too' (107). One cinemagoer remembers the notorious Monty, 'riding his bike across the stage during *Yield to the Night* at the Majestic' in Derby (Breakwell and Hammond: 124), while Ray Gosling recalls that part of the pleasure of cinemagoing was recognising familiar voices, catcalling from the young audience, ('Whopper's in tonight – be some fun'); 'films were things that were put up for us to barrack at the entire time' (31). Only *Rebel without a Cause* was exempt from such treatment.

Some of the contradictions at play in the mid-fifties can be seen in a juxtaposition of comments on another X-rated film, *The Blackboard Jungle*. In December 1955, *Films and Filming* used the film as an example to argue that the cinema audience was changing for the better. It cited a letter from the Home Office to licensing authorities about X certificates which makes the traditional argument about audiences: 'the cinema is regarded as family entertainment and an increase in the number of films to which children cannot be admitted, even if accompanied, would not suit the social habits of the majority of regular cinema-goers.' The leader refutes this by suggesting that there are a minority of filmgoers who 'who rightly regard films as of greater significance than a convenient way to kill time.' The success of *Rififi* and *The Blackboard Jungle* are 'evidence that there is a widespread demand for a more adult, intelligent entertainment.' Demand there may have been, but Ray Gosling remembers *The Blackboard Jungle* being received rather differently: 'a cheap film at a cheap cinema about a high school in America where the teenagers beat up the teachers ... it was a jolly good boo, clap and foot-stamping film' (32). Perhaps not quite the adult response that *Films and Filming* had been looking for.

By the mid-sixties, however, mainstream cinema with its 'half-slumbering, kissing and canoodling audience' (Breakwell and Hammond: 124) seemed to be confirmed as a 'semi-private place' (Schofield: 143) for the young to make love. Sociologist Michael Schofield, in his sympathetic report of research in the early 1960s, *The Sexual Behaviour of Young People*, found that 51 percent of those surveyed went to the cinema on a first date (55), and two-thirds of the boys and three-quarters of the girls went more than once a month (143). Young adults had always been an important sector of the audience but, as *Films and Filming* had feared in the mid-fifties, they now moved into a position of dominance (Laing: 110). What was unusual was not that the young were going to the cinema but that increasingly they seemed to have the place to themselves. A Welsh reader in *Picturegoer* reported a liking for sexy films like *Room at the Top* and *Passport to Shame*; if more came out like that, 'the boys in our village will pack out the house' (5 March 1960). Those looking back on their cinemagoing days in the 1960s associate the final fling of the teddy boys with the decline of the cinema. Roger Wakeling remembers the early 1960s as 'a time of the last drain piped leg of the Teddy boy era' and recalls 'a gargantuan Ted' disrupting the final performance at a closing cinema in Nottingham (Breakwell and Hammond: 30–1). Another cinemagoer, who remembers a matinee of *A Hard Day's Night* at which the 'Teds and greasers and hard-faced girls' made up the audience, commented on the 'rows of lads [who] have put their winklepickers on the backs of their seats' (21), proclaiming themselves to be dominant in the space of the cinema. Such memories, like those of 1940s cinemagoers interviewed by O'Brien and Eyles or Stacey, go back into childhood and youth but conjure up a very different set of cinemagoing associations.

The ideal of 'the cinema' for a mass audience was under threat in other ways. While the main circuits, Rank and ABC, remained dominant there was, as Murphy shows, a tendency towards fragmentation and more specialist audiences among the smaller circuits and independent exhibitors; these cinemas provided some kind of rather shabby space for programmes of 'popular classics, foreign sex and art films and the "X" films which the circuits were reluctant to show' (1992: 105). In January 1963, *Films and Filming* celebrated the 'dramatic and sustained support for cinemas showing as a regular policy, only films of genuine artistic merit', which were largely European in origin. But the nature of the cinematic space for such a screening policy was a problem and *Sight and Sound* argued that the mix of art and sensation in some venues was putting the serious cinemagoer off since 'cinemas … get a bad name' (quoted in Murphy 1992: 71). In addition, cinemas were disappearing. A reader's letter to *Films and Filming* in March 1963 criticised Rank for closing cinemas and transforming the cinema audience into mindless dupes: 'if Rank has its way we'll soon be a nation of bingo and TV maniacs.' Alternatives seemed to be possible, and there were some indications of what the future might hold for cinemagoers. A report in *Films and Filming* in December 1963 described a boom in cinema building in America, with two or three auditoria being provided for 'people who are selective in their film going and want a wide selection of films at their disposal', while a prescient reader described the delights of watching 'distinguished films' on the BBC – the American *High Noon*, the French *Hiroshima Mon Amour* and the Italian *Bicycle Thieves* among them – and remarked, 'I would rather stay at home and watch good films than join the peanut munching idiots at the local flick-house' (November 1963). Multiplexes and video, here we come.

The changes in the meaning and importance of the cinema as a social space affected how it was understood in the context of mass culture as a whole in the late fifties. *Films and Filming* was pressing for cinema to be considered an art form for adults and the heterogeneous audience enjoying a regular night out was no longer the dominant way in which the cinema audience was conceived. Its view of the traditional audience is once again summed up with the assertion that 'cinema is no place in which to kill time' (January 1963). The fate of *Picturegoer* gives a sad indication of what had happened. In pursuit of a young readership, the magazine abandoned its general audience and sought the youthful reader, who was believed to be more interested in other forms of popular culture. By 1960, the magazine had combined with *Disc Parade*, and the first cover of that year (2 January) featured a young girl who did not even want to be a film star but instead aspired to be 'a television hostess or an advertising model'. Articles on 'Which pop star will be the star of 1960?' confirmed the new approach, and four months later the magazine announced that next week it would become *Date*, a 'sparkling new magazine for the teens and twenties' with 'utterly luxurious feminine features' (23 April 1960). *Picturegoer* had been overtaken by new forms of popular culture in which cinema began to look rather old-fashioned. Tony Bennett sees the late 1950s as 'the critical turning point in the trajectory of popular culture' with the advent of 'a new type of popular culture which, owing to its specific association with youth, marked the development of pronounced generation division within the culture of the popular classes' (9). As cinemas closed all over the country, it was clear that cinema was not that new type of culture and could no longer claim to be the most significant and modern of the mass media.

Cinema and popular culture

This decline is reflected in the way in which cinema begins to be bypassed in sociological accounts of mass media effects. Although Fyvel associated his teddy boys with the cinema, the more heinous causes of juvenile alienation lay elsewhere, in the culture of consumption generated by television and advertising. He suggested that 'One could argue convincingly, if a little fancifully … that the sharp rise in juvenile delinquency in Britain from 1955 onwards was linked with the arrival in that year of commercial television' (194). The pop singer who was 'fabulously successful' (222) without having to work was a problematic role model, and Fyvel linked the boredom and disaffection of significant groups of young people with the 'growing subordination of life to the advertisements and sale of consumer goods' (313). For Richard Hoggart, it was the juke box boys, 'putting copper after copper into the mechanical record player' (248) to hear American records, who were at the forefront of the decline in British working-class culture. Harry Hopkins borrowed the term 'Admass' from J.B. Priestley to describe the way in which the mass media melded with PR and advertising in a huge selling exercise. It was Admass that created the teenager and ensured that the traditional rebellion of youth was 'institutionalised' (425) in a commercial exercise in which fashion and music, rather than cinema, were the major appeals. Fyvel was entirely typical in his assignment of causes. Bill Osgerby's survey of sociological literature on youth confirms Bennett's comments by also seeing the late 1950s as 'a critical turning point in the development of British youth culture' and points to the key role given to the media, particularly television, in spreading youth consumption (90).

   If cinema no longer provided a scapegoat for delinquency or an explanation of youth behaviour, it was even more firmly excluded from sociological accounts of their parents. Its place was largely taken by television. Thus, Young and Willmott, in their study, first published in 1957, of the consequences for working-class families of a move to a new housing estate, give an account of television viewing in the mid-fifties that is vivid in its description of the capacity of television to dominate domestic space. The nearest cinema was several miles away and, instead of going out to the cinema or the pub, the family sits night after night around the magic screen in its place of honour in the parlour:

> In one household the parents and five children of all ages were paraded in a half circle ... the two month old baby was stationed in its pram in front of the set. The scene had the air of a strange ritual. The father said proudly: 'The tellie keeps the family together. None of us ever have to go out now.'
>
> (1962: 143)

Another sociological study, *Education and the Working Class*, first published in 1962, provides a further instance of television's capacity to transform the domestic space; in the working-class homes visited for the study, 'television sets were almost universal', and if 'they had gone into the front room then the special function of that place was much altered. The television drew it into the living space of the family' (Jackson and Marsden: 63). Hopkins, in his popular account, uses the same idea of television dictating the organisation of even the furniture of family life: 'gathered before the hypnotic screen on the low "television chairs" that now made their appearance in the shops, families took their food from large "television plates", gropingly, in the half-darkness' (331).

Television was not the only attraction in the home, however, and sociologists and commentators emphasised a more general interest in the home being taken by men and women as the 1950s wore on. Willmott and Young returned to questions of domestic leisure in a study of a more middle-class suburb, for which the field work was done in 1957 and 1959. Rather surprisingly, television hardly featured there, but the authors claimed to have found a shift to leisure activities that revolved around the home for husbands as well as wives. The emphasis on do-it-yourself, gardening and home decorating ensured that 'more money is used for the house, more leisure used for work' on it (33). Television watching was thus one of a number of activities that tended to associate leisure with the home and worked against entertainments that, like the cinema, involved adults leaving the domestic space of the home.

As the debate about mass culture continued in the 1950s, there is a sense in which cinema began to be detached from the more general strictures applied to the popular mass media. Just as the change in the use of cinema as a public space opened the way for more specialist art cinema, so there was an increasing emphasis on the specificity of film within the mass media. Murphy has traced the development of this trend in his account of the 'critical debates' (1992: 58) in small magazines devoted to a discussion of film criticism and the qualities which should be valued in particular films. Highly polarised positions were developed that drew on broader debates about popular culture, Americanisation and art and the aim on all sides was to identify criteria that would permit certain kinds of film (precisely which was subject to debate) to be differentiated from the standard products of the mass media. In particular, the identification of personal style and intelligence in films was strongly valued, even though there was disagreement about the assessment of particular directors. As Ian Cameron pointed out in the second issue of *Movie*, 'everyone accepts the cinema of directors for France, Italy, Japan, India, Argentina, Sweden and Poland … It is only over American movies that the trouble starts' (September 1962). The other omission from his list was Britain, and *Movie*'s contributors shared with the critics with whom they disagreed a sense that British cinema as a creative institution failed to provide its audience with the best that cinema could offer as an art form.

Outside this specific debate, though, cinema could claim to straddle the divide between mass culture and art in a distinctive way. Roger Manvell argued in a book aimed at children that the 'large, unthinking audience has transferred the major part of its habitual attention to television', which meant that cinema could have 'some success with films that appeal to the intelligence of audiences' (1961: 30). Education was seen as particularly important in opening up the cinema to those intelligent audiences. Concerns about the influence of Admass led the National Union of Teachers to organise a conference in 1960 under the title 'Popular Culture and Personal Responsibility' to 'examine the impact of mass communications on present-day moral and cultural standards' (Thompson: 7). Not surprisingly, the conference tended to conclude that what was needed was education, but Albert Hunt, whose paper on 'The Film' was subsequently included among those published, had a less difficult task than some of his fellow speakers in arguing that the study of film could be part of a liberal education. In doing so, Hunt distanced film from the other mass media being discussed – 'film is distinct from the rest of the new media in that so far it is the only one to have developed into an art form' (100) – and allied it with more traditional subjects: 'Nobody asks why we teach music and drama: and nobody should ask why we teach film' (120). Like the film critics involved in the critical debate above, Hunt's assertion hinges on an understanding of 'the film' as 'the concrete expression of the director's imagination' (104). Using detailed textual analysis, he argues against the formulaic quality of much commercial cinema, providing examples from Kubrick and Bunuel as indications of 'what an imaginative director can do, even when he is forced to work with economic limitations' (117). It is significant that Hunt refers to 'film' rather than 'cinema' in his essay, since the object of study is to be the individual film/director and it is the experience of understanding a film that is to be the basis for education. This emphasis can be contrasted with other papers from the same conference. Philip Abrams' essay on radio and television places much greater emphasis on the institutional arrangements for broadcasting and Frank Whitehead's essay on advertising argues that education on advertising had to be negative, inoculation rather than appreciation (48). This shift in discussions about film and cinema was indeed important. It made it possible for film studies to be incorporated into education at various levels through the interpretative strategies associated with the teaching of literature and drama. But it tended to remove films from debates about popular culture more generally and to under-play questions about cinema as an institution.

Representing mass culture

These debates about mass culture and cinema's role within it can be found in the films of the period. Sometimes the issues are addressed directly and polemi-cally; sometimes they are implicit in the settings, characterisations and narrative actions that the films are drawing on. The specificity of cinema as a mass medium with a popular but declining following affects the way that particular issues around mass culture are addressed and, while the films do not present a sustained or consistently articulated view, a recognisable set of attitudes emerges that confirms the somewhat beleaguered role of cinema, particularly towards the end of the period. We can divide this account into three main areas: the representation of British popular culture, especially in relation to British national identity and the particularities of British society; the role of the mass media, including the press and advertising; and the impact of television, as a special case, in cinematic representations of this most challenging rival.

At the beginning of the period in particular, there is considerable emphasis on various manifestations of popular culture. Cinema's contribution to the post-war entertainment boom was to use entertainment itself as the basis for a large number of stories. Sometimes this manifests itself in particular settings such as holiday camps, fairgrounds, holiday resorts, pubs, race tracks, the dogs, boxing's 'square ring' and music halls, and in the activities that the characters are involved in: beauty competitions, gambling, sporting activities, dancing, the pools. Sometimes, popular culture is critical to the plot, as in *The Blue Lamp*, when the crowds at the dog track come together to entrap the criminal, or *Easy Money*, in which four stories revolve around the possibility of a win on the pools, or the beauty contest in *Lady Godiva Rides Again*, which propels inno-cent Marge into the dangerous world of show business. Generally, the reference is to contemporary popular culture, though in some films, such as *The Wicked Lady*, *Trottie True* and *Esther Waters*, activities like a winter fair, music hall and horse racing contribute to the historical setting. This culture may take place on a small scale (a game of darts or a cycle ride in *It Always Rains on Sunday*, for instance); more often it involves crowds coming together, as in *Holiday Camp*, *Derby Day* or *The Blue Lamp*. Even when it has a mass setting, though, the emphasis is on the contribution that people make to their own entertainment, the role individuals play in the bustling activity that surrounds them.

One important element of this stress on the popular is the prominence given to the Britishness of such cultural activity. One method of achieving this identi-fication of popular culture with national identity is by continuing the wartime convention of bringing different classes together, in this case in pursuit of fun. Thus, *Holiday Camp*, though it is largely populated by working-class families, has room for the upper middle-class Esther (Flora Robson); and the appeal of sports such as horse racing and boxing in a number of films is that it can involve the aristocrats and the working class. *Derby Day* features a mixed group of characters enjoying a day at the races, including Lady Helen; a respectable working-class couple, Gladys and Joe; a murderer and his mistress; and a film star accompanying a lady's maid whose employer won the trip in a raffle. In *Cage of Gold*, Bill and Judy are in the crowd for a boxing match in glamorous evening dress. The music hall also provides a communal venue in which the traditional mixing of classes (exemplified in the liaison between aristocrats and dancing girls in the historical *Trottie True*) engenders a sense of national community, which is maintained in the more exclusively working-class venues shown in *The Blue Lamp*. The rather later *Ring of Spies* calls on this tradition ironically when it has the two spies going to the theatre to enjoy the classic British humour of the Crazy Gang on one of their trips to London.

It sometimes assumed, partly because of the dominance of Ealing films in the immediate post-war years, that such representations of British popular culture are necessarily cosy and warm-hearted. I would suggest, however, that these settings and activities provide a good source of narrative drama because they have a strong element of danger. *The Woman in Question*, *Wall of Death* and *The Woman for Joe*, for instance, call on the solidarity and comradeship of the fairground to different degrees but also emphasise the elements of risk and cheating in this traditional way of life. The attraction of racing is in the gambling and the Derby Day crowd in *Esther Waters* and *Derby Day* depends for its traditional character on the sharks and showmen who seek to gull the day trippers. Even in a seaside beauty contest it pays to keep your wits about you, as Doll (Diana Dors) demonstrates in *Lady Godiva Rides Again*; Doll lets newcomer Marge into the backstage tricks of the contest and, having been set up to win, shrewdly assesses what is in her best interest and throws the contest. Popular culture in these films therefore involves not only the communal solidarity of the crowds but also the active use of wit and humour so as to know what is going on in those crowds.

This seedier side of popular culture is confirmed in the crime films of the late 1940s, which feature bars, clubs and other dives in notorious areas such as Soho and Brighton (Murphy 1989). These generic venues survived into the B movies of the early 1960s, with examples like the Night Owl club in *The Gentle Trap* and the Blue Baboon club in *Pit of Darkness*. While these British crime films clearly draw on the generic references of American gangster films, they also seem to have their own British characteristics in the documentary emphasis on London low life, the contrasts between the brightly lit West End and the mean back streets, and the mix of the rich and the criminal who are drawn to the basement clubs and backroom bars. The American sources are thus reinforced by a Dickensian awareness of the perils and fascinations of those who live on the fringes of respectable society.

The fear of Americanisation in opposition to indigenous British popular culture can be seen more clearly in cinematic representations of mass culture, which are a particularly important feature from the mid-fifties. A key characteristic of the presentation of mass culture is the emphasis on the imposition of ideas or products, often though not necessarily from a foreign source, on to a largely passive audience. This can be seen in terms of individual artefacts – American comics take over the imagination of the teenage boy in *London Belongs to Me* and popular music has an insidious effect on any number of British adolescents from *I Believe in You* to *Beat Girl*. In addition, the industries that make such mass products are deemed to be corrupt and interested only in money and profit, even though some individuals who work for them may be honourable. The treatment of the press offers a good example of this. Individual journalists, such as those in *Murder in Reverse*, *Noose* and *The Long Memory*, may pursue a story in the interests of undoing a wrong but the institution as a whole is presented in terms of big business out to make a quick buck by promoting sensational stories. Thus, in *The Long Memory*, the journalist Craig protests that the hero, a man wrongly convicted of murder, 'should be left alone to work things out for himself', but the editor promptly puts another journalist on the story with instructions to pursue it vigorously. In *The Oracle*, the newspaper proprietor insists on misusing the traditional prophetic abilities of the oracle to produce banner headlines, disregarding the havoc caused among the mass of readers.

A similar differentiation between the individual and the business can be found in the handling of popular music, although here the emphasis on the American sources of the industry is stronger. Individual singers may be honest and appealing but the industry as a whole is exploitative. In films with a dance or music setting, this contrast is often expressed through a clash between the down-to-earth values of British popular culture and the slickness of American mass culture. In *Dance Hall*, for instance, the impending Americanisation of the Palais is hinted at in the jiving that occasionally breaks out but the big bands are British, the orchestra players chat in a friendly way with the local girls, and the glamour of the dance hall is tempered by shots of the cleaners. Later, British lads aim to be pop singers in the American vein but both Terry Dene in *The Golden Disc* and Tommy Steele in *It's All Happening* need the quick-witted skills and amiable good humour of the cinematic Cockney to counter the malpractices of the music companies.

Television, particularly when it was linked with advertising, offered cinema the most ready example of the bad effects of mass culture.[3] Cinematic representations of television consistently pull together audience addiction, silly content and commercial selling as a way of identifying cinema's rival with the excesses of Admass. *Meet Mr Lucifer* (1953), Ealing's attempted comedy that identifies television as an instrument of the devil, was made before commercial television was available in Britain but it lays down some of the key tropes in quite a perceptive way. Television is seen to speak directly to its audience, who literally reply to the announcers and performers who address them; the lonely hearts singer (Kay Kendall) uses this intimacy directly when she appeals to her audience as individuals who have an assignation with her; domestic arrangements are literally upset as neighbours come around to join the viewing circle or the furniture is pushed back to enable the viewers to join in television's barn dance; the TV programmes seem to be a bizarre mix that eschews drama (presumably as the property of cinema) but includes dancing, which manages to be both old-fashioned *and* American, demonstrations of impossibly fancy dishes and impenetrable discussions of mathematics and science. The television audience is presented as weak and vulnerable through age, nationality or gender. The television set is first given to Mr Pedelty as a retirement present. It then passes to the newly wed Kit, who uses sex to persuade her husband that they should take it on and watches any kind of programme indiscriminately. Its final recipient is Hector (Gordon Jackson), whose Scottish Presbyterian priggishness is no match for the seductive, feminine charms of the television singer.

Ironically, *Meet Mr Lucifer* goes some way towards indicating what the attractions of television might be. This is partly because of Kendall's filmic presence in the dramatically large close-ups of her 'television' performance. In addition, the possibilities of the new medium in terms of domestic comfort and communal watching are indicated, but in the end the film emphasises both domestic disruption (Kit's marriage is nearly wrecked by television) and the falseness of the community that television creates. In the most convivial scene, the most unlikely characters join in the dancing inspired by the television – neighbours, relations, sailors, ragged children and prostitutes. It is clear that this community is inauthentic – some cannot even get into the room where the television is – and once the television is gone its members cold-shoulder their erstwhile host, not wishing to know him now that he is televisionless.

The notion of such an ersatz community was particularly problematic for an Ealing film but, as television ownership became more common, cinema continued to be critical not only of the disruption of community and family relations but also of television's association with mass culture and commercialism. This surfaced most sharply in 'new wave' films towards the end of the period, when television comes to be associated with consumption (the use of television advertising in *The Loneliness of the Long Distance Runner*, for instance) and with the mindless absorption in light entertainment that Arthur Seaton berates his father about in *Saturday Night and Sunday Morning*. Although strikingly expressed, this contemptuous attitude to television was not new to cinema, although in the 1950s it was often expressed through comedy. Arthur Askey's *Make Mine a Million* parodies both the stuffiness of the BBC and the gullibility of the public, who will only buy a product when it has been advertised on 'the telly'. *Simon and Laura*, a film in which two stars of the theatre and cinema (Peter Finch and Kay Kendall) are persuaded to feature in a daily television serial, plays off the characteristics of theatre, film and television against each other, largely to television's disadvantage. Television's technical limitations are illustrated in the opening scenes of this colour film, when a vivid dance sequence is reduced to black and white on the small screen. And throughout the film, interference and loss of sound consistently mar the broadcasts. The connection between television and consumption is also made early on, when the BBC's 'Controller of Television' links the repetitions of successful series on television to those of advertising and declares that it is 'rather like advertising. Repeat a thing often enough and everyone has to buy it.' The viewers are represented by a family – grandma, husband and wife, brother and sister – which is gathered around the set in the manner described by the sociologists cited above. The serial fits into the domestic routines of eating and family chat, and when a fight breaks out in the televised serial its effects can be seen in the quarrel that is sparked off between husband and wife watching at home. The theatrical style of acting and the dramatic arguments between the 'real' Simon and Laura are contrasted with the cloying family intimacies of the television script. When the producer discovers that Simon and Laura have hidden their warring tendencies from him, he is shocked that television's fundamental claim of intimacy has been breached. 'Insincerity is the one thing you can't get away with on television,' he complains. 'We seem to have managed pretty well up till now,' Simon responds sardonically.

However, it is significant that, despite this patronising attitude to television, British cinema increasingly offers a problematic representation of itself. Although television is the enemy, it is apparently difficult to contrast it with a popular and vibrant version of cinema. Instead, cinema represents itself in ambiguous and self-deprecatory ways. Two examples are typical of this. In *The Blue Lamp* (1950), cinema is contrasted with a nostalgic reference to another example of popular culture in the use of Tessie O'Shea's music hall performance as an alibi for a robbery. One of the crimes of Tom (Dirk Bogarde) and his gang is that they misuse and pervert this wholesome entertainment by using it as a cover. Moreover, the act of robbery and the subsequent murder of PC George Dixon (Jack Warner) take place in the cinema. The cinema is the place for teenagers – a young couple on a date are quarrelling about the film as they leave – so it is an appropriate place for the young delinquent. The virtues of indigenous popular culture are reaffirmed when the young killer is caught by the communal action of the crowds at the greyhound track.

Later on in the decade, *The Smallest Show on Earth* (1957) presents an apparently affectionate view of cinema, which the trade press, *The Cinema*, suggested reflected on the industry as a whole: 'an industry that can afford to laugh at itself in this way can't be in such a bad way after all' (quoted in Chapman: 200). But the film goes some way to demonstrating the ambiguous pleasures now typical of cinemagoing. Matt (Bill Travers) and Jean Spenser (Virginia McKenna) inherit a rundown cinema, the Bijou. They attempt to prove that it is a going concern so that they can sell it to the owner of the rival cinema, the Grand. The film features a number of versions of 'the cinema'. The Grand is the successful cinema – smart, orderly, plush – but it is strongly associated with the values of big business and commerce. It lacks heart. The lost past of the cinema is referred to in a wonderful vignette in which the ancient retainers at the Bijou rerun, for their own pleasure, the silent British film *Comin' Thro' the Rye*. But the recurring image of cinemagoing offered by the film is the unruly audience of the Bijou. In one sense, the Bijou is successful. It gets in a heterogeneous crowd, including a mix of children, teddy boys, respectable middle-aged women,

families and old men, who enjoy the characteristic pleasures of the cinema –
viewing, eating, drinking, kissing in the back row. In some ways, this is the mass
audience described in *Picturegoer*. But the point of the film is that this version
of cinema is not just unsustainable but may also be undesirable. It is not only
that the equipment is ancient and the building regularly shaken by passing
trains. More importantly, the cinema crowd has the characteristics of the mob;
the audience throws things at the screen, consumes cheap films and ice cream
with the same lack of discrimination and rushes out in an unstoppable flood to
avoid the traditional standing for *God Save the Queen*. All of this is played as
comedy and is now very evocative but it is clear that the modern young couple
cannot be expected to carry on in this old-fashioned way. In the end, they get
their money from the owner of the Grand and leave not only the cinema
industry but the country.

Murphy argues that the 1950s were a time of relative stability for the British
film industry, when despite the usual crises 'film production enjoyed greater
health and stability than might have been expected given the competition from
television' (1989: 230). This stability is evident in a number of successful mainstream films that were very popular with audiences and in the development of
key genres, particularly comedy and the war film, which were an essential part of
British culture in the period. Nevertheless, I want to suggest that the relatively

"THE SMALLEST SHOW ON EARTH" . A Frank Launder - Sidney Gilliat Presentation
Starring BILL TREVORS and VIRGINIA MC KENNA   with Margaret Rutherford · A TIMES FILM CORP. Release

Figure 1.2 The Smallest Show on Earth (British Lion Films, 1957).
Courtesy of the Ronald Grant Archive.

stable position of the industry needs to be put into the context of the changing attitudes to cinemagoing and to the sense of cinema as a shared space. At the beginning of the period, cinema could still be considered as entertainment for all, a prime example of the modern, mass media and one that situated itself within the day-to-day experience of popular culture more generally. Len England, looking back on his cinemagoing days in south London, links his work for Mass Observation, which he joined at the beginning of the Second World War, with the importance of the cinema in everyday life: 'Mass Observation were pioneers of trying to get at what real people did and thought and felt. Cinema was at the centre of this – it was everywhere, in the back streets and everywhere else. It was the pop culture in those days' (O'Brien and Eyles: 38). By the end of the 1950s, that centrality was no longer the case. Cinema was being thought of and presented itself as a medium that was old-fashioned, uncomfortable and associated with past pleasures. For the general audience, cinemagoing was changing from being the quintessential modern form of popular entertainment to an old-fashioned and somewhat marginal pursuit. This contradiction between a relatively stable industry and an increasing marginalisation in terms of its social significance offers a crucial context for understanding the stories, images and ideas that British cinema offered its audiences in the period.

2 Modernity, the modern and fifties Britain

'Funnily enough, I couldn't get used to the *newness* of things,' Mrs D.S. told a researcher about her move to Harlow New Town in the 1950s (Attfield: 222). 'Newness' is not a word much associated with the 1950s. Instead, the period after the Second World War is characterised first by austerity and then by a secure, rather complacent, affluence. The 1950s is, after all, the half-remembered childhood of those millions born in the immediate post-war period and has tended to assume the aura of a safe and stable golden age. It sits quietly between the upheaval and dangers of the Second World War and the social revolution of the 1960s. But those living in the 1950s often experienced a feeling of change and newness, which they both welcomed and worried about. In this chapter, I want consider how this experience of modernity might have been understood in the 1950s and to present a brief account of the terms that are going to be brought into play in the analysis I offer of certain themes and topics that appear and reappear in films of the period. At various points in this book, I will be arguing that British films of the 1950s offer a view of the world that is at odds with what were understood, at the time, to be progressive notions of change and modernisation. In this chapter, therefore, I will consider, first, the term 'modernity' itself in order to offer a useful framework for thinking about Britain in the 1950s and then give two specific examples of how being modern and new was conceived of in the period.

Obviously, this is in itself a task that could fill another book. The development and elaboration of the term 'modernity' is the subject of both complex debate and a vast literature. One recent lengthy account, John Jervis' *Exploring the Modern*, concludes by stressing the impossibility of pinning down the meaning of the term: 'perhaps, modernity has always existed as a story that exaggerates its own unity and distinctiveness ... At the end of this book, we can no longer be entirely sure what it was about' (338). Therefore, I want to stress that I am not attempting to offer a definitive account of modernity but something more modest. This chapter seeks to provide a sketch of some of the key aspects of modernity so that its terms may then be used to look more productively at the films under discussion. What is provided here is a somewhat abstract account of terms chosen not because they are necessarily the most important with respect to debates about modernity but because they can do theoretical work in the film analysis in subsequent chapters.

Modernity – a project and an experience

It is helpful to consider modernity in terms of two rather different aspects: as a project that has developed over time and that helps to explain the development of modern society and as the experience of living with and against that project. Marshall Berman began his hugely influential work *All That Is Solid Melts into Air* (1982) by defining modernity as 'a mode of vital experience – experience of space and time, of the self and others, of life's possibilities and perils'. The experience is one of living in 'a maelstrom of perpetual disintegration and renewal, of struggle and contradiction, of ambiguity and anguish' (15). Initially, the emphasis is on feeling but this maelstrom is the product of 'social processes' that are driven by 'an ever expanding, drastically fluctuating capitalist world market' (16). Jervis also offers an initial definition of modernity as 'the experience of the world constantly changing, constantly engendering a past out of the death of the here and now, and constantly reproducing the "here and now" as the present, the contemporary, the fashionable' (6). But he also draws attention to 'the other sense of modernity' (6) involving a project 'at the heart of Western culture' (8) in which the central dynamic of society is 'an orientation to rational and purposive control of the environment (both natural and social), thereby both understanding and transforming it' (6). This drive for control is manifested in the extension of industry, science and technology into all parts of society and in developments in education and politics that seek to civilise and control this process. Modernity as experience and modernity as project are clearly related, although, as Jervis comments, they seem to 'point in opposite directions' (9), the former to rupture, change and instability, the latter to an attempt to impose order, civilisation and progress. It is the tension between the two, he argues, that results in a 'distinctive "modern attitude": one of simultaneous involvement and detachment, immersion and distancing, fascination and repulsion' (9), a 'reflexive' attitude that is 'self-aware, self-conscious' (10).

Berman gives a powerful summary of the social processes that are at the heart of the project and that feed into the 'maelstrom of modern life' (16). These include:

> Great discoveries in the physical sciences, changing our images of the universe and our place in it; the industrialization of production, which transforms scientific knowledge into technology ...; immense demographic upheavals ... rapid and often cataclysmic urban growth; systems of mass communication ... enveloping and binding together the most diverse people and societies; increasingly powerful national states, bureaucratically structured and operated, constantly striving to expand their powers; mass social movements of people, and peoples, challenging their political and economic rulers.
>
> (16)

This is a powerful account, which emphasises the dynamic process of change as well as the different strands that contribute to it: the drive to understand and control nature; the bringing together of people through demographic movement from one country to another; the shift of populations from country to town, which premised industrialisation; and the urges to both bureaucracy and democracy, which characterise the development of the nation-state.

Alan O'Shea, in his consideration of Berman's work, confirms that modernity can be seen as a project in which reason and science should free mankind from poverty and ignorance. He adds an important dimension by stressing that the acceleration of modernisation in the late nineteenth century relied on the raw materials provided by the expansion of European empires and the development of ideologies premised on assumptions about European rationality and progress compared with the primitive behaviour and organisation of the backward peoples being discovered and taken under European control in an extension of imperial power. O'Shea also emphasises other factors: lives speeded up by 'faster transport systems and easier communications' (15); spatial distances compressed and dispersed through the experience of mass migrations; and the rationalisation of the labour process though the development of factory systems and time-and-motion studies. O'Shea identifies the growth of state power and the engagement of the state with new demands for democracy as an important factor but also identifies the development of new modes of scientific study such as psychiatry, psychology and medicine, which sought to apply the criteria of science and reason to new areas of human behaviour. One does not need to take a Foucaultian approach to see these new sciences as important in the way in which they claimed new knowledge about personal relationships and the family, which was disseminated and popularised through newly developing media systems such as the popular press and cinema.

In reflecting on the 'consequences of modernity', Anthony Giddens identifies three main sources of the 'dynamism of modernity' that might be considered as drivers of the project. First, he comments on the 'separation of time and space' (53) which also involved the 'separation of *space* from *place*' (18). The rationalisation of time, through the development of clocks, calendars, dating systems and timetables, removed the connection between time and place and modern telecommunications also removed the link between place and space in the sense of the need for a specific geographical location for social activity. It became possible to develop social relations that were 'locationally distant from any given situation of face-to-face interaction' (18). Social relations no longer depended on being in the same place and modern organisations are both able to break free from the 'restraints of local habits and practices' (20) and make connections across space, reconstructing what counts as local. Giddens links this to his second feature of modernity, the development of 'disembedding mechanisms', which ' "lift out" social activity from localised contexts, reorganising social relations across large time–space distances' (53). One such mechanism of particular importance is the expert system. Modern life, Giddens argues, depends on the willingness of people to trust in 'systems of technical accomplishment or professional expertise' (27), of which they have very little direct experience, which produce goods such as cars that can be used without being understood. Trust in experts is both necessary and possible because of the way in which modernity relies on knowledge rather than tradition as the basis for activity. The third mark of modernity, for Giddens, is the way in which knowledge is continually gathered, examined and re-formed in the light of new evidence. On one level, this would seem to be an example of modernity's rationalist project to examine and control the world. However, Giddens argues that modernity is characterised by the 'reflexive appropriation of knowledge' (53), so that knowledge itself is continually publicised and re-examined in a way that is profoundly unsettling. This activity is not confined to public debate about how society is organised but extends into the most intimate, private relationships, which are continually the subject of analysis: 'marriage and the family would not be what they are today,' Giddens comments, 'were they not thoroughly "sociologised" and "psychologised"' (43). Expert comments on and explanations of private relationships become an intrinsic part of the relationships themselves.

In thinking about modernity as a project, then, certain key features emerge. Modernity is defined by an emphasis on the possibilities of reason and science in controlling forces that might otherwise spin out of control; the driving force of capitalism in developing mechanisms to exploit raw material and labour; the pre-eminence of the nation-state, which controls and supports its citizens through its bureaucratic arrangements; the replacement of local place by global space, so that 'social and physical worlds were no more co-terminous' (Clarke: 4); the need for trust in technical and professional knowledge and the expertise and systems that dispense them; and the development of new modes of knowledge that take for their object of study the public and private lives of their fellow citizens. But the project is also intimately bound up with the experience of modernity; these changes and transformations are felt viscerally as both exciting and frightening. This experience is not uniform – differences in gender and race, for instance, profoundly affect how modernity is experienced – but it is nearly always deeply unsettling.

The experience of modernity is thus ambivalent. Even in its more optimistic modes, modernity involves a duality of feeling that O'Shea, for instance, describes as engendering a belief in rationality, the benefits of technology and the possibilities of a more prosperous and stable life and 'the desire for excitement, risk and the unknown' (20), an eagerness to transcend the everyday. As Berman argues, it is possible to welcome both these aspects, 'to make oneself somehow at home in the maelstrom' (344), to relish that 'the process of modernization, even as it exploits and torments us, brings our energies and imaginations to life, drives us to grasp and confront the world that modernization makes, and to strive to make it our own' (348). Elizabeth Wilson remembers how her mother introduced her to the city and 'planted within me … a conviction of the fateful pleasures to be enjoyed and the enormous anxieties to be overcome in discovering the city' (1991: 1). This response is ambivalent in its fear and excitement but wants to engage with danger. For others, an anxiety about the modern world may be expressed in the 'passion for continuity' and the 'desire to preserve and retain' that Alison Light finds in the popular 1930s newspaper column *Mrs Miniver* (145), or in the interest in national heritage that Patrick Wright describes as 'the backward glance which is taken from the edge of a vividly imagined abyss' (70). In this sense, a yearning for the parochial and the pleasure sought in imagined pasts can be as significant a response to modernity as the breathless excitement of the committed modernist.

'Modernity' is a conceptual term and not one that was available in the 1950s. But words like 'new', 'modern' and 'contemporary' were widely used. New towns, the new look, modern art, contemporary furniture, the new Elizabethans were all discussed, promoted and sold to the public. As another Harlow ex-resident remembered: 'we had a purple carpet … an orange wall … it was very modern' (Attfield: 227). In trying to get a sense of why there was the emphasis on the modern, why being modern mattered in the 1950s, I will look at two idealised figures who seemed to crystallise feelings about change: the expert and the new woman.

The expert and new Britain

In providing a sketch of the expert as a modern phenomenon, I am going to turn to the account given in *The New Look: A Social History of the Forties and Fifties*, written by Harry Hopkins at a point in the early 1960s when he could look back over the period. Hopkins has a tendency to patronise what he describes as if looking back over past naiveté with the more knowing eye of the 1960s. Nevertheless, his book is revealing as the work of someone who lived through the period and is imbued with many of its assumptions. He defines social history as exploring a process and since this is '*contemporary* social history' he is, as he says, 'exploring the process from inside it' (11). In *The New Look*, we find not just a host of anecdotes and incidents but also a viewpoint, a sensibility that provides us with a modern account of the very modernity that it is seeking to describe. He offers a polemical account of the post-war period in which the expert transforms, for good or ill, the familiar landscape.

Hopkins provides the reader with a grand narrative through which to understand ' "the social revolution" of the last twenty years' (11). He acknowledges that the trends he is describing originated earlier, but he considers that during the post-war period 'the pace of their development accelerated so greatly as to produce differences of kind rather than merely of degree' (11). In his introduction, Hopkins lays out clearly the two motors that drive his narrative: the influence of science and technology and the relationship between the 'concept of public good and the drives of private profit' (12). In taking these themes, Hopkins is working with two of the key concepts of modernity: the role of science in understanding and controlling the world and the organisation of citizens and the state within a modern social democracy. In addition, Hopkins, as he so often does, uses the metaphors of modernity – speed, acceleration, drives, forces, travelling, the harnessing of power, the directing to specific ends.

As Hopkins describes it, there are two key periods in which these modern themes are worked through. The first is in the late 1940s, in post-war 'New Britain' (360), when the Labour government took the state controls, necessary in war, and continued them into peacetime. The wartime emphasis on planning, government control and large units of organisation became the way in which the Labour government carried out its programme of nationalisation, reform in education and health, and economic management. A bureaucratic network set up to implement this programme was both pervasive and consensual. Working parties were set up 'to run the modernising rule' (84) over British industries; wages councils to determine pay in key areas; boards to run the nationalised industries; joint production councils; and works committees to bring together unions and management in both the public and the private sectors. Reason and rationality were to be brought to all sectors of the British economy and, despite the severe economic difficulties, the Labour government continued to believe that expert planning could solve the problems.

Hopkins sees this emphasis as being at odds with the needs of democracy; even the organisations of social democracy are losing contact with individual voters and workers, so that 'the newly nationalised industries … were proving to be merely one more means by which the economists, technologists, the managers, the experts entered yet further into their kingdom' (94) and 'at the grass roots of British democracy, local government, the technocrats and centralisers were now taking over in force' (122). Even in the new National Health Service, the development and greater availability of new scientific methods had an alienating effect, creating 'narrower and narrower circles of specialists' so that doctors had difficulty handling 'the appalling burden of technical detail that now appeared necessary' (142). The countryside offered no respite from the continual pace of change, for farmers were working to a 1947 four-year plan to raise output and the agricultural engineer had taken over from the farrier in mending the machinery that ensured targets could be met (178).

Later in the book, Hopkins moves on to the mid- to late 1950s and considers further changes in society from the same perspective. But this is 'Newer New Britain', which is, 'psychologically at least, really new', because the machinery of modernisation is now making its own pace and Americanisation is becoming a real factor (360). Despite the change to a Conservative government, 'planning was tacitly accepted as a routine task of government' (364). The government was advised by experts, ' "scientific" economists' (365), so that 'Ministers began to look more and more like public relations officers for economists, passing down their verdicts translated into suitable baby-talk' (366). However, the government planner is overshadowed by the scientist and technologist. In the 'bright, new factory', Hopkins asserts, 'technology … was taking much of the dirt and sweat out of work'; the labourer was giving way to 'blue-collared attendants upon machine processes' (340), and the foreman to the white-collared supervisor. The office became more like a factory as 'the "machine revolution" ' removed distinctions between roles and turned everyone into 'operators and "data processors" ' (343). Personnel managers, 'busily grading and labelling' (343), joined the raft of experts who would manage the work process. Outside work, the same technological planning, this time of specifically transatlantic origin, was evident in the arrival of the supermarket and the laundrette: 'here again was the classless, mechanical servant. Here again the bright clean-cut functionalism, the carefully planned lay-out ... the "know-how", the automatic, all-embracing, "technological classlessness of the times" ' (353).

In this analysis, technology works closely with science, often with a capital 'S'. Here, indeed, the figure of the individual scientist almost disappears into the personification of science itself. Science was transforming transport, reducing distances so as to bring, for instance, 'Tokyo within 36 hours of London' (389). Medical science was producing 500 new drugs a year (388), and new specialisms in psychiatry and social medicine were encouraging work on preventive health practices. Society itself could be scientifically analysed, since the 'younger social sciences, sociology in particular, could now offer diagnostic instruments opening up a view of the living social body that was wider and more sharply focused than before' (380). But the most dramatic evidence of the crucial way in which science was transforming the world and how it was experienced was in atomic science and space research, in which scientists and technologists were advancing into 'the Unknown with the precision and assurance of civil engineers' (386). In a classic statement of modernity, Hopkins comments that through science:

> ground that had been familiar beneath the feet for centuries was being cut away, it seemed, in weeks. Time was telescoped. Memory was lost. The picture, a semi-abstract, had no perspective, existing only in the single plane of the Present.
>
> (388)

Hopkins is again concerned about the effect of this on democracy, on the accountability of experts to ordinary people, and he argues that politicians and voters can barely keep up with the advances being made. Indeed, Science cannot be contained within the boundaries and controls of the nation-state. 'Technological advance developed a momentum of its own, transcending men and nations' (391), Hopkins suggests, citing the example of co-operation between world scientists at the 1957 Peaceful Uses of Atomic Energy Conference as evidence that science's threat to the democratic structures of government had to be set against its 'power to unify' (398) across national boundaries. Despite the fact that scientists are using the world as their laboratory, Hopkins finds that 'Western Man' still has trust in science: 'he watched the scientists at work with calm – possibly tranquillized? – gaze in confident expectation of greater wonders to come' (389).

It is clear that what Hopkins is describing in *The New Look* is a modernising project in which the experts reorganise society into a shape determined not by the people but by the dynamic force of their own expertise and even political leaders 'dare no longer disagree with [the expert]' (375). Hopkins describes what it feels like to live in the middle of this great experiment, emphasising both the excitement and the uncertainty. The book is characterised by hyperbole and exaggeration, by scare quotes around words like 'scientific', 'new' and 'modern', as Hopkins stretches his prose to describe a society in which familiar rituals and everyday practices are being changed dramatically by discoveries that the layman cannot understand. Hopkins makes a comparison with the nineteenth-century upheavals of the Industrial Revolution. The difference, he suggests, is that the Victorian discoveries of evolution and engineering were 'human' and could be enjoyed by anyone who could look at a fossil in a microscope or travel on a train. In the 1950s, science had become abstract, had passed into 'the realm of pure mathematics', so that

> for the layman, all contact with 'reality' was lost. For the non-scientists – that is, for most people – life in the Fifties often seemed to resemble an endless ride on a roller-coaster in which the landscape rushed by as a blur and a scream.
>
> (392)

The drive towards the modern thus has the crucial effect of drawing a sharp distinction between the expert and the layman. It is the effect of this that helps to explain Hopkins' tone, the attitude he takes to change. For, although as we have seen, Hopkins expresses concerns about the pace and direction of modernisation, nevertheless he broadly supports the project because it is helping the British people to shake off their undemocratic, class-obsessed, cramped past. Emphasis is often placed on rising affluence as the mechanism by which the working class is deemed to be reaching up into the middle class in the 1950s, but for Hopkins affluence is not a cause but a result of technological and scientific changes, which have forced the changes in education, in work practices, in wages, in leisure and indeed in manners, which meant that British class divisions were losing their meaning. The expert requires a particular kind of worker, a particular kind of consumer, and organises the world so as to get them. All classes are changed by this process and the only worthwhile distinction is between those who have knowledge and those who do not. The new experts, 'builders of a new world … were not so foolish as to expect its divisions to coincide with those of the old one' (159). Nor indeed, according to Hopkins, were those below. When in a Gallup poll, about half the British people described themselves as middle-class, Hopkins sees this as a rejection of old stereotypes:

> by which, of course, they meant NOT 'working-class'. What else they meant was not yet very clear … they were … simply making the half-instinctive recognition that in this England of the Fifties it had finally become impossible to describe the social present in terms of the social past – even though they were the only terms that currently existed.
>
> (346)

If the technological drive to break down class barriers could be linked to the social democratic promise of full citizenship for all, then the modern might have much to offer.

Hopkins' book is a work of high rhetoric. His expert is an imaginary figure who combines almost magical powers in science and technology with a bureaucratic emphasis on planning and detail. The book offers not so much an accurate account as a polemical vision of the experience of being modern in the 1950s. Its descriptions fit precisely the more theoretical accounts of modernity with which this chapter began. In his emphasis on science and technology, on the role of the expert, on the pace of change and the compression of time and space, Hopkins vividly expresses some of the key concepts of modernity. Hopkins' vision is of a classless citizen who is able to understand and live comfortably in a transformed world. For Hopkins, there is in the end no alternative but to throw in one's lot with the modern, despite all the doubts and misgivings, because it is inevitably the future.

The new woman

Hopkins' expert is male, dressed in a white coat or grey pullover rather than the flowing skirts and tight-waisted jackets of Dior's famous 'new look'. The other figure I want to look at, in exploring the way in which being modern was thought about in the 1950s, is the new woman. Again, this figure is a construction, this time taken from a range of sources. Whereas the expert is single-minded, rational and committed to the future, the new woman embodies some of the contradictions at stake when the modern is pitched against some of the more natural connotations with which women are traditionally associated. The constructions of womanhood at play in the 1950s focus on four main areas: motherhood, sexuality, paid work and consumption. Although they emphasise different things, taken together they provide an ideal figure – the new woman who is the 'touchstone for the social revolution' (Wilson 1980: 12).

The 1950s is commonly associated with the notion that women went back to the home after the war and settled down to bring up children. This conception, which is in some respects a misconception, is based on the way in which the developing professions of social work and psychiatry produced a rhetoric of motherhood that was a powerful force in public debates about women in the 1950s. This discourse emphasised the biological imperatives of mothering and the development of psychological understandings of the relationship between mother and child. Motherhood, it was argued, was rooted in biology and natural feelings and should bring women deep rewards. John Bowlby, a child psychologist whose ideas were widely popularised and sometimes exaggerated, stated forcibly that the key bond in the family was that between mother and child which could be established only by the continuous presence of the mother. His best seller, *Child Care and the Growth of Love*, first published in paperback in 1953, stressed 'the absolute need of infants and toddlers for the continuous care of their mothers' (18). D.W. Winnicott drew attention to 'the immense contribution to the individual and to society' made by 'the ordinary good mother ... *simply through being devoted to her infant*' (10) and claimed that as an expert he was hoping to give young mothers 'support in their reliance on their natural tendencies' (11). The mother is fitted to her task 'in its essentials by her biological orientation to her own baby' (189), he argued, and, in a direct address to mothers, he stressed the loving pleasure that a mother could get from her child, 'the richness of her minute-to-minute contact with her own baby' (25). Enjoyment was essential for mother and child, for 'if you are enjoying it all, it is like the sun coming out, for the baby' (27). The mother's power lay in the home, since a mother was internal to the family; she represented closeness, security and love, while the father was the doorway to the outside world, society's representative, the breadwinner. Winnicott stresses the rewards for the mother in this arrangement: 'only in her own home is she free, if she has the courage, to spread herself, to find her own self' (120).

To some extent, a mother's natural feelings gave her the specialist skills she needed to bring up her child well. According to Winnicott, the mother was 'a specialist in this matter of her own children' (175) who should not be dominated by teachers and other professionals and Haste has emphasised that during the 1950s 'motherhood ... acquired specialist status' (152). However, despite the emphasis on the natural development of the woman's instincts, it was felt that some women at least needed direction and the discourses of education and social work encouraged women to learn the skills needed for their role. The Newsom reports on education in 1948 and 1963 stressed the importance of educating girls into the work of housewife and mother. The 1963 report, *Half Our Future*, made recommendations on the education of children of average or less than average ability and did suggest that some domestic crafts lessons might be useful for boys. But the emphasis was on encouraging girls to see that 'there is more to marriage than feeding the family and bathing the baby and that they will themselves have a key role in establishing the standards of the home and in educating their children' (137). The British Medical Association produced a magazine, *Family Doctor*, which advised women on the physical and psychological aspects of childcare and the more popular women's magazines provided specialist advice on mothering. Sociologists found that middle-class mothers were becoming more aware of the existence of theories of childcare, more willing to do things differently from their own mothers, 'in general, more self-conscious about the whole business of bringing up children', and that there was some evidence of this 'rather introspective approach ... gradually spreading down the social scale' (Newson and Newson: 170). An increasing array of professional help was prepared to intervene in family life, with a particular emphasis on psychoanalytic approaches. In social work, there was a move to concentrate on personal development and the achievement of secure and balanced relationships within the family. The Family Welfare Association shifted its focus away from welfare support to therapeutic case work with the aim of making 'the quality of family life and the personal happiness of its clients its primary concern' (L. Pincus, *Social Casework in Marital Problems*, quoted in Wilson 1977: 87)

For the modern woman, though, motherhood was not enough; it was also necessary that she should be a good sexual partner in marriage. Winnicott stressed that the mother also needed 'the devotion of a husband, and satisfying sexual experiences' (9). The marriage guidance and psycho-sexual counselling services that were developing after the war began to emphasise the importance of a satisfactory sexual relationship within marriage. In a 1948 report for the Marriage Guidance Council, the 'simultaneous orgasm' was set out as 'a desirable ideal', and husbands were deemed particularly responsible for learning the techniques that might assist their wives to this goal (quoted in Weeks: 237). While women's pleasure was seen as important, her role was seen as essentially seductive; she was to be desirable rather than desiring, and she was to be fulfilled sexually by her husband's attentiveness. Wilson suggests that by the 1950s a typically complementary ideal was emerging: 'sexual potency in men and sexual responsiveness in women began to be seen as explicitly desirable qualities' (1977: 66).

As with motherhood, sexual experience for women was the subject of expert advice. Discussion of female sexuality was popularised in the press and through manuals about marriage and sex. The Kinsey report on *The Sexual Behaviour of the Human Female*, published in Britain in 1953 and known in the popular press as the 'K-bomb', was seen as being somewhat explosive in its claim to have studied women's behaviour and to have revealed the extent of premarital sex and masturbation (Wilson 1980: 87). More prosaically, women's magazines and handbooks were a source of advice for women; a survey published in 1956 reported that 'three-fifths of young married women had read books on sex and marriage' (Chesser, quoted in Haste: 155). And again, part of the effect of this was to bring psychoanalytic interpretations of sexual behaviour into the popular domain and give women particular responsibility for understanding their own sexual behaviour. Thus, Doctor X in *Woman's Companion* tells a reader who is worried about her lack of sexual feeling that 'You have to go back to your childhood to find the real reason for this unhappiness' and encourages her that while 'it is no easy matter to overcome the repressions of a lifetime ... it can be done' (28 January 1956).

The advice offered to women about motherhood and sexuality seemed to put traditional roles into a modern context, a context which emphasised that a woman could become expert in these areas, which were particularly her concern. But the biggest debates about the new woman centred on her role in the public world of work and the psychological effects on children of the working mother. Jeffrey Weeks comments on the 'absence of any single coherent strategy to send women back to the home' after the war (233). Labour shortages and the development of paid caring roles (teachers, nurses, childcare officers) within the welfare state created a demand for women's labour. The position had not changed by the end of the decade, despite the growing emphasis on motherhood. A study of working mothers and their children in 1963, which reviewed post-war policy, argued that the government was either 'ambivalent or without policy' on the matter of working mothers, so that 'one minister may denounce working mothers as contributors to juvenile delinquency at a time when another department is seeking to attract them into teaching or into hospitals' (Yudkin and Holme: 27). During the 1950s, the percentage of women working outside the home increased marginally but the dramatic increase (partly fuelled by earlier marriages) was in married women working: in 1931, the census showed that 16 percent of married women were working; in 1951, the figure was 40 percent and in 1961, 52 percent (Bourke: 100). Figures for 1959 show that 44 percent of women with children aged between 5 and 10 were in some form of paid work, and the figure rose to 66 percent for those whose children were between 11 and 15 years old (Roberts: 122).

Despite this evidence of women entering the public world of work by necessity and choice, it is important to note that women's paid work was viewed as being different from that of men. Employment literature emphasised women's differences as employees in terms of the work they could do and when they could do it. The increase in women's employment was largely an increase in part-time work and studies showed that women themselves felt that part-time work 'had to fit around family demands on their time' (Summerfield 1994: 63). Debates raged about the point at which a mother might be able to go out to work (when the child was 3 years, 5 years, 15 years old?) and for how many hours a week she should work. The number of women recorded as working part-time rose from 12 percent in 1951 to 26 percent in 1961 (Lewis: 74) and there were indications that married women left and rejoined the workforce more frequently than other women, often because childcare arrangements broke down (Yudkin and Home). The tendency for women to be in part-time, segregated work was reinforced by 'the loss of occupational status' that many women suffered when returning to work after having children, making an enforced move from white-collar office work to part-time domestic or factory work (V. Klein: 36). All of this encouraged a view of women's paid work as being different and inferior. Where men aspired to a working life which was full-time and continuous, women were encouraged to see their work as part-time and interruptible so that it could be fitted in with the needs of the family.

Despite all this, some sociologists reported that for women themselves paid work was an important source of income and personal satisfaction. Viola Klein's 1965 study, based on a survey carried out in 1957, found that the overwhelming incentive for working outside the home was financial but other reasons given included enjoyment, mental stimulus and the need for company; over half wanted to work even if the family income was larger (V. Klein: 36–7). A later study found that 88.5 percent of women in the study 'expressed positive enjoyment in their work' (Yudkin and Holmes: 48). In 1957, a local paper reported, more colloquially and significantly using the popular psychology of the time, that women in Harlow were 'going out to work in ever-increasing numbers ... They need the stimulus and interest of outside work, and in fact many women grow quite neurotic if they are deprived of it' (*Harlow Citizen,* quoted in Attfield: 229). These incentives to work were felt even among those not in employment: 47 percent of the full-time housewives in Klein's sample would have liked a job, but the majority of these cited childcare as the main difficulty (44–5).

Women's paid work, although hidden, was helping to contribute to the production of the goods that were part of Hopkins' modernising project. Much more visible was their role in the purchasing and use of the new goods coming on to the market. The technology that Hopkins lauded entered the home through labour-saving devices, and the new woman was seen as the key to the consumption of domestic goods such as refrigerators, ovens, vacuum cleaners, furniture, irons, convenience foods and new fabrics such as nylon and rayon. Women's earnings could be seen as 'pin money' that paid for these supposed luxuries. Klein's sample saw their earnings as supplementary to their husband's income and used them to buy what they called extras – holidays, furniture, better clothes, a nicer home (39). Yudkin and Holme found that married women were working not for themselves but to improve the standard of living for their family (44), and the purchase of domestic equipment followed a consistent pattern: 'the electric iron, vacuum cleaner and television' were bought first followed later by 'the fridge and the washing machine' (Roberts: 29). Not all the goods purchased were so practical. In the late 1940s, the fashionable 'New Look' was both welcomed and criticised for reviving a 'lost glamour and femininity' (Wilson 1980: 84), and the gradual demise of rationing and the emphasis on a new sexuality were reflected in purchases of clothes and makeup. New fabrics contributed to the vogue for home dressmaking. The new woman could express her femininity through fashion and fashion was becoming more widely available.

As with motherhood and sexuality, the new woman, in her home-making role, had to learn to handle her new powers, to know that orange and purple were the modern colours and to appreciate the value of new man-made fabrics and convenience foods. The expansion of advertising in the media was one way in which women were educated into consumption, and the close connections perceived between advertising and brainwashing help to explain why women's shopping was often viewed with suspicion. As Harry Hopkins notoriously put it, 'it sometimes seemed that this new New Woman played her role of heroine of the People's Capitalism with a dangerous facility', being vulnerable to 'impulse buying' and 'naturally attracted by bright packaging' (335). More soberly, women's magazines sought to place purchasing in the context of home management and even Hopkins had to admit that 'the pages that mattered [in the magazines] were the practical pages' (328). The magazines provided recipes, knitting patterns, decorating advice and do-it-yourself information, and

> where attention was paid to new products on the market it tended to be heavily informative and educational. The visual layout often resembled a trade catalogue. Many features were meant to 'test' housewives on their

ability to 'choose wisely', and there were regular 'shopping guides' informing the reader of what was available in the shops and offering advice on what to look for.

(Partington: 207–8)

According to sociologists, the new woman, with her various and complex roles, was to be found most readily in what came to be called 'the companionate marriage', a marriage in which the wife, because of her expertise, was accorded a balanced and equal status with her husband even though the nature of their responsibilities differed. The term 'companionate marriage' was used to mean different things in different contexts,[1] but it indicates a shift away from a marriage in which one partner plays the dominant role (usually the man, but sometimes the woman in working-class communities) to a relationship in which a sharing of responsibilities is the norm. This may mean a supposedly equal but complementary division of labour in which the wife manages the housework and children and the man is the breadwinner and handyman, or it may mean a blurring of boundaries in which women make a financial contribution to the household while men take on more of the caring roles. Willmott and Young reported on changes in the organisation of male leisure time which, they claimed, the husband increasingly spent at home. In a study of working-class families in Bethnal Green carried out between 1953 and 1955, they observed that the reduction in working hours had created

> the 'weekend', a new term and a new experience for the working man. With it has come the new sight of young fathers wheeling prams up Bethnal Green Road on a Saturday morning, taking their little daughters for a row on the lake or playing with their sons on the putting green.
>
> (1976: 24)

In a later study of suburban Woodford, Willmott and Young reported that husbands 'hurry back from their offices and factories' and spend the evenings and weekends helping with the housework and children and taking on their 'own specific tasks within the family economy, particularly in decorating and repairing the home' (1976: 29–30). Roberts, in her post-war oral history, found that husbands had their own tasks within the household: 'carpentry, working with metal, doing repairs and gardening' (40) and comments that 'the trend was for fathers to be more involved with their children' (156). Feminist commentators have been critical of the readiness with which sociologists of the 1950s such as Young and Willmott believed that husbands had changed their role, but for our purposes we need only to note that the companionate marriage was deemed to be the place in which the new woman could best flourish. It was the balance of activities that was deemed important in the modern marriage, but activities were largely organised on gender lines. As a father, the man was assigned the external, adventurous, playful role with his children and, in the house he took on the heavy work role of builder, carpenter, electrician and handyman to parallel his wife's role as a knowledgeable mother, consumer and home economist.

From this complex formation of the new woman, it is worth picking out a number of factors. First, it is through her that science and technology enter the private world of the home, in terms of both material technologies and psychological explanations. It is through her that the home is to be modernised, marriage 'psychologised' (Giddens) and children socialised. Second, although the new woman is undoubtedly the subject (if not the creation) of experts, she is herself expected to become the expert in her own sphere. The adoption of terms like 'home management', 'domestic science' and 'applied household science' seeks to express that approach and to give the housewife a new status. Third, it is clear that these different roles clashed, and the nature of the clash was commented on by sociologists in, for instance, the debate about working mothers or in the description of the middle-class wife who is 'supposed to be a social asset to her husband' but who finds that the 'arrival of young children inevitably restricts her horizons rather drastically' (Newson and Newson: 221). The new woman, for all her associations with frivolity and glamour, was, like Hopkins' expert, actually underpinned by a whole battery of social discourses through which modern society was being transformed and reorganised.

'Going travelling'

I will return to a number of these issues in the studies of the films that follow: to issues of mothering, childcare and the 'psychologising' of the family; to the new woman and her complex role; to the question of expertise and trust, particularly in relation to the bureaucracy of the state; to the compression of space and the relationship between the local and the modern world; to the disappearance of class; and to the whole question of the experience of change and how it can be managed. It is appropriate to look at British cinema in the context of how it handles the questions posed by modernity since film itself has been seen as a particularly modern art form. Cinema was established in the maelstrom of industrialisation and urbanisation, bringing together the masses for a form of entertainment that precisely depended on crossing the boundaries of space and time so that, in Benjamin's phrase, in the cinema 'we calmly and adventurously go travelling' (229). Films could show what was not there, edit time and space, use impossible angles, change the scale of objects through close-up or long shot and generally offer a dizzy experience of the modern and the new. Film, Benjamin argued, could explore the internal and the external world, presenting material for close, psychoanalytic analysis by isolating it and showing it 'from more points of view' but also opening up 'an immense and unexpected field for action' (229). Films used the urban experience as a major theme and reflected it back to those who were experiencing it for the first time. US cinema in the 1950s continued this engagement with the modern. In its genre variations, a number of the themes discussed here can be seen. Film noir expressed, in its stories and *mise en scènes*, the ambivalences of city life and the ruptures and discontinuities of modern sensibilities; the gangster genre turned its attention to the hidden organisations and syndicates that parodied modern business systems by rationalising crime and murder; melodramas combined psychological and social discourses with strongly expressive aesthetic modes to tell stories of troubled marriages and wayward children; even the western took a psychological turn in the father/son dramas of directors like Anthony Mann.

It is perhaps also relevant that modes of reading that emerged in the institutionalisation of academic film study also bear the hallmarks of the reflexive destabilising of knowledge that Giddens associates with modernity. Such methods, summarised in an influential article by Commolli and Narbonni in *Cahiers du Cinema*, involve reading 'against the grain' of the text, responding to moments of discontinuity and disruption as if they were psychoanalytic symptoms that could be analysed for darker and truer meanings:

> if one reads the film obliquely, looking for symptoms; if one looks beyond its apparent formal coherence one can see that it is riddled with cracks; it is splitting under an internal tension which is simply not there in an ideologically innocuous text.

(27)

This approach has produced the remarkable bodies of theoretical work on, for instance, fifties melodrama and film noir in which the text and the method seem to spring from the same modernist dynamic.

Such an approach is fruitful for British cinema and it is one that I will be adopting in the pages that follow. But I am also aware of its limitations in analysing a cinema that is, in many ways, stubbornly resistant to the maelstrom of modernity and curiously unperturbed by the changes that are being described in the sociological, psychological and educational literature of the period, which I will also call on. This earnest work, which often appeared in popular paperback form, assumed that Britain was inevitably becoming a modern society. Mainstream British cinema, though, demonstrated a blithe resistance to change, a comic affection for tradition and a sceptical attitude to modernist claims about social and technological transformation. This position of resistance to modern society was established by the early 1950s and was popularly successful, underpinning some of the key genres of the 1950s, in particular the domestic comedy and the war film. It is marked by an attachment to the local and parochial; an (often comic) mistrust of the state and its bureaucracy; a firm attachment to class and hierarchies as a given in any institution and as the basis for characterisation and action; a mistrust of expertise or authority in, for example, science or education and a mocking approach to planning and state intervention; an unwillingness to use or develop psychological explanations for action; a pervasive silliness in its handling of sex and marriage; and a recourse to tradition rather than knowledge as a justification for action and hence a resistant attitude to change. The old-fashioned cinemas provided films that celebrated such a stance and the popularity of many British films during this period lies, it seems to me, not so much in any attempt, conscious or otherwise, to expose the anxieties of modernity or to look back nostalgically to the past but in their success in giving audiences a rest from the stress of being citizens in the grip of modernisation. These films refuse to take the ambivalences and fears of the modern experience seriously and instead sport a bland common sense, a pragmatic, 'don't let's worry about it' approach. There are moments of anxiety and doubt, of course, some of which we will explore. Nevertheless, I would contend that it is the blithe refusal to deal with modernity that makes much of fifties popular cinema so hard to contend with now. While I do not accept that 'staring at British cinema in the 50s is like staring into a void' (Brown: 193), I recognise the feeling. By setting the films in a different kind of context, I hope to explain why many of them now look as if they come from another world.

3 Rural rebels and the landscape of opposition

On VE Day, 8 May 1945, Nella Last wrote in the diary that she kept for Mass Observation about the trip she had made that day with her husband and son to Coniston Water. 'It was a heavy, sultry day,' she recorded, 'but odd shafts of sunlight made long spears of sparkling silver on the ruffled water, and the scent of the leafing trees, of damp earth and moss, lay over all like a blessing … I felt I'd kept a tryst with the quiet hills and fells' (279). Such a response to nature was not uncommon among those trying to express in poetry and novels a sense of the Britain (or more commonly, perhaps, England) that was being fought for. Angus Calder notes unsympathetically that 'many writers who should have known better implied that the soldiers and airmen were dying to preserve an essentially rural Britain' (419). Popular novelists like Ernest Raymond and Neville Shute drew on such sentiments in novels like *The Last to Rest* (1941) and *Pastoral* (1944), linking the immediate privations and sacrifices of the war to a timeless sense of the country (in both senses) enduring.[1] In film, this rhetoric of the countryside had a well-established tradition; as Andrew Higson observes, in his discussion of the 1924 film *Comin' Thro' the Rye*, it involved 'the construction of a very specific rural vision of the national landscape and the national character' (1997: 43) that was developed in response to the increasing industrialisation of Britain in the late nineteenth and early twentieth centuries. In particular, Higson argues that the establishment of this rural idyll involved a displacement in which a particular landscape and setting derived from the south of England came to stand for the nation as a whole, creating a 'a new vision of the nation as England, which was itself reduced to a particular vision of the South Country' (43).

In some senses, wartime cinema was less concerned with nature and the pastoral than the literature was. Reviewing *I Know where I'm Going* in November 1945, Dilys Powell commented that

> regional films have not been common in our cinema … Films of English character (I speak again of the fiction film) have dwelt chiefly on urban character … only within the last year or so have country character and country scene begun to play a considerable part in the entertainment film.
>
> (*Sunday Times*. 18 November 1945)

If we stick to the fiction film of the early 1940s (and thus rule out Jennings' weaving together of images of the country and the city in *Listen to Britain*) *Went the Day Well* stands out for making the English countryside an emotional signifier of what the war was being fought for; the threat of invasion is powerfully invoked by the way in which the sunlit fields and hedgerows surrounding the village become a site of death for the Home Guard. But in 1944, two films, *Tawny Pipit* and *A Canterbury Tale*, used the landscape in the pastoral way described by Higson, drawing on the idyllic English countryside not just as a backdrop to a story but as an expression of national sentiment. Both films are set in southern England; the landscape is farmed and fruitful; children play safely in the streams and meadows; the woods are dappled. The order is not just in the symbolic arrangement of the narrative but also in the visual expression of the countryside, which seeks an emotional and aesthetic response from the audience. The countryside, in Jeffrey Richards' words, enshrines 'freedom, stability, tradition, peacefulness and spirituality' (1997: 102), values that are expressed in the way in which the camera moves over the landscape of cultivated fields and picks out farm workers in the orchards or hay meadows. It is this tradition that film critic Roger Manvell continued to espouse after the war in his description of the 'green, sweet and rain-quenched landscape', which he felt was one of the reasons why the British Isles were 'a fine country for a film-maker' (1953: 222).

In this chapter, I want to examine how this sense of the countryside as a repository of fundamental values was expressed in British cinema in the post-war period and look, in particular, at how rural narratives placed an emphasis on highly local geographies that triumph over the global connections associated with modernity. In these post-war versions of earlier tropes, national sentiment, a rural setting and an insider/outsider narrative structure combine to create a story of resistance, not to the wartime enemy but to modernisation and the future. I shall argue, first, that, despite the emphasis in pastoral tradition on southern England, this narrative of rural resistance was easier to work with in films that were set elsewhere, in rural Ireland or Scotland. Second, I shall look at how attempts, in the early fifties, to use English rural settings in this way proved more difficult to incorporate into this anti-modern thematic. In a final coda, I shall suggest that a rather harsher version of the English landscape did, however, offer a site of metaphorical opposition even when the narrative structures of disruption and rural resistance, outlined in this chapter, were not being deployed.

Rural resistance and Celtic tales

Films set in Scotland and Ireland offer particularly clear versions of a narrative of rural resistance. The stories of films set in Ireland, such as *The Oracle* (1953) and *Happy Ever After* (1954), and in Scotland, such as *I Know where I'm Going* (1945), *Whisky Galore* (1948), *Laxdale Hall* (1952), *The Maggie* (1953) and *Geordie* (1955) use clear national stereotypes that combine nationalist sentiment with a more general anti-modern position. Building on the work of McArthur, Richards and Barr in their studies of some of these films, this section looks at the way this opposition is expressed through an examination of three key motifs: the communication methods, which construct a web of relationships within and outside the community; the outsiders who intrude into the community; and the nature of the rural community that repels them.

The telephone has a significance in theories of modernity, since it is an example of modern technology that 'lets you be in two places at once' and thereby abolishes 'temporal and spatial distance' (Jervis: 211). For this reason, the telephone also has a dynamic narrative function in many films. David Bordwell and Kristin Thompson, in their study of cinematic narrative organisation, point to the significant use of the telephone as a device that brings protagonists together and provides the cause-and-effect links that drive the narrative along. The telephone's capacity to connect different spaces made it an invaluable means of linking characters in different cinematic spaces and allowing them to issue the instructions or invitations which can take the story further. However, the films that I am discussing represent the telephone and other modern communications technologies rather differently. Far from making connection easier, the films work to make the telephone and the radio seem strange, inefficient devices. Transplanted from their urban surroundings, telephones appear in strange and inconvenient places. Thus, in *I Know where I'm Going*, the telephone is positioned in an isolated spot halfway between the house and the village and is placed next to the waterfall, so conversations are drowned out by the noise of the water. As one critic commented, *The Oracle* is set on 'a one-telephone island' (*Sunday Dispatch*: 17 March 1953), and in that film and *Whisky Galore*, the telephone is in the local post office, as is the radio used to contact the island in *I Know where I'm Going*. In *The Maggie*, the American businessman, Marshall, tries to keep in touch with his organisation while trying to ensure that his furniture is safely transported by the broken-down puffer to his Scottish home. But the *Maggie* is out of radio contact with the shore so, when the boat stops, Marshall is forced to chase from bar to post office in search of a telephone. 'I've never seen such a man for the telephoning,' comments Mactaggart, the captain of the *Maggie*, 'it will be the American way. Everything in a rush.'

One feature of modern communications methods in these circumstances is that they cease to be private. 'Trouble for all of you in the post today,' the postman tells the laird in *Laxdale Hall*, while in *Happy Ever After* the manservant delivers his master's letters with the sardonic comment, 'Not a word of good news in any of them.' In *I Know where I'm Going*, Joan has to conduct a conversation with her fiancé in public; she finds his voice strange and is embarrassed at having to make private arrangements in front of others. The impersonal mechanics of telephoning are subverted by the personal interests of the operators who control its use. Roache, the postmaster in *The Oracle*, admonishes one of his telephone users for 'cluttering up the public services', while Peggy in *Whisky Galore* advises Waggett not to make a call so early in the morning – 'he'll be in bed, surely.' Telegrams are easy game; Roache in *The Oracle* monitors the instructions that the journalist Blake receives from his editor through the telegrams he is sent and knows, for instance, when he has been sacked.

In addition, far from being an efficient means of conducting business, the use of modern communications often results in difficulties and unforeseen consequences. In *Whisky Galore*, Waggett's use of the telephone consistently ends disastrously. His attempts to speak to George on the phone are thwarted by his mother, who will not permit its use on a Sunday; the colonel is indeed angry at being woken by the telephone when Waggett tries to warn him about the islanders' activities; in the end, the telephone signifies his downfall, as we cut from a phone call that summons Waggett back to the mainland to a shot of him on the boat, under arrest for smuggling and being miserably borne away from the island. Similarly, in *The Maggie*, the initial mistake of hiring the *Maggie* is made because Marshall thinks a brisk phone call will ensure that his instructions are followed. Throughout the film, Marshall's frantic attempts to keep in touch with civilisation by telephone fail; his wife cuts him off, the manager of the shipping company laughs at him, and his subordinates can never quite manage to do what he wants. A striking example of the misunderstandings generated by modern communications occurs in *Geordie*. Towards the end of the film, the hammer thrower Geordie is participating in the Olympic Games in Melbourne. Despite being on the other side of the world, Geordie can hear his girlfriend, Jean's whispered message of encouragement – 'Come on now, Geordie' – and makes the winning throw. Jean, however, has to rely on the radio and is appalled to hear the commentator describe Geordie embracing the Danish female shot putter. On his return, she describes her embarrassment – 'the whole glen listening on the wireless' – and is only won over by Geordie's personal demonstrations of love.

Modern methods of communication are thus systematically disrupted in these films and fail to achieve their aim of greater control and order. More generally, the representative of the modern world who is trying to use them is presented as an intruder. As Richards has argued, although this intruder figure is frequently English, nationality is less important than the associations with 'modernity, individualism and secularism' (1997: 249–50). The narrative structures of these films hinge on the entry of the intruder into the rural community with a view to transforming or controlling it. This basic structure allows for two rather different kinds of intruder figure: the bureaucrat, representing the modern state and the industrialist, representing modern industry. Both figures can be seen in the films under discussion.

The state bureaucrat is by the late 1940s a familiar figure in British cinema. The organisation of Britain for war had been a huge administrative task, which continued after 1945 with the development of the welfare state and the continuation of rationing and other restrictions. The figure of the bureaucrat embodied the state's interest in every aspect of daily life and the expectation that everything could be officially organised. It is this role of control on behalf of the state that Waggett in *Whisky Galore* proudly assumes when declaring himself 'responsible for the defence of this island.' In *Geordie*, the bureaucratic role is taken by the representatives of the British Olympic Association, who are alarmed by Geordie's blunt straightforwardness ('I'm not sure we haven't bitten off more than we can chew with that lad') and have to send a telegram to the committee in London over Geordie's determination to wear his Scottish kilt at the games rather than the British (English) blazer and slacks. In the usual muddled way of bureaucracy, the committee's telegram in reply arrives too late to be acted on. The clearest association between bureaucracy and the modern state is presented in *Laxdale Hall*. The film's first scene is in the Houses of Parliament as Samuel Pettigrew MP is asked to lead a parliamentary delegation to Scotland to deal with an 'outbreak of anarchy', the refusal of key members of a small community to pay a road licence fee. The delegation is sent to impose order and collect revenue but this bureaucratic function broadens into a more fundamental discussion about how life should be lived in modern Britain. Pettigrew, whose own mother came from the village, prides himself on having moved beyond the limited horizons of Laxdale and specifically associates himself with a modern version of society. 'People in the twentieth century have more to think about than chasing rabbits,' he remarks, taking a side swipe at a traditional sport, and he opens up the debate about road tax into a broader discussion about what a modern society can offer these 'backward' folk. Pettigrew promises them a modern, capitalist future, 'clean hygienic homes, profitable work and a decent standard of living … a glorious future of hard work and high wages.'

This association of the intruder figure with modernity is even clearer when he/she is a representative of industrialisation and business. In *I Know where I'm Going*, Joan is a young working woman, independent and self-confident, who is about to marry the manager of Consolidated Chemical Industries; indeed, on the journey to Scotland, she dreams that she is to marry the business itself. She appears to believe that money can solve most problems, including that of the weather, and, in her determination to meet her fiancé on the island, puts lives at risk by offering an irresistible sum to a young fisherman to get her across the strait. If Joan is aspiring to the higher reaches of capitalism so, in a comic mode, is O'Leary, the intruder in *Happy Ever After*, who arrives in Rathbarney to take over his dead great uncle's estate. O'Leary arrives on the train in the pin-striped suit and bowler hat of the bureaucrat but it is his attempts to exploit the estate in the manner of modern business that upsets the locals. He plans changes, what he calls 'reconstruction' or squeezing 'the lemon dry'. He does so by relying on formal agreements rather than tradition or personal arrangements. He insists on collecting the rent on the cottage of his ancient bailiff by calculating ten years of arrears and giving him a week to pay; he seeks to charge interest on debts the estate is owed but refuses to pay his predecessor's gambling debts because they were not put in writing; he refuses to honour the dying wishes of his great uncle because they were only 'deathbed ramblings'.

Even more dynamic are the full-blown industrialists who appear in person in

The Oracle and *The Maggie*. In both of these films, a double structure presents an initially fairly harmless intruder, who is then backed up by his more effective boss. In *The Oracle*, a young journalist, Blake, is the initiator who visits the island for a holiday but the exploitation of the oracle's accurate predictions – for weather forecasts, racing results, the problem page – is driven by his editor back in London, who prints them in his newspaper. While clearly pursuing profit, the editor also claims to be driven by a modern concern for the future, telling his reluctant staff that Blake has 'a source of truth, ... a key that can open the doors to social and scientific advancement.' The editor insists on asking questions that will have a major impact on the mass readership, culminating in the momentous 'Will there be another war?' The oracle's predictions, formerly confined to the mundane queries of a small island, are now major issues made known to the nation and the world.

In *The Maggie*, the confrontation between old and new is even more direct, for here the industrialist Marshall is gradually drawn into face-to-face dealings with cunning and obdurate Mactaggart and his crew. Initially, he tries to leave the negotiations with Mactaggart to Mr Pusey, an English bureaucrat complete with bowler hat, umbrella and brief case. Pusey, who hired the *Maggie* accidentally in the first place, ends up so embroiled with the crew that he is arrested on a poaching charge. With the failure of this delegated approach, Marshall is forced into enemy territory and has to board the *Maggie* himself in an attempt to control what is going on. Marshall, like the editor in *The Oracle*, is a representative of the modern global business. As the general overseas manager of World International Airways, he is used to moving goods and people quickly across continents and presenting a good public image to the press and the world. Marshall believes in efficiency, legal agreements and getting what he pays for. None of this is of any help to him in his dealings with Mactaggart. 'Doesn't the job you're supposed to be doing mean anything to you?' he asks, as Mactaggart takes another detour in the extended journey to make the delivery. 'Don't you think you should fulfil your contract?'

The intruders in these narratives thus share certain characteristics. They embrace the modern world and have high expectations about the benefits it can deliver. They operate a network of mechanised communications that enables them to cut across local and national boundaries and to leap over the natural obstacles of water, wind or mountains. Their outlook is not entirely mercenary, but their ideals are based on an expectation that good organisation and rational behaviour mean profit as well as progress. The intruders are single-minded and direct; they know where they are going. Set against them, though, are rural communities that communicate in an entirely different way and have different expectations about relationships with the outside world. The communities vary in size and organisation, but they have certain key characteristics in common.

First, it is important to note that the communities are not homogeneous, particularly in terms of class, and they do not operate formally through democratic or equal relationships. As McArthur (49) notes, 'quasi-feudal' hierarchical class relations are central to the villages depicted in *Laxdale Hall* and *Geordie*.

In *Happy Ever After*, the Irish yokels depend on the Anglo aristocracy for their way of life, and O'Leary's behaviour is disastrous for the village precisely because he will not adopt his assigned role as the benign master and offends both the aristocracy, by refusing to support the hunt, and the servant class, by withdrawing his favours and his employment. Torquil, the laird in *I Know where I'm Going*, clearly has authority, which relies on position as well as charm, and in the much smaller community of *The Maggie*, a clear hierarchy is established from Mactaggart as the skipper down to Dougie, the ship's boy. In these films, each member of society has a specific role, which, even when it is outside the law, as in the case of poaching, is nevertheless part of the established order of things: in *Laxdale Hall* and *Happy Ever After*, 'official' poachers are allowed to operate openly within certain local rules.

Nevertheless, by focusing on the formal framework of class relationships one misses the fluidity that also characterises these communities; the intruder finds them difficult to get a grip on as the people in them flow like water through and around the traps meant to fix them. This fluidity is made possible by the different way in which they communicate and their different relationship to space and place. Communication depends not on one-to-one conversations in which orders are given and received across distance but on the spreading of information by many within a recognised space. The countryside in *Geordie* provides an open space in which the laird, vicar and gamekeeper meet and argue as equals. The village setting, used in most of these films, provides a space that has boundaries, allowing intruders to be recognised, but internally allows for mixing and a flowing together. The village green, the pubs, bars, shops and post offices operate as communal spaces in which news and information can be exchanged and hierarchical differences eroded. The bars he drinks in provide Mactaggart with more information about Marshall's business than Marshall's own phone calls; in *Happy Ever After*, the major is a good member of the community because he drinks in the pub, and it is there that he sorts out amicably the fight between rival poachers. These informal spaces are reinforced by the more formal coming together of the community in meetings to discuss problems (*The Oracle, Laxdale Hall*) or to celebrate with dance and music (*I Know where I'm Going, The Maggie*).

At its most extreme, the community evades the attempts by the intruder to impose order by scattering out over the land and taking over the whole space. In *The Maggie*, Mitchell never quite knows who he is up against as Mactaggart's ever-shifting allies flow on to the bridge to cheer the stranded puffer or distract him in bars in remote coves. *Whisky Galore* offers the best and most joyous examples of the way in which the community can feel and act on its instincts without the need for spoken communication. Barr has analysed the scene in which the villagers hide the whisky from the excise men, commenting on the 'sense of urgent intuitive teamwork' (1977: 113) created by the montage of urgent hands and ingenious hiding places. There are other examples in the film of the people acting in this way: when the news of the wreck first comes through the men spill on to the streets, flowing from door to door, the throng becoming bigger as the news spreads; similarly, the whisky is lifted from the ship in a joint effort emphasised by the swarm of small boats and the swift editing, which makes individual actions into a co-ordinated activity. Something similar, though less well executed, occurs at the end of *Happy Ever After*, when the community converges on the hall with the intention of getting rid of O'Leary under cover of the traditional 'O'Leary Night', when the ancestral ghost is meant to appear. The rival poachers unite in an attempt to ambush O'Leary in the woods, while two different groups of villagers wander through the grounds and invade the house. Unknown to each other, both the major and Thaddy, the manservant, dress up as ghosts to frighten O'Leary. Finally, the whole village arrives to put out a fire, and the local priest and lawyer make up an official delegation to announce the discovery of a new will which does, in the end, lead to O'Leary's expulsion. As Father Cormack tells O'Leary, 'In an emergency, the whole village acts as one man.'

'In an emergency …'. The reference is surely to be understood by the audience in terms of the Second World War. *Whisky Galore* is set in 1943, and the rationing of whisky is described as a 'desolation worse than war'; the islanders use road blocks, barbed wire and passwords in the attempt to defend their haul. In *The Maggie*, the old puffer slips through the canals and inlets as if evading enemy detection, particularly when Marshall tries to follow it by air. In *Happy Ever After*, references to the war may be more ambiguous: when one of the villagers remarks, of the O'Leary night activities, 'It was like old times while it lasted …', Irish independence may be a reference as well. But wartime references persist in the action of these films, which is reminiscent of the resistance portrayed in wartime films like *Went the Day Well*. Small groups work together in unspoken concert, and rural rebels prove themselves willing if not capable fighters. In *Laxdale Hall*, the laird leads the community into hand-to-hand combat with poachers and inadvertently the police as well, while in *Happy Ever After*, the villagers are quite ruthless in their plans to murder O'Leary: 'it will be a pleasure to see his face when he finds it no longer attached to his body' says one as wire is stretched at neck level along the road, while another seizes a sten gun, declaring, 'that will be humane enough for the likes of him.' In their defensive attitude to the modern world and its representatives, the communities act out a guerrilla warfare that translates wartime images of a small, tightly defined island resisting the massed forces of the enemy into a peacetime rebellion against the modern world.

Two forms of resolution can be found in these films. In one version, the intruder is won over to the virtues of the local and the rural and recognises the need to retreat from the modern world. Joan in *I Know where I'm Going* recognises that she was lying to herself as well as to Torquil and embraces the countryside as well as the true laird rather than the industrialist, who has merely rented the island. In *Whisky Galore*, *The Oracle* and *Laxdale Hall*, the gentler representatives of the modern world, the sergeant, Blake and Marvell, fall in love and are taken into the community. But the other form of resolution is to humiliate and expel the intruder. Waggett in *Whisky Galore* loses all control and is taken off the island under arrest; O'Leary leaves Rathbarney penniless; Pettigrew, the leader of the delegation to Laxdale, is blackmailed into agreeing with the villagers; Marshall walks away alone, despite having enabled Mactaggart to keep the *Maggie* afloat. In neither type of resolution do we get the classic narrative model where both parties change to accommodate or move towards each other. The *Maggie* may change her name to the *Calvin B Marshall* but it remains the dirty old puffer; Geordie resolves never to compete again and returns to Jean and his rural way of life. Village life does not change. Instead, the ongoing significance of the landscape is stressed as rural order is restored, and the natural world provides the final image.

Such an intransigent attitude is possible only because national sentiment makes it explicable and acceptable. Richards has rightly argued that films set in Celtic communities appeal across national boundaries, but it is the expression of different national sentiments that makes this rural rebellion acceptable. Geordie may throw his hammer for the British team, but the film endorses his insistence on a Scottish identity. Such films demand something of a double somersault for English audiences. The stereotypes of Englishness (Waggett, Pusey, O'Leary, the Olympic officials) are made into figures of fun at best, at worst killjoys and spoilsports who fail to understand traditional values, so English audiences are not invited to identify with their own national identity. Instead, as if to recognise that the bulk of the audience is looking in from the outside, the films position the viewer as an outsider who has to be drawn into the community as well as the film. This is often done through scenes celebrating traditional national customs at which the language and the music proclaim the binding together of a community marked by national difference. In *Whisky Galore*, the sergeant acts as the audience's entry point into the community and is given information, for instance, about the *reitiach*, the traditional celebration of a wedding. At the *ceilidhs* in *I Know where I'm Going* and *The Maggie*, the camera is initially positioned outside, viewing through a window with Joan and Marshall, until invited, with them, to join in. In both cases, the documentary elements of the celebration sequences reinforce the positioning of the audience as outsiders, observing the weather-beaten local faces, the bardic speeches in Gaelic and the haunting music.

These films set in Scotland and Ireland purport to tell tales of Celtic resistance and McArthur identifies their ideological work as masking the nature of post-war realities from Scottish audiences: 'the disabilities of being tied to a post-imperial geriatric with undiminished ambition for maintaining great-power status' (49). But the films also seek to offer a version of national identity for English audiences. By refusing a contemporary national identity for Scots, the films work to present a national unity based on opposition to the modern world that the English can join by proxy. Local/modern dichotomies are fitted into a further pattern of difference that allows victory for the local and traditional to be presented not as a parochial and doomed struggle but as an expression of feeling which is comparable to that summoned up during the war. The assertion of Celtic identity, although it is drained of its political resonances, is important because, through its resonances with wartime nationalism, it makes possible the unlikely victory of the rural and the local.

English rural rebellions

We can see how important national identity is to the assertion of rural rebellion when we look at the difficulty of translating similar themes to English settings in three films of the early 1950s: *Green Grow the Rushes*, *Time, Gentlemen, Please* and *Conflict of Wings*. All three films were made by groups with left-wing aspirations, *Green Grow the Rushes* by ACT and the other two by Group Three. All try to ally stories of rural resistance to concepts of Englishness in the same way that the Celtic films use national sentiment to express local resistance. But the films that take these themes into the English countryside had more difficulty in asserting unambiguous support for traditional rural values. Without the sense of difference provided by Celtic national sentiment, it proved hard to create convincingly the traditions and the sense of the local on which the narrative depends.

Of the three films set in the English countryside, *Green Grow the Rushes* (1951) comes closest to the Celtic versions. The film opens with three officials, with umbrellas, briefcases and, on this occasion, trilbies rather than bowler hats, perhaps indicating their slightly lower status as members of a sub-commission from the Ministry of Agriculture and Fisheries. They have come to look at why the people refuse to recognise 'the supreme authority of the Ministry' and devote their land to growing food for the nation. With the coastguards and customs men, they form what one of the rebels calls an 'assorted rabble of bureaucrats' in trying to close down the local smuggling trade. The outsiders are thus heavily marked as bureaucrats and representatives of the national rather than local interests. The village asserts its historic independence from the nation through a charter of independence granted by Henry III, a charter that recognises the significance of local geography in its acknowledgement of how the people claimed their land from the sea. It is this local knowledge of the creeks and rivers that enables the locals to engage in smuggling, an activity that, as *Whisky Galore* illustrated, usefully combines the pursuit of pleasure with resistance to authority. The village organisation has the hierarchical but informal structure of the Celtic communities; Colonel Gill takes the lord of the manor role, but the defensive action is co-ordinated through a variety of characters, including a young sailor, Bob, the boat owner, the eccentric Captain Biddle and the journalist, Meg, who, as befits a locally born 'marsh girl', soon becomes an accomplice. Like the Scots and Irish, these English rebels use national identity to fight bureaucracy, but here they have to use the trappings of Englishness itself. Captain Biddle wears a bowler-hat, as if in subversive demonstration of his own authority, and he knows how to use his shipping law as pedantically as a bureaucrat; the official procedures of the charter's petty sessions are as laborious as any devised by Whitehall, although the villagers are able to use them in their favour. In the dénouement, however, the informal organisation of the people saves the day as they swarm through the public spaces of the village. The local men are called together to Biddle's boat to drink away the evidence of smuggling and the crowds at the pageant celebrating Charter Day act instinctively to ensure that the officials are thoroughly thwarted. 'These people don't deserve to be governed,' announces one of the ministry officials as the sub-commission retreats, defeated.

But if the narrative follows a similar pattern to *Whisky Galore* and *Laxdale Hall*, *Green Grow the Rushes* lacks the resonances that might give a similar emotional credibility to its rebellion. The main problem is that, while the local myths and stereotypes used by the films set in Scotland and Ireland have an existence outside the films, Anderida Marsh's Charter Day is invented for this film, and Henry III is a king about whom no legends or national myths accrue. The early 1950s did see some attempts to mark the Festival of Britain and the Coronation with pageants of English history but, like them, the glee singing and medieval fancy dress at the Charter Day fair lack any sense of genuine engagement with a past that is still a factor in how the present might be lived. Without this foundation, the rebellion of the smugglers in *Green Grow the Rushes* remains a half-hearted fantasy. As the credits at the beginning suggest, 'Any resemblance to any living persons or actual events would be more than coincidence. It would be a miracle.'

Time, Gentlemen, Please, a year later in 1952, follows a similar narrative pattern to *Green Grow the Rushes* but has interesting differences in the historical references it is calling on. At first sight, it would seem that the film is drawing on the paradigms outlined above. The rural village of Little Hayhoe is to be visited by a government representative, in this case the prime minister himself, and he is preceded by a ministerial envoy who requires of the pub landlord 'a large pale sherry' and 'the best room'. The village is picturesque with its ancient church, guildhall and almshouses and is populated by a number of ancient characters who flock to the pub and the square when informed on the village grapevine of important events such as the possibility of free beer. The resistance is led by an 'Irish rebel', Dan Dance, a tramp who refuses the regime of work and who likes to be free, sleeping under stars and hearing the birds in the early morning. He is punished by being confined ('it's like shutting you in a cage,' his grand-daughter protests) but, with the help of a new vicar (who is also Irish) and the rest of the community, he continually evades and subverts his punishment.

But the organisation of these now familiar elements is rather different in *Time, Gentlemen, Please*. The ancient village is, in fact, linked to modernity. The prime minister is visiting because a new factory has given the village the highest employment rate in the country; as the newsreel voice-over puts it, 'once a sleepy rural retreat, now a hive of industry.' And the restrictions that Dan fights against are those imposed not by officialdom from outside but by the leaders of the village – the lord of the manor, the old vicar, the landlord and the leading spinster – who act as the local councillors, magistrates and general keepers of law and order. Here, the hierarchical structures are not supported by the looser, less formal social interaction that unites the village in other rural films; the villagers resent those who govern them and pelt Sir Digby, the council leader, with eggs and fruit when the opportunity arises. Nor is liberty to be found, as it is in *Green Grow the Rushes*, in ancient laws and customs. Dan's confinement is in the 400-year-old almshouse, and the rules that restrict him – a 9p.m. curfew, a bath once a day, poor food and a hard bed – are imposed by the will of the sixteenth-century founder, whose malevolent picture looks down on Dan as he sleeps. Moreover, it emerges that the ancient rules have been exploited by the members of the council, who are using the funds improperly to restore the ancient buildings of the village which they just happen to own – the manor house, the church, the weaving barn.

Dan and the new vicar turn the rules to Dan's financial advantage ('You Irishmen with your odd ideas of right and wrong,' complains Sir Digby), and the resolution of *Time, Gentlemen, Please* makes it clear that this is a rural rebellion in alliance with modernity rather than against it. This involves an alliance between Dan's generous democratic instincts and the work and prosperity offered by the modern factory. Mr Spinks, the owner of the factory, who has been patronised and looked down on by the local dignitaries, suggests to Dan that they unite to 'kick this lot out'. They stand in the council elections and, supported by the people and with the help of a group of local tramps, they sweep the board on election night. Outside the guildhall, the crowds in the square celebrate both Dance's victory and Sir Digby's ignominious tally of one vote. Dan and the vicar have already agreed that the money from the almshouse should be put to a 'use more in keeping with the times', and on the night of his election Dan deliberately breaks his curfew rules and promises that the 'money will go somewhere more useful' – the almshouse will be turned into a day nursery for workers at the factory. But Dance and the factory owner both have to compromise to achieve this unifying victory. Dance has to get a job, but the factory regimes are adapted to give him one that suits his desire to sleep all day – that of mattress tester. The prime minister visits the village, and rural Little Hayhoe is clearly and productively established as part of the modern state. Like *Green Grow the Rushes, Time, Gentlemen, Please* has a strong air of fantasy and whimsy. But its references to an idea of Englishness based on medieval charters, local knowledge of the land and successful rebellion against state bureaucracy disguise its attempts to use a more contemporary rhetoric. In its ending, the film draws on more recent references to the post-war election of 1945 and the promise of social change created by people working with a modern and reformed government rather than against a bumbling and petty-minded one. In this, *Time, Gentlemen, Please* is a rare example, almost despite itself, of the possibility of harmonising local aims with those of the contemporary state rather than to local geography and history.

The final film of rural England to be considered, *Conflict of Wings* (1954), also pays sympathetic attention to the demands of modernity but returns for its resolution to the local legends and natural landscapes that are a feature of the Celtic films. The conflict of the title refers to this, directly setting the wings of the seagulls against those of the planes of the RAF, which needs to use the area for practice low-level bombing flights. Although the film does feature bureaucrats from the Ministry of Land Acquisition, the main outsiders are the representatives of the RAF, whose arguments are given more than usually sympathetic weight. Their main representative, Captain Bill Morris, is in love with a local girl, Sally, and tries to describe to her the excitement and the importance of flying. He links it to 'man's gradual mastery of the land, sea, now the air ... getting closer to something.' Bill thus links flying to the future: 'I want progress,' he tells Sally, 'and you ...' His visions of tomorrow are backed up by the arguments of his squadron leader, who emphasises that local needs must give way to the nation's global responsibilities. Patriotism means 'seeing that your country is safe and prosperous,' he tells one of the leaders of the resistance to RAF plans. 'Sometimes we haven't as much time as we think.' At the end of the film, when it is clear that the RAF will have to move its practice range elsewhere, he confirms that they are in training to go to Malaya: 'now we have to move to another range and someone else will have to wait too.'

Opposition to the RAF is led by Sally and Harry, a local character who gets drunk on Thursdays as a protest against his 'paltry, cheese-paring' state pension: 'I swallows it all down to blast their eyes.' They are supported by a mixed group of villagers, including the landlord of the pub and the eel catcher. The resistance is based on two themes. First, there is a reference to the past and to the notion that the land's association with the past should protect it in the present. Sally argues that the land in dispute is 'a world of its own with all sorts of tales and legends about it.' In particular, she tells Bill about the respect the local people have for the Island of Children, where, legend has it, the Romans buried their dead children. Associated with this myth-making are a variety of devices to protect the land as sacred ground – at various points the villagers try to prove that Henry VIII granted the fishing rights to local fishermen and hence to the eel catcher, that the land belongs to the Church and cannot be put to secular use and that it is a protected bird sanctuary. Such arguments, which are comparable to the use of the medieval charter in *Green Grow the Rushes* and the almshouse legacies in *Time, Gentlemen, Please*, are, in *Conflict of Wings*, linked more firmly to the workings of nature. The old legend of the Island of Children reaches into the present, making a link through the timelessness of the natural world and the local belief that the birds represent the souls of the lost children. The first RAF run over the disputed site is called off when Sally's favourite seagull flies into the squadron leader's windscreen.[2]

The second mode of resistance is the guerrilla attack on modernity through the same kind of popular local action that we have seen in other films. At a mass meeting, the local people decide to take their boats on to the disputed waterways and defend them by occupying the space. The RAF's modern methods of communication do not detect this activity. The 'place is absolutely deserted,' reports the radio operator at the site, 'I feel like Robinson Crusoe,' while the camera reveals the flotilla of small boats sliding through the inlets. One of the boats damages the telephone lines, leaving the squadron leader, in the clouds, with no information about what is happening on the site. An accident is only averted when the villagers are sighted from the air, waving red kerchiefs, and orders are given not to fire. Both sides are thwarted and depressed. The commanding officer is furious about his men's safety, while Sally cries and Harry retreats, remarking 'we might as well go home.'

This ambiguous resolution is a far cry from the triumphant expulsion of outsiders in, for instance, *Whisky Galore* and *Happy Ever After*. The RAF is driven away from this locality but it must find a place elsewhere. In an irony the film does not acknowledge, it is the bureaucrats who triumph with the establishment of an inquiry. The film tries to paper over the cracks through the romance between Sally and Bill. The final words of dialogue indicate the difficulty of resolving the problem:

Sally: You don't gain anything without losing something.... We had to do it.
Bill: So did we.
Sally: We were both right.
Sally then tries to break through this impasse by an appeal to national sentiment
Sally: Such a little island, isn't it?
Bill: You mean the Island of Children.
Sally: No. I was thinking of England.

A final shot of them kissing as both planes and birds fly overhead attempts a visual resolution, but this nationalist discourse undermines rather than supports Sally's position, even leaving aside the problem that England is not an island. The predicament occurs because associating modernity with the RAF makes it clear that the vision of England that Sally and Bill aspire to must include the national and international responsibilities of a modern state (hence the reference to Malaya). In an English context, denying modernity means denying national identity, importance and influence in the post-war world. Whereas the repulsion of outsiders or making them surrender to a different way of life contributes to the bringing together of local and national identity in the films set in Ireland and Scotland, in the English versions the outsiders are themselves English, and their defeat has a cost. *Green Grow the Rushes* resolves this by accepting the parochialism of the local and opting for the medieval rather than the modern; *Time, Gentlemen, Please* finds the outsiders in its own community and joins with the modern state through the local activity of ejecting them; *Conflict of Wings* cannot reconcile the local and national and reverts to nostalgia for the wartime imagery of the beleaguered island.

The resistant landscape

I have examined how these films work with a common set of themes and narrative structures in which the question of local, national and global loyalties in the modern world are inserted into narratives of resistance that draw on wartime references. The rural setting is crucial to this in that it associates the local with a sense of rootedness and natural order, which makes an opposition to the modern and the global seem natural rather than parochial. In addition, the portrayal of landscape is a significant selling point for the Celtic films and is often picked out as a source of pleasure by the critics. *Monthly Film Bulletin* praised *I Know where I'm Going* for its 'affectionate and sympathetic handling of the Highland setting' (December 1945: 147); *The Star* praised the 'wild beauty of scenery' in *Whisky Galore* (17 July 1949) and remarked of *The Oracle* that 'the scenery is lovely' (15 May 1953); *Geordie* was commended by *Picturegoer* for its 'fresh tang of heather' and the 'beautiful settings of the Highlands' (3 September 1955).

Despite the importance of the rural setting, the landscape is often treated as an attractive backdrop rather than integrated into the story. In *Laxdale Hall*, *The Oracle* and *Happy Ever After*, village life is set within a pleasant rural setting that is understood and controlled by the locals, if not by the outsiders, and that is represented, often through sets and backdrops, in a picturesque manner. *I Know where I'm Going* and *Whisky Galore* are the exceptions here; in the former, as Dilys Powell pointed out, 'landscape and seascape are handled as if they had personalities of their own' (*Sunday Times*: 18 November 1945), while the documentary approach of *Whisky Galore* presents a natural world that has a stubbornness, a physical presence that claims an existence separate from characters and narrative. Nevertheless, even in these films the forces of nature, so treacherous to the outsider, can be understood and to some extent controlled by those who live there. The achievement of *Whisky Galore*, in particular, is to create a sense of people drawing their skills and purpose from an understanding of what it means to live in that spectacular landscape. The visual organisation of nature (the light of dawn on the sea, the open windy skies, the whiteness of the sands) is linked to the activity of the islanders, who scud across the sea in their tiny boats or conceal their secrets (whether it be whisky or romance) in the caves and dunes of the shore. The community's victory comes from that understanding in a way that it does not elsewhere even in *The Maggie*. In the later film, Mactaggart is presented as a man who knows the local geography and understands the weather but in the end this serves little purpose – Mactaggart wins through a combination of cunning and pathos – and the visual beauty of the landscape that the puffer trundles through serves as a beautiful backdrop.

If the Celtic landscapes are not as wild as is sometimes supposed, the English settings are generally even tamer. In his discussion of the English pastoral tradition, Higson suggests that 'the nation was thus represented as a rural space, but its landscapes were also crucially populated and cultivated, not wild and sublime' (1997: 43). *A Canterbury Tale* and *Tawny Pipit* offered wartime versions of this pastoral landscape, and the films I have discussed here share their emphasis on the cultivated and controlled. *Conflict of Wings* draws on the pastoral tradition of the country as a place of peace and refuge and uses colour and camera movement, in a limited way, to establish the function of the landscape as a safe place in which to hide. In *Time, Gentlemen, Please*, the landscape helps to define the country/city contrast that underpins the narrative, but its aesthetic significance is relatively weak. Love of nature is one of Dan's distinguishing characteristics, and he tells his granddaughter that in the almshouse he will miss 'the stars and the birds in the early morning', but the visual representation of the landscape is set-bound and unimaginative. This tendency to use the setting as a pretty backdrop in rural narratives can be seen elsewhere in, for instance, Ealing's use of the green fields of *The Titfield Thunderbolt* or the beautiful Yorkshire setting in *Lease of Life*.

In the English films, then, the landscape tends to operate as a safe place, a conservative and nostalgic site for the opposition to modernity. However, I want to note that a rather different kind of English landscape can also be found in films of the period, landscapes that are not 'populated and cultivated' and that suggest different meanings for the English countryside. Side by side with the pastoral strand runs a view of the countryside as a much less safe place. In such films, the landscape has a more ambiguous role, if not 'wild and sublime', at least more obdurate and unyielding. We can see a little of this in *Green Grow the Rushes*, where on occasion the location work carries a symbolic and aesthetic value that departs from the usual whimsy. Thus, at the film's opening, the three ministry men leave their car and stumble across the open fields as low camera angles emphasise their vulnerability to the open skies and wide fields that stretch before them. This is contrasted with the closed creeks of the marsh, which hide, beneath dark skies, the smuggled drink and the secret journeys of the locals. Here we get glimpses of the closed world of nature, which is protective but also dangerous; much more than just a setting for action, its workings impinge on those who live there. But the film backs away from this view of the natural world, and rural order is restored by returning to the fake pageantry of the Charter Day fair.

This use of landscape as a dangerous site of ambiguity and opposition runs like a thin thread through fifties cinema, in films that do not otherwise have rural rebellion as their central motif. Two thrillers, operating in very different generic modes from the films we have been discussing so far, offer examples of this. In *The Clouded Yellow* (1950), Somers, an off-duty secret service man played by Trevor Howard, takes up with Sophie (Jean Simmons), a young girl who is falsely accused of murder. She lives in an idyllic rural retreat in a pastoral landscape that is sunlit, orderly and peaceful; but it is, as Somers identifies, 'a trap' from which she must escape. The pair flee to Newcastle and thence to Liverpool, but on their way they are tracked across the Lake District by the police. The film thus moves from the traditional hiding places of the urban streets to the bleak landscape of the uncultivated fells, where the rocks and vegetation both shelter and expose them. The fugitives try to adapt themselves to the landscape by working with the terrain as they hide in the bracken and the caves in the rock, and their efforts to become part of the landscape contrast with the mechanistic attempts by the police to impose order on it; a helicopter surveys the land from the air, while the police walk in lines across the moor so as to cover every inch of the ground and create invisible lines of communication through their radios. The physical harshness of the landscape is emphasised – Somers is injured and captured as he tries to jump a stream – but so is its beauty in long shots that set the tiny figures of police and fugitives into the sweep of the fells. It is in this exposed and bleak place that Sophie recovers her memory, making the psychological breakthrough that will allow her to prove her innocence. The film uses the landscape metaphorically to express the resistance of the protagonists to the state and the stripping away of confusion and deceit in Sophie's mind but the physical presence of the terrain itself is also strongly expressed.

This double use of metaphor and physical presence is also a feature of the use of landscape in *The Long Memory* (1953). The hero of the film, Davidson, is, like Sophie, a victim of injustice and has been made an outsider by the forces of the law. He, though, has actually served a term of imprisonment for a murder that he did not commit and from which he emerges determined on revenge. Homeless and friendless, he retreats to the coast of Kent and lives in the cabin of an abandoned barge on the beach. Excluded from society by his 'crime', Davidson seeks isolation in order to avenge himself on those he blames for his imprisonment. The landscape expresses both his isolation and his despair. The vast spaces of the sky dominate the image, and the beaches and marshland are empty and flat. This is not a conventionally beautiful landscape in which nature offers a comfortable retreat. Human attempts to populate and cultivate it have failed; the vegetation is scrappy and windblown, the beach is littered with the hulks of abandoned boats, and the few residents live in broken-down shacks and railway carriages. The landscape makes those who try to live in it seem small and insignificant; the film is punctuated by shots in which characters walking along the slightly raised path between sea and land are pushed to the side of the screen, dwarfed by the terrain. Metaphorically, the bleak landscape represents Davidson's isolation from humanity and it is only in that setting that he can be restored. But this is more than a metaphorical landscape. While Davidson is capable of redemption, the windswept bleakness of the terrain underlines that the land itself remains obdurate and untransformed.[3]

Films like *The Clouded Yellow* and *The Long Memory* stand out because they use the English rural landscape expressively and transform it into a bleak and hostile environment, not just a space for resistance but a form of resistance itself. In most films of the mid-fifties, the countryside acts as a backdrop for car rallies, country house hideaways and state institutions. This expressive use of the rural setting goes underground. Perhaps that is why the use of landscape was celebrated as one of the distinctive features of a number of films of the New Wave in which the trip to the country was a frequent narrative sequence, allowing a respite from urban life and the opportunity for reflection. And if that use of the countryside rapidly became a convention, it is worth noting that the obduracy and resistance of the landscape still finds expression, as it had done ten years before, in the harsh moors and bleak fields of thrillers and B films such as *Hell is a City* (1960) and *Serena* (1962).

4 Resisting modernity
Comedies of bureaucracy and expertise

Between the local communities and the international systems discussed in the last chapter there intervenes the national state. One of Harry Hopkins' key signifiers of modernity was an increase in state intervention, initially sanctioned by war but continuing in peacetime and accepted as a necessary and legitimate activity by the post-war Labour government and the Conservative governments of the 1950s. It was through the state that the modern citizen could be created and controlled and it was through the state's bureaucracy that the excessively dynamic forces of modernity could be channelled. The state was entrusted not only with the welfare of its citizens – the cradle-to-grave protection of the welfare state – but also with harnessing the expertise of the scientists, architects, designers and planners who would develop the modern Britain. In the process, the state needed its own experts, civil servants and government officials of all kinds, some of them in newly developing professions, such as sociologists, psychologists and social workers. For Hopkins, one contradictory feature of the modern world is that the streamlined, driving force of science and technology is paralleled by and requires an increase in the bureaucracy and paperwork associated with planning. The emphasis could no longer be on the individual but only on the 'complementing specialisms' (Hopkins: 160) that had to be fitted together like cogs in a wheel and that needed systems to enable them to function. This emphasis on impersonal bureaucracy was a feature not only of the state and its own civil service but also of the institutions associated with it – the police, the education system and the law, for instance.

The traditional institutions associated with the state not only had to be remodelled for the new order but also had to be staffed differently. As we have seen, Hopkins sees the expert taking over from the generalist, the manager from the professional. Such a change was summed up in the term 'meritocracy', a key word used to describe the process whereby 'the old mandarinate was increasingly out-flanked' (174) by those receiving a modern education in science and technology which was markedly different from the traditional liberal arts education provided by Oxbridge and the public schools. Hopkins pictures the sons of manual workers coming through redbrick universities and the 'provincial "Tech"', working as engineers and technologists, 'shamelessly talking in miscellaneous accents their unintelligible shop' (159). If Hopkins felt some qualms at the takeover of power by 'a competitively selected elite who managed', he had no sympathy for those they were replacing, the 'hereditary class who ruled' (175). Sociologist Michael Young's satire *The Rise of the Meritocracy* also expressed doubts about the outcome of the change but its basic assumption was that a 'fundamental change' was taking place whereby 'the talented have been given the opportunity to rise to the level which accords with their capacities' (14). The classless society was envisaged as being one in which merit was the criterion for getting on.

This emphasis on institutions and bureaucracy comes as no surprise to viewers of British film comedies of the 1950s, in which the civil service, hospitals, army barracks, schools, universities, prisons and ships, both naval and commercial, provide just some of the settings for comedy. Sarah Street has suggested that comedies of the late 1940s and 1950s derived their impetus from 'fears about state power and a mistrust of bureaucratic structures in general' and that the institutions that are critiqued in the films 'serve as microcosms of British society as a whole' (64). In this chapter, I examine in more detail what is at stake here and reflect on the way in which mainstream comedies that lampooned the traditional classes and hierarchies also served to support them in the face of modernising threats to blow them away. In this sense, I want to suggest that these comedies have the curious quality of being both stultifying and rebellious and that, when faced with a conflict between the traditional and the modern, they revert to the traditional in a way that blocks off the challenges and risks that comedy can present. The first section of this chapter looks at how the role of the state is handled in films that use the device of a fantasy state for its comic potential. In the second section, I look at the role of the expert and at the opposition between systems that depend on trust in expertise and those that are underpinned by tradition. The final section looks at how comedies about criminals provide an unlikely opportunity for issues of class, hierarchy and merit to surface.[1]

The fantasy state

One of Ealing's most famous and definitive comedies, *Passport to Pimlico* (1949), uses fantasy to imagine what it would be like to live outside the post-war British state. As Barr analyses the film, the apparent desire to be freed from the burden of post-war rationing and restrictions is replaced by 'a more potent dream ... of a return to wartime solidarity' (1977: 104). The people of Pimlico become the people of a misplaced bit of Burgundy – foreigners in their own land – so that opposition to the British state is no longer a question of grumbling but is legally demanded. The film's major fantasy is, as Barr indicates, a return to wartime unity, which of course involves an increase in restriction. But this fantasy is predicated on another: that the state can be restored to its wartime role of representing and protecting the people rather than bullying them. *Passport to Pimlico* mourns the loss of Ealing's wartime myth that the people were the state and offers a reluctant recognition, through its use of fantasy, that this equation can no longer be assumed. Although in the end reconciled to and welcomed back by the state, Pimlico persists as a 'romantic vision of a community that can stay safe and happy and cut off' (107).

Passport to Pimlico tends to be criticised for the cosiness of this fantasy, for its nostalgic celebration of wartime unity, which is no longer appropriate even in 1949 and certainly makes no sense in Ealing's later comedies of the 1950s. But perhaps the film's complex formulations of what is at stake are better appreciated when we look at some of the fantasy states in films that followed it. Unlike *Passport to Pimlico*, these state fantasies are set outside Britain but like it they can tell us much about how the British state itself is thought about and represented. The fantasy state is not confined to comedy, although significantly it always tends to lead to comic scenarios. We will note some of its features in two 1950 comedy thrillers, *State Secret* and *Highly Dangerous* and in *King's Rhapsody* (1955) a romantic musical produced and directed by Herbert Wilcox for his wife, Anna Neagle. Generally though, the device is used in comedies either as the mainspring for the plot (*Penny Princess* (1952), *The Mouse that Roared* (1959) and its sequel *The Mouse on the Moon* (1963)), or as an important site for action (*You Know What Sailors Are* (1954) and *Carlton-Browne of the FO* (1958)). It is this group of films that will be looked at in this section.

Passport to Pimlico is a fantasy that gets much of its effect, as Barr suggests, from the realist detail that it invested in its imaginary state. In part, this was because the film's location was still the familiar streets of Ealing's London. The later films move to imaginary settings – Vosnia, Grand Fenwick, Agraria – which are not Britain and they are therefore required to imagine the trappings and regimes of a state in a rather different way, opening up questions about the desirable and not so desirable characteristics of a fantasy state. One model on offer for thinking through these possibilities was the communist-controlled states of Eastern Europe. This is the model used in the two thrillers, *State Secret* and *Highly Dangerous*. In both these films, a Westerner enters a tightly controlled state in Eastern Europe, and the plots centre on scenes of chase, hiding and evasion until a successful exit is achieved. In *Highly Dangerous*, Frances (Margaret Lockwood) is sent to a tightly controlled Eastern European country by the British authorities as a spy to find out about a dangerous scientific experiment. Her contact is murdered but Frances, inspired by the fictional exploits of a spy in a radio serial and helped by an American journalist, Bill, manages to enter the tightly guarded laboratories and escape with the evidence. In *State Secret*, the hero John Marlowe (Douglas Fairbanks Jr) enters Vosnia freely; invited for his medical expertise, he decides to go because 'here are a people who open a window, lift a corner of the curtain and let in a breath of fresh air. I don't feel like slamming a window in their faces.' But once Marlowe recognises the patient as the dictator who runs the country, his own life is put at risk and he spends the rest of the film evading the state authorities until he can escape with Lisa, the woman who has helped him.

Although *State Secret* offers a more detailed account in comparison with the deliberate comic-book style of *Highly Dangerous*, the films offer a similar version of the state. In both films, the state is represented as all-powerful and pervasive. Frances meets the chief of police on her train journey into the country, and from then on he or his representative shadows her, turning up at the checkpoint that guards the laboratories, or, apparently off-duty, when she lunches in a cafe. When he captures her, this pervasive power is emphasised by his use of a truth drug; it is 'more efficient', he tells her, because with it he 'can search into the hidden parts of the mind'. In *State Secret*, this aspiration to total control is represented by the colonel and, although Marlowe temporarily escapes from him, loudspeakers and radio broadcasts pursue him, and soldiers and police roam the streets looking for him. Even when Marlowe thinks that he and Lisa have crossed the border, a poster of the dictator looks down at him, emphasising that he cannot escape. In a cynical way, the state manoeuvres to control the population, to keep secrets and to control information so as to produce what the Colonel calls 'spontaneous, mass demonstration[s] of loyalty'. The state is bureaucratic. Papers and passports are checked continually, and is movement curtailed and proscribed. The state is inhuman; its representatives have what the chief of police describes as 'inexhaustible patience' and, as the colonel tells Marlowe, his life counts for little when set against 'the survival of the whole state'.

All of this draws on Cold War rhetoric and, in the case of *Highly Dangerous* in particular, apparently draws sharp distinctions between the corrupt and dangerous chief of police and the good intentions of the British government. But when Frances returns successfully from her mission, she comes up against the red tape of quarantine regulations and food rationing and the censorship of the British officials, who are insistent that Bill cannot send a scoop story of their escapades to his newspaper editor. All this is played for humour of course; nevertheless the re-entry into British society is marked by some of the same problems with the state that Frances experienced in Eastern Europe. The more cynical *State Secret* begins by raising the question of comparisons in a parody of the usual disclaimers: 'you won't find the state of Vosnia on any map,' the opening credits tell the audience, 'Still let's face it – Vosnia exists and any resemblance it may have to any other state, past or present, living or dead, is hardly coincidental.' While the resemblance to Eastern Europe is clear, the film's tone suggests that the fixing of the democratic process, the manipulated crowds and the devious politicians may offer some comparisons with a state closer to home.

The more benign fantasy states of the comedies tend to be set in a Ruritarian middle Europe, although Agraria (*You Know What Sailors Are*) has distinctly Turkish elements. They tend to be rural enclaves, protected by mountains, in which a peasant culture supports a traditional way of life. Lampidorra (*Penny Princess*) and Grand Fenwick (the two *Mouse* films) are tiny states in the Alps, while Laurentia (*King's Rhapsody*) is a mountainous state further east. Gaillardia (*Carlton-Browne of the FO*) is exceptional in that it is an island, but its old king sports the uniform favoured by cinematic middle European generals, all epaulettes and tassels. These states take some elements from the Eastern European model. Their rulers tend to have dictatorial powers, and the crowds that frequently line the streets and squares are easily manipulated. Cheering crowds generally greet the ruler's appearance on a balcony and, while there is a distinct folk element to the dancing and singing that accompanies such displays, it is also clear that on such occasions the crowds can be swayed by more devious politicians. In *King's Rhapsody*, for instance, the crowds gather outside the palace to sing a welcome at King Richard's return from exile but are quickly turned against him, reappearing outside the palace to threaten him with violence. *Carlton-Browne of the FO* takes the Eastern European parallels the furthest when the island is divided (by a white line rather than a wall) and subject to 'spontaneous' uprisings. These states then have a populist rhetoric but the people can be circumvented or exploited if the government seeks to do so.

In other ways, though, the point of reference for these fantasy states is a particular version of the British state. Thus, the rulers tend to be members of a royal family whose claim to govern is based on tradition and inheritance. The Duchess of Grand Fenwick is descended from an English knight and even Lindy, the American girl who inherits the throne in *Penny Princess*, is given the trappings of royalty – a charter, a throne, red robes and a title – and the band plays 'Rule Britannia' as a form of celebration. The ruler is generally advised by some form of council or parliament, which is meant to represent the people and which gets to debate problems, although voting is rare. This is partly because government is generally by collusion between ruler and council and/or between the different parties in the council. In *King's Rhapsody*, this works against the king as the prime minister and the queen mother are in alliance to remove him. Similarly, on Gaillardia, the prime minister, supported by two other ministers, who just happen to be his cousin and brother-in-law, plots against the new king, whom he regards as a dangerous modernising influence. In other cases, the arrangement works more harmoniously and the ruler is supported by the council. Thus, until Princess Lindy arrives, Lampidorra is ruled by a Council of Three – the blacksmith, the cobbler and the policeman – and they continue to advise her when she takes over. In Grand Fenwick, a form of parliament with opposing sides exists but in *The Mouse that Roared*, the 'hereditary' prime minister is supported throughout by the opposition leader of the Party of the Common Man (played as a parody of Ernest Bevin), who speaks against the establishment but works to sustain it. These comedies then offer a version of the state that parodies the British system of parliamentary democracy within a tradition of royal inheritance. But the state, even in these benign formulations, is marked by a lack of democracy and collusion between the various elements of the establishment, which removes the state from the people.

If royalty and government provide one form of reference to Britain, the other main reference point is invoked by the wartime rhetoric of defiance by a small state facing up to the Great Powers. This is a complex scenario, since Britain features in a number of these films as a great power, but it is also possible to see Britain figured in the small fantasy states that are trying to rescue themselves from financial disaster and to avoid being caught up in the Cold War. Financial bankruptcy, particularly in the face of American wealth, is a feature of *Penny Princess* and the *Mouse* films, and the small states have to resort to unlikely measures to survive. The ideal for the fantasy state is that described by the voice-over in *Penny Princess*: 'no taxes, no quotas, no tariffs, no forms to fill in' – but that leads to bankruptcy. One way out is to seek American aid: in *Penny Princess*, the Lampidorrans sell their country to an American businessman, while in *The Mouse that Roared* Grand Fenwick declares war on the USA in an attempt to get the goods and money that, the prime minister points out, America pours on its defeated enemies. But neither ploy works and the vulnerability of the small state is made more acute by the rivalry of the Cold War, which is systematically parodied. In *You Know What Sailors Are*, the president wants a knockout weapon so that he can win the arms race with a neighbouring state, the Russian-sounding Smorsnigog. In *The Mouse on the Moon*, Grand Fenwick gets money for space research as part of a US attempt to outmanoeuvre the Russians. Both the *Mouse* films have scenes in which representatives from the Great Powers try to win Grand Fenwick over to them, while *Carlton-Browne of the FO* features the Russians intervening at the United Nations with their notorious 'niet'.

The films thus offer a potentially anxious scenario in which some of the trappings of the state, particularly its bureaucracy, are mocked and the nation is beset by financial problems and vulnerable to both America and Russia. However, the resolution of these problems is through the use of traditional resources, so the technology of the modern world is treated as if it were reclaimable by a local, pre-industrial folk culture. Thus, in *Penny Princess*, Lampidorra's economy is saved when it turns to exporting the local cheese, laced with berries and known as 'the happy cheese'. When, in a parody of a contemporary preoccupation, this causes a trade war and exports are hit by the imposition of tariffs, the Lampidorrans successfully resort to their old methods of smuggling, a familiar way, as we saw in Chapter 3, of reasserting the local in the face of global attempts at control. The mad professor in *You Know What Sailors Are* successfully makes a rocket out of a pawnbroker's three balls and a pram in a laboratory that is so full of experimental clutter that he has to climb in through the window. In *The Mouse on the Moon*, Grand Fenwick enters the space race, with the help of American money, but the rocket is fuelled by the 'mysterious, explosive, unstabilising wine of Grand Fenwick' and, in its ramshackle state, cluttered with strings of onions and a chicken, the rocket is more like a peasant's home than a streamlined example of modern technology. *The Mouse that Roared* offers the most consistent working through of this determination that modernity can be outflanked by the traditional. War having been declared on the United States, in the hope of reaping the rewards of defeat, the small army, in its medieval chain mail and armed with longbows, crosses the Atlantic. Unknowingly, they arrive in a New York which is deserted because of a national air raid drill in connection with work on a new and powerful bomb.

The medieval army is thus unopposed and by accident manages to capture the bomb and its inventor and take them back to Grand Fenwick. Thus, the small state both 'defeats' the prime modern state and seizes the main symbol of the Cold War. Inevitably, though, in the dungeons of Grand Fenwick, the bomb is found to be a dud, thus suggesting that modern technology and the politics of the Cold War are based on a fraud.

Trust, expertise and tradition

The fantasy state in these comedies presents a version of the state that has some of the elements of the modern British state in its bureaucracy, its semi-democratic arrangements and its obsession with trade and foreign relations. The effect of the comedy is to reduce this powerful state to a small medieval kingdom in which muddle and good will triumph. Something similar occurs in the handling of other aspects of modernity in fifties comedies. We saw in Chapter 2 how Hopkins' vision of modern Britain in the 1950s was inextricably linked to the rise of the scientific and technological expert and how Giddens, for instance, argues that the organisation of modern society requires trust in 'systems of technical accomplishment or professional expertise' (27). Such systems require trust in 'the authenticity of the expert knowledge' (28), which cannot be checked by those depending on it. This trust in expert knowledge is contrasted with the trust in tradition that had sustained earlier societies. This question of trust in the expert is at the heart of many comedies of the period and the relationship between the new expert, the traditional professional and the ordinary man is the source of much humour.

It is possible to find the white-coated scientists of Hopkins' modern polemic in fifties films, and in science fiction films or contemporary thrillers such as *80,000 Suspects* (1963) they are treated with ambivalent respect. While, as Durgnant points out, they are frequently blamed for what goes wrong, they clearly represent a pursuit of knowledge and a sense of the future that is recognisably within a modern framework. However, the scientists and technologists of the mainstream comedies work in a different way: 'You're always exploding things,' comments the prime minister of Grand Fenwick to his resident scientist; and rockets, moon shots, destructive weapons and explosions feature in many comedies, often providing an absurd or explosive ending (*Bulldog Breed*, *Watch Your Stern*) or a comic character study (David Kossof in the *Mouse* films, Robert Morley in *Go to Blazes*). Even when played relatively straight and in the most modern of contexts, as when Kenneth More plays Webb, the planning engineer in *Next to No Time* (1958), the comic scientist draws on a number of features that form a recognisable stereotype based on a particular view of science. The scientist is generally male, although an eccentric female like Hattie Jacques (*Watch your Stern*) may take on the role. He is totally absorbed by knowledge, which consumes him and causes explosions of enthusiasm comparable to the unstable experiments he works on. This makes it so difficult for him to live in the ordinary world that he forgets to eat (*The Mouse that Roared*) and dresses haphazardly. It also means that because the scientist is absorbed in his work he is free of other commitments, either to the state (the professor swaps national allegiances in *The Mouse that Roared*), big business (*Next to No Time*) or even the pursuit of crime; 'fire-raising is an art, a science,' the professor in *Go to Blazes* explains to the criminals who want to use fire-fighting as a cover, and he is shocked that they want to 'extinguish the sacred flame'. The scientist sometimes tries to explain what he does, but his work is so advanced that it cannot be understood by either the audience in the film or that watching: Vincent falls asleep listening to the professor's explanations in *The Mouse on the Moon*, while Webb in *Next to No Time* is reduced to arm waving and hand gestures when he tries to explain his discoveries. Not only is their knowledge obscure, it also frequently seems to fly in the face of common sense and to work in the opposite way to what might be expected. This is reinforced by the fact that discoveries, although supported by a battery of plans, formulae and diagrams, often seem to be made by accident. The plans are interchangeable (*Watch your Stern*), and the experiments themselves are chaotic and unstable, characterised by bubbling test tubes, coiled springs and red balls in molecular models. The equipment looks like, and frequently is, everyday objects, reconfigured by the scientist's eccentric vision of the world. Webb in *Next to No Time* is forced to recreate his model on a luxury liner and so builds it from champagne bottles, cigars, table tennis bats, light bulbs and bedsprings; the professor in *The Mouse on the Moon* uses shower heads and old clocks to build his rocket.

All this is drawing on stereotypes about the mad scientist, well established in Hollywood and elsewhere, but in this context they have a particular inflection. The scientist does win some trust, and he may indeed, as in the *Mouse* films and *Next to No Time*, act as the moral centre of the film. But he does so only insofar as his allegiance is to his work rather than to big business or the state, and the trust depends on his personality rather than his knowledge. Through these figures, science is presented as something that is potentially dangerous but is actually rather ineffective, and indeed the less 'science' there is, the more effective the outcome is likely to be. This is made explicit in *The Mouse on the Moon* when Grand Fenwick wins the space race because the professor refuses to behave like a proper astronaut. There is no countdown because 'we just go', the rocket travels slowly because 'we are in no hurry' and they are first by accident because a chicken sits on the accelerator handle; 'how nice and how modern too,' the professor remarks of the food in tubes being eaten on the moon by rival astronauts from the USA and USSR and sighs contentedly as he tucks into his own freshly cooked fried chicken. The clinical, impersonal nature of science, stressed by Hopkins, is replaced by science as a more traditional form of magic that is unpredictable, chaotic and human. The limited trust placed in it is not trust in expert systems but on more traditional modes of relying on a person.

The transformation of the scientist into a magician is effective when the plot presents him as an individual, working on his own. It is much more problematic, even in the comedies, when science is indeed presented as part of a system. *The Man in the Moon* (1960) presents science as part of a government institution (NARSTI) and as a system of knowledge in which technology supports a regime based on experiment and data. Into this strolls the common man, William Blood, played by Kenneth More, who already knows about the ways of science through being a guinea pig for the Common Cold Research Centre. Blood is taken on by a trio of scientists to be the first man on the Moon, paving the way for the better-qualified astronauts, who cannot be risked on a first run (British sensibilities not allowing the more usual dog or monkey to be used for these purposes). Blood goes through a series of experiments and tests, which he passes successfully, despite the efforts to sabotage him by the other aspiring astronauts. A 'textbook launching' is hailed by the scientists as a great success and they are all set to send up the others until Blood returns to the launch station to inform them that he had in fact landed a few miles away in the Australian outback. Blood tells the scientists, 'It's back to the old drawing board,' while he returns to more failed experiments, this time in family planning.

The institutionalisation of science is made clear in *The Man in the Moon*. The research institute is housed in large, modern buildings with plate glass windows, open staircases and contemporary furniture. Banks of equipment, rows of instruments and automated systems support the experiments, and the launch is conducted with the full panoply of the countdown that the professor eschews in

Figure 4.1 Kenneth More in *The Man in the Moon* (J. Arthur Rank, 1960).
Courtesy of the Kobal Collection.

The Mouse on the Moon. The three main scientists – Professor Davidson, Dr Stephens and Dr Wilmott – have some of the characteristics of those in the other comedies. Professor Davidson dresses eccentrically with scarf and waistcoat, Dr Wilmott refuses to pay attention to conversations that do not interest him, and the trio are so remote from the everyday world that they do not know who Billy Butlin is, despite his national celebrity as a holiday camp entrepreneur. But it is also clear that they are part of a government bureaucracy, funded by public money and eager to avoid questions in Parliament; the leader of the team, Dr Stephens, is a manager as well as a scientist, dressing in smart suits and concerned about finances.

The film emphasises throughout that these modern scientists see themselves as more knowledgeable and more rational than ordinary people and that they prefer others to remain ignorant. At the Common Cold Research Centre, one of the doctors is thoroughly alarmed at the thought of patients taking their own temperatures. The scientists at NARSTI pride themselves on being outside normal life and treat other humans as further elements in the experiments. As Dr Wilmott says of his astronauts: 'there's no need to confuse them with the exact literal truth.' When one of the trained astronauts becomes jealous of Blood, the scientists decide to treat him with 'psychological detergent' to leave his brain 'washed whitest of all'. And in a perfectly pleasant way, the trio's work is underpinned by the different value placed on the elite, who have knowledge, and ordinary people, who do not; Blood, as Dr Wilmott puts it, is 'an ordinary chap … Ordinary in the sense that he's expendable.'

Blood, who carries ordinariness to extremes, uses it as a weapon against this system of expertise. Kenneth More's star image exuded a cheerful breeziness, 'redolent of robust good health and exuding self-confidence' (Spicer 1997: 151), which is drawn on extensively here. From the beginning of the film, his determinedly cheerful refusal to act in a useful way, by catching a cold, upsets the scientists; the superintendent of the Common Cold Research Centre tells him to 'take your health elsewhere … it's a subversive influence.' Although for plot purposes his immune system is represented as exceptional, he gets through the experiments as if he were 'an ordinary chap' on holiday. He takes his thermos, picnic and *Daily Sketch* into the temperature-testing chambers and passes off the rise in heat as if it were generated by the picture of a pretty girl ('What a scorcher'); he treats the G-force testing machine as if it were a fairground ride ('better value than the big dipper') and approaches the impact-testing equipment with the remark, 'I always like playing on trains.'

In the final scenes of the launch, it would seem that Blood has been taken over by the expert systems of the scientists. They emphasise the importance of regime and order: 'stick to the procedure and nothing can go wrong,' 'remember the drill.' Blood is dehumanised in his space suit and helmet; his face is blank and his limbs stiff as he is transported by automated pavements and cranes to the rocket entrance. Thinking that he has landed on the Moon, Dr Stephens tells Blood what he *must* be seeing – the key features of the lunar landscape – not paying sufficient attention to his rather pragmatic comments about the persistence of gravity and the heat; by definition, the scientists' expertise is beyond checking by the ordinary man. The scientists rely on their own instruments and therefore look to Blood for emotion rather than knowledge: 'your feelings, William?' Stephens asks him when they think he is on the Moon. To fulfil the demands of the plot, Blood could presumably have radioed back with the information that he is still on Earth but the film needs the physical disruption caused when Blood returns to the space centre, crashing through the gates, setting off the alarm systems and breaching the security cordon. 'Nobody outside this room has authority to interrupt,' protest Dr Stephens, but Blood's return with knowledge to prevent scientific disaster embodies the return of the ordinary man to the controls.

The Man in the Moon is one of many films of the period that appear to offer 'a critique of British institutions' (Street: 64), but it is unusual in that the institution is a modern one. More usual is a structure in which a traditional institution, what we might call, following Giddens, a system of tradition rather than expertise and knowledge, is entered by someone who is at the very least ignorant of its traditions and may indeed have a plan for change. Traditional institutions are the focus, as Street (70) points out, of two popular series, the *Doctor* series and the later *Carry On* films, and of a number of popular comedies made by the Boulting brothers. Such comedies take as their basis the clash between the traditional professions (medicine, the law, education, for instance) and those who are subject to them (patients, litigants, pupils), but they often use a hero who is seeking to enter the profession as an intermediary between them and as a point of identification for the audience. Education, which was one of the key modernising instruments in the rhetoric of meritocracy, provides an interesting example of how modernity and tradition are worked through in the context of systems of tradition.

Bachelor of Hearts (1958) takes these issues head on and resolves them in a conservative way, which seems particularly significant given the strong liberal leanings of the German-born director, Wolf Rilla. Filmed in colour, *Bachelor of Hearts* is a Rank comedy in the style of *Genevieve* and *Doctor in the House*. It tells the story of Wolf, a German student who comes to study at Cambridge. The early parts of the film deal with Wolf's difficulties in dealing with traditional Cambridge manners, manners that must have seemed just as strange to the audience and that are held up for mockery. He is confused over how to address the porter, wrongly calling him 'sir' and trying to shake his hand; the college necessities list tells him that he should have a set of 'one dozen sherry glasses'; he is puzzled by the 'bedder's' offer to make his bed and scathing about the old furniture in his rooms – 'perhaps here Oliver Cromwell has just moved in.' Gradually, Wolf settles down. He gains a girlfriend, Ann, who becomes his guide, translating terms like 'rag week' and 'mucking in', and he learns to offer tea on all occasions. The film settles into a series of set pieces based on the pranks of the students' Dodo Club. Although Wolf never joins the club, he make friends with Hugo and the others and gets involved in their world. Eventually, Wolf graduates with a Class 1 and the film ends with Wolf and Ann drifting at dawn along the river in a punt after the May Ball.

The film is organised around the clash between Wolf's modernising tendencies and the traditional values of Cambridge. From the beginning, he is energetic and assertive, refusing to be put down by peculiar English behaviour and confident in his own abilities. He literally will not give way and learns to stands up for himself by turning English manners against the English, patronising Hugo as 'old boy' and offering the cleaner tea. Wolf makes it clear that he is in Cambridge to study, and he criticises the other students for being 'a lot of school children'. He starts with a meritocratic determination to work hard, and he is indeed successful, although the point is made that Hugo also passes his exams despite doing no work at all. Wolf is eager to learn but puzzled when what he is told seems contradictory; 'there's no logic in this country,' he protests.

However, Wolf's single-minded determination is at odds not only with the film's emphasis on the importance of fun but also with the values associated with his two key teachers, Ann and his tutor, Mr Murdoch. Both are to a limited extent associated with more modern attitudes than some of the upper-class students; Ann is seen reading a magazine *Modern Woman*, while Mr Murdoch has something of a northern accent and is president of the jazz club. The film flirts with the possibility of Cambridge changing and being brought up to date but consistently returns to the view that it is Wolf who must change to accept what Cambridge offers. Ann, despite her status as a modern young woman, reminds Wolf that 'we're old-fashioned'; she is there to tell him about the traditional rules of the Dodo Club, the conventions of courtship and the beauty of Cambridge, which is emphasised in a number of montages, drawing attention to the way the architecture combines with nature to make a perfect film setting. Murdoch, like Ann, is committed to Cambridge as it is and sets the rich experience it offers against Wolf's more narrow concept of what is needed to get on. Murdoch's function is to underpin the idiocies of the Dodo Club and other Cambridge excesses by giving them an educational rationale. He criticises Wolf's work as being unoriginal and tells him that he has 'a notebook mind', 'an electronic brain' that needs 'broadening'. The German education system is associated with mechanistic learning (Murdoch admits that Wolf has been well taught), while Cambridge offers a whole experience beyond lectures and supervisions. Wolf cannot control this experience but must wait for it to come to him: 'leave the door open,' Murdoch tells a puzzled Wolf, 'let Cambridge knock on it if you want to get the best value out of us.' In the end, Wolf takes the advice and learns to trust that the traditions of the institution have a value beyond logic.

Bachelor of Hearts closes with Ann and Wolf in the punt, benignly overseen from the bridge by Wolf's tutors. Appropriately, the final shot of the energetic Wolf is of him asleep, finally won over to Cambridge's gentle ways. The modernising hero has been changed but the traditions of Cambridge roll on.

This resolution followed the model provided by *Doctor in the House* in 1954. This very popular comedy centred on a group of medical students and offered an account that was praised for its realism and freshness. The hero, the middle-class Simon Sparrow, who is committed to his work to qualify as a doctor, falls in with a very mixed group of medical students more interested in women and sport. After a series of scrapes and incidents, Sparrow does qualify as a doctor and wins his girlfriend but also has learned, largely through the example of the more upper-class Grimsdyke, that 'there is more to life than ... diagnosis.'

Durgnat assigns *Doctor in the House* to his 'affluence cycle' of mid-fifties comedies, which have an 'air of gay, youthful, relatively modest contentment and sauciness' (44–5), while Street takes a more gloomy view, seeing the young hero Simon Sparrow as 'an awkward, powerless character who is petrified by women and frustrated by the institutions in which he works' (70). What this draws attention to is the contradiction between the plot of much of the film, in which Sparrow is indeed frequently rendered ineffective, and the tone, which is light-hearted in its episodic construction, bright colours and cheerful music. In addition, these rather different critical evaluations draw attention to the film's ambivalent attitude to the more modern attitude to the Health Service that Sparrow represents. Unlike Grimsdyke, Sparrow has no family money to support him and has arrived at St Swithins on merit. He is training to be a GP rather than the more traditionally powerful surgeon and his major success is in helping with a home birth. One of the striking features of Sparrow's medicine is that his patients want him to do well. They are more experienced with their illnesses than he is and give him the knowledge he needs: the pregnant mother has had at least three other babies and is being looked after by her own mother, while in the hospital Sparrow regularly encounters Mr Briggs, a patient who helps him out with 'excellent' diagnoses of his own condition. In some senses, Sparrow is their representative, providing a different model of the doctor for the new NHS.

But *Doctor in the House* makes clear both that this new kind of professional has been nurtured by the old traditions and that the traditions will not and should not be changed. A key figure here is Sir Lancelot, characteristically played by James Robertson Justice.[2] Sir Lancelot makes his first appearance sweeping up the steps of the hospital with a group of nervous officials and students in his train. He shouts at the students and takes as little notice as possible of the patients, telling Mr Briggs 'you won't understand our medical talk' and reassuring him that the details of his operation are 'nothing whatever to do with you'. But Sir Lancelot's traditional ways support the new students and Sparrow, in particular, as they learn not only to be doctors but also to understand the institution. Unlike the dean, who appears to believe only in discipline and work, Sir Lancelot, like Murdoch in *Bachelor of Hearts*, asserts that being a medical student is about more than medicine. Sir Lancelot likes Sparrow because he is 'a very promising young lad' and 'the finest rugby foot-baller we've had for a generation'. He enjoys the students' escapades and saves them after a brawl with the rival school by paying the fine imposed by the dean.

He then saves Sparrow from expulsion by using the history of the institution against the dean: recalling a particularly scandalous episode from the dean's own student days, Sir Lancelot muses that it would be a 'pity these stories should be allowed to die. I think I shall have to retail that one to the students as a little light relief.' His jovial blackmail works, and Sparrow is reprieved to sit his exams. As in *Bachelor of Hearts*, what is emphasised is not changes in the institution but in the apprentice, who has to learn what it has to offer.

But it is not merely in tales of upper-class education that the *status quo* and its traditional systems are vigorously preserved. *Carry on Teacher* (1959) offers a rather less elevated account, which also hinges on tradition. This film, refreshingly set in a secondary modern school, starts with an announcement to the teachers by the headmaster that he plans to leave for another post at the end of term and that to facilitate this the school must do well in the forthcoming inspection. The inspection team, consisting of an appropriately modern duo of a career woman and a child psychiatrist, arrives. Mayhem is let loose in the school as the pupils set about wrecking the inspection. Rockets explode in chemistry lessons, awkward questions about under-age sex are asked in a lesson on *Romeo and Juliet*, the school play falls into chaos and itching powder and glue on the chairs cause panic even in the private meetings of staff and the inspection team. All this is highly disruptive and appears to be a challenge not just to the discipline and insights of the inspection team (the child psychiatrist comes in for relentless lampooning) but also to the traditional authority of the teachers. Resolution is achieved when the teachers learn that the children are behaving badly because they want the school to get a bad report so that the head will stay. When at the end he waves to the children gathered in the playground and tells them 'See you next term,' they cheer uproariously at the maintenance of the *status quo*. While the film, like many in the series, may challenge sexual repressiveness and middle-class manners, it does so within the framework of an established and traditional hierarchy.

Class and hierarchies in the crime comedy

Carry on Teacher gives us an indication of what is at stake in the reassertion of the importance of traditional systems in these films. What I am suggesting is not that comedies of the period necessarily bow down to the superiority of the traditional forms of authority (the upper-class regimes of Cambridge colleges, the middle-class teachers) but that they present hierarchies in the traditional systems that are deemed to give everyone a role. Thus the meritocratic and scientific systems of expertise that see the common man as expendable are not to be trusted, but the systems that depend on tradition can be because their hierarchies require people at every level. This helps to explain why class continues to be such a strong and powerful signifier in films of the period, despite the modern political, sociological and educational discourses that were proclaiming its rapid demise. It is through class that characters in these films are assigned a place that can be clearly identified by the audience. In a traditional system, people may then know their place and operate successfully without appearing to be kowtowing to those above them. It is this emphasis on class and hierarchy that gives the comedies their curious mix of rebellion and stultifying conformity.

Carry on Teacher demonstrates this by making the children powerful agents in their own right who act effectively in the hierarchy of the school with the aim of defending that hierarchy. In order to analyse this phenomenon further, we can look at a number of films that deal with another group, which is arguably at the bottom of the pile – criminals – to see how notions of class and hierarchy can be understood through this highly popular sub-genre, which flourished particularly towards the end of the period under discussion. Despite the well-known fears of the teenage criminal expressed in social problem films, this group of films is characterised by a remarkably tolerant and benign view of the adult criminal. Looking at this genre in the context of class and hierarchy helps to explain why this might be so.

The Ealing comedies, *The Lavender Hill Mob* and *The Ladykillers*, had as the basis of their plots a gang perpetrating an elaborately planned crime. Barr argues that the former is among 'the set of Ealing comedies that enlist our sympathy with a form of law-breaking' (he is comparing it to *Whisky Galore* in particular) but suggests that it operates as a form of daydream in which 'the good humour has the effect of continuously endorsing the "social" values even while the plot is ostensibly defying them' (1977: 117). It is not so much the conventionally moral ending that reasserts order but the comedy, which imagines an escape from that morality without the risks involved. *The Ladykillers* is perhaps rather tougher. The gang, Barr suggests, represents the social mix of post-war society: it is led by Alec Guinness as the fiendishly clever professor with his confident Establishment manners but also includes an upper-class ex-officer who is sliding down the social scale; working-class One-Round claiming his rights to be counted; Harry, the representative of modern youth, and even a foreigner, the ruthless Louis. Working together, the gang hope to defeat the Establishment by pulling off a big robbery but are in the end defeated not by the law but by 'the Nannyish authority and the Victorian Baggage' (173) compressed into the figure of their landlady, Mrs Wilberforce.

Barr argues, in his analysis of Mackendrick's work, that *The Ladykillers* exposes the cost of Mrs Wilberforce's survival to show the damaging consequence of the triumph of 'the inertia of the *status quo*' (173). But perhaps the film was also hijacked by 'Mrs W.' and emerged as a celebration of tradition and the tenacity of the past. If that is the case, then, both *The Lavender Hill Mob* and *The Ladykillers* offer challenges to authority that are less than first appears. In addition, *The Ladykillers* brings together a number of features of the comic criminal gang that will reappear in later comedies. The gang is seeking to commit the victimless crime, as the professor tries to explain to Mrs Wilberforce. In that sense, the crime does not harm anyone at a personal level, only the bureaucratic systems of the insurance company. Because of this, the gang's actions do not exclude its members from society. The social mix of the group and the nature of the crime indicate that it is a reflection of society, a slightly skewed but recognisable version of the social systems to which it is notionally opposed. The gang has a leader and clearly allocated roles; it has different class positions, which determine those roles, and methods of dealing with decision making and conflict.

Peter Sellers played the somewhat bewildered representative of youth in *The Ladykillers* and, although Durgnat suggests that he is a star of the 1960s (174), the groundwork for his star image was laid in the 1950s. By the early 1960s, Sellers was emerging as a major star, and two crime caper comedies, both written by John Warren, provided Sellers with leading roles that he played with uncharacteristic nuance. Both used the format of the gang setting up and carrying out an elaborate crime. In *Two Way Stretch* (1960), Sellers plays Dodger Lane, who leads a comfortable life in prison with his two cell mates until a former but untrustworthy accomplice, Soapy (Wilfred Hyde-White) persuades them to join in the robbery of a huge cache of diamonds. The three secretly break out of prison for the night to commit the crime, thus providing themselves with an excellent alibi, and successfully steal the jewels from under the noses of the army. However, when they are officially released from prison the plan begins to unravel, and the film ends with the diamonds returned to the rightful owner, the sultan, although the trio, disguised as Arabs, appear to be set for another try.

The Wrong Arm of the Law (1962) brought many of the same actors together in a more elaborate tale featuring Sellers as the gang leader Pearly Gates, who has a double life as Monsieur Jules, the manager of a fashion house. The criminal world of London is being reduced to chaos by an Australian 'IPO mob', who, acting on information provided by Gates' girlfriend, impersonate police officers and take the spoils of the true criminals after the crime has been safely committed. Gates is instrumental in getting a deal between organised crime and Scotland Yard, which eventually results in the capture of the rogue gang, which is lured into carrying out a fake van robbery. Pearly, who had his own plans for the robbery, tries to flee the country with the loot but discovers that the money is fake and ends up on a desert island designing grass skirts for his new fashion house.

Both films draw on similar characteristics to present the crime, the criminal and his gang. *Two-Way Stretch* offers a less complex account. Here the crime is a fantasy that involves no violence in its execution, offers a fabulous reward (£2 million worth of diamonds) and is committed against a stock figure of British comedy, a foreign potentate. The gang itself is hierarchical, with different skills provided by its different members. It is typical of this genre that the hierarchy is indicated by nicknames: the brains are provided by Dodger, who reads the *Investor's Chronicle* and takes an interest in stocks and shares; the safe breaking is done by Jelly Knight; and Lenny the Dip is the apprentice, still learning the relatively junior role of pickpocket. Outside the prison, Lenny's mother provides surveillance and Ethel, Dodger's girlfriend, has the sex appeal to stop a dustcart in its tracks, an integral part of the scheme. The problem here is that

Figure 4.2 Peter Sellers in *Two Way Stretch* (British Lion Films, 1961).
Courtesy of the Kobal Collection.

leadership of the gang is disputed by the confidence trickster Soapy (Wilfred Hyde-White), who disguises himself as a vicar in order to get into the prison to speak to his 'parishioners'. But it is Dodger who looks after the gang members, both in terms of their comfort in the prison and organising the escape. He has got himself a position of some power in the prison as a 'trusty' and uses it to protect and further the interests of the gang. He does this not out of selfless motives but because it is the best way of looking after his own interests.

The film emphasises that collusion between the apparently opposing sides – the prison authorities and the prisoners – provides a stable situation in which both sides can pursue their own concerns. The liberal attitudes of the prison governor are certainly mocked; practical classes, considered by the governor to be a progressive experiment to give the prisoners a possible trade in the outside world, are used by them to develop handier safe-breaking skills. Nevertheless, the prisoners are careful not to undermine the governor in public and the sharing of authority in the prison leads to a comfortable life for all. The chief officer shares chats and cups of tea with the prisoners, and the governor is left to get on with his passion for gardening. It is not the prisoners who disturb this order but the arrival of a new chief officer, Crout (Lionel Jeffries), who insists that the prison be run much more strictly. Ironically, this has as much effect on the governor as the prisoners when his roses are uprooted by Crout's hunt for an escape tunnel and his prize marrow is destroyed by a flying rock from the old-fashioned quarry, which Crout has insisted on reopening. Crout's efforts to control the gang have no success and only lead to his being persistently the butt of the film's key moments of humorous humiliation. Bedraggled by crawling through tunnels and blown up by his own explosives, Crout, by the end of the film, is reduced to paranoia and delusion. Hunting for Soapy, he attacks a group of vicars, crying 'You're taking the mickey out of me' and 'They're all crooks.' He gets no support from the governor and the trio, escaping on the train with the diamonds, call out mockingly to him.

The Wrong Arm of the Law works with a similar structure. Again the crimes are relatively victimless, involving jewellery thefts from the rich or robbery from institutions such as banks and post offices. No violence is used and the major crime of the film is a fake, organised by the police themselves and carried out by Gates and his gang with their approval. As in *Two-Way Stretch*, the gang has a hierarchical structure, although this time it is more elaborate and apes the procedures of a big company. Gates is clearly in charge of planning and organisation, providing information, which he gleans from the rich clients in his fashion house and, for instance, checking out a high-class jewellers to set up a robbery for others to carry out. He sees himself as an old-fashioned, kindly boss who provides overtime on Sunday, a 'fortnight's holiday on the Costa Brava, luncheon vouchers' and other perks. Other members of the gang have their own specialist skills, although expertise may have to be brought in from abroad for major jobs. This hierarchical model with Gates as leader is confirmed at the meeting that he arranges with other criminals to discuss the problem. Here the model is the trade union meeting, with Gates in the chair, while the other gang leader, O'Toole, acts as secretary, checking rules and procedure.

The collusion between the opposing sides is also on a grander scale and is conducted in a more knowledgeable way on the Establishment side. Gates, who describes his proposal to bring the rival criminals together for a meeting as 'a United Nations plan', acts with their authority as their delegate to raise the problem of the rogue gang with the police. After initial misunderstanding, he is recognised by the police in this role and welcomed with 'a nice pot of tea and a couple of fairy cakes'. A meeting is arranged between Gates and the assistant commissioner 'on neutral ground' at a children's fair. Each is accompanied by henchmen in mackintoshes, and the editing emphasises the parallels between the groups as they enter the fairground and have a go on the rides while the negotiations take place through an intermediary. While neither side exactly trusts the other, both want the same end – the restoration of the norms of criminal behaviour – and both Gates and the assistant commissioner act in similar ways to try to ensure that the deal tilts in their favour.

In *The Wrong Arm of the Law*, the initial disruption is caused by the gang of Australians who confuse the relationship between the two parties by posing as policemen when they are in fact criminals. But much of the comic disorder during the action of the film is caused by Nosey Parker, the officious inspector played by Lionel Jeffries, who played Crout in *Two-Way Stretch*. Parker shares Crout's self-importance and his determination to uphold the dignity of authority but, like Crout, he is continually humiliated as his attempts at control fail. Parker is the intermediary between the two sides, but both Gates and his superiors in the police force treat him with amusement and contempt. His position is further undermined when he is 'lent' to Gates to look after the police interests in the robbery. Trying to stop Gates escaping with the money, Parker handcuffs himself to the bag: 'Now what are you going to do?' he challenges Gates, 'take me with you?' But this is false bravado and he is lured by the money and, like a good working-class comedian, the thought of escaping from his mother-in-law. He flies off with Gates, only to find that the money is fake. The final shot of the film and its parting joke reveals him working for Gates, making grass skirts on a treadle sewing machine.

Criminal comedies such as these provide fruitful material in considering how questions of class and merit are being made sense of and joked about in popular culture in the late 1950s. Merit is actually taken more seriously in these films than in the comedies about education discussed earlier, since crime is presented as a more open profession than education and the law. The gang leader is no longer the academic professor of *The Ladykillers* but a working-class lad who gets the position because of his ability. As leader of the gang he has to be intelligent as well as cunning, and much emphasis is placed on his ability to plan and organise.[3] Dodger and Gates have both made their way up the profession, so they match their opposite numbers in the system despite the class differences between them. Sellers' performances also have moments when he looks for approbation and appreciation as if aware, like the scholarship boy, that he is moving beyond his social position. In *The Wrong Arm of the Law*, he is vulnerable to his girlfriend's betrayal of his plans because he wants to impress her with his clever ideas and cosmopolitan ways and he is bashful when the extraordinary general meeting of crooks and criminals sings 'For He's a Jolly Good Fellow'.

Class, though, remains of crucial importance. It is the way in which characters can be understood and quick judgements made about them and the comedies are full of stereotypes based on rather precise class positions. Class characteristics indeed give the working class criminals an opportunity to outmanoeuvre those who are apparently above them in the system. The rich, who are so snobbish as to show off their jewellery and furs to Monsieur Jules, deserve to be robbed in schemes masterminded by Pearly Gates. The patrician languor of the governor in *Two-Way Stretch* and the assistant commissioner in *The Wrong Arm of the Law* leaves space for working-class energy and initiative to be applied to the organisation of the prison and the pursuit of crime. Class is identified through speech and manner and is therefore not entirely fixed, since class positions can be copied. Sellers' well-known 'talent for mimicry' (Murphy 1992: 245) means that accent and manners can never be entirely trusted. His role as a French dress designer gives scope for these talents but other instances are used more subtly in these films. In *Two-Way Stretch*, for instance, he adopts a rougher, working-class accent in front of the prison visitors as if to conform to their stereotypes about working-class prisoners, while in *The Wrong Arm of the Law* his tone is modulated in discussions with the assistant commissioner.

But the fact that class differences can be misleading does not mean that they are not important. It is class that explains why the behaviour of Crout and Perkins is so disruptive, for they are working-class characters trying to impress and pattern themselves on the Establishment. Jeffries' strangulated vowels, his over-emphasised aitches and ingratiating smiles and gestures when talking to the boss all indicate that he is trying to be something that he is not, while his zealous pursuit of order is undermined precisely because he lacks the 'natural' calm and control of even the unsuccessful members of the Establishment such as the governor. Thus, while Sellers' characters illustrate that it is possible to adopt the manners of a different class, it can only be done successfully as a piece of acting, a knowing deception that does not undermine a character's basic position. When it is done without self-awareness, it leads to the humiliations experienced by Crout and Perkins.

These criminal comedies, then, although they recognise the possibilities of movement based on merit, continue to take class as the basis for decision making and action. They have a rebellious air, which arises from the way in which the heroes challenge Establishment manners and find ways of getting around rules and restrictions; the highly conventional endings mete out a comic punishment to the gang leader, but the upper classes do not impose their own sense of order. But the generally conservative tone of these comedies can be traced to the way in which they rely on the continuance of a class-based hierarchy. The criminal gang fits cosily into the established pattern of society by setting up parallel structures into which the working class can fit without challenging the established order. Their personnel and hierarchies match those of legitimate organisations, and they have their own bureaucracies and inefficiencies. Prison cells are transformed into comfortable living rooms with cuckoo clocks and pet cats. Men are nagged by their mothers and wives and betrayed by their girlfriends. When the normal (albeit criminal) order is disrupted, they expect, like everyone else, to be able to turn to the proper authorities: 'I want to know what the police are doing about it,' demands one criminal at the extraordinary meeting in *The Wrong Arm of the Law*, 'We pay our rates.' The suggestion that criminal organisations are indistinguishable from their Establishment equivalents can have its cutting edge, as in many an American gangster film, or it can lead to the cynical satire that was to come later in the 1960s. But in British cinema of the period, the trope works in reverse: far from being outside society, in its methods and organisation the gang operates as a parallel structure, embedded in the society and operating symbiotically as a mirror image of more legitimate institutions. British comedy imagines that the criminal, like other professionals, works within the hierarchies of a traditional system and so draws him into the traditional, class-based world of the British state.

5   The post-war settlement and women's choices

Melodrama and realism in Ealing drama

In their introduction to the British Film Institute's 1983 monograph *Gainsborough Melodrama*, the editors, Sue Aspinall and Robert Murphy, suggested that Gainsborough melodramas had been rendered invisible because of initial critical derision and later neglect by film theorists. 'We would like to put these films on the map,' they argued, 'and to redress the critical imbalance which has made British film culture of the 1940s seem synonymous with Ealing Studios' (1). Julian Petley included Gainsborough melodramas in his assessment of 'the lost continent' of British cinema, which had been systematically overlooked in critical writing still marked by a 'dominant realist aesthetic' (98). Ten years later, Pam Cook continues to argue that Gainsborough costume romances have 'consistently been marginalised, ignored or subsumed into the consensus in discussion of British cinema' and suggests that the films have been treated as 'marginal aberrations' in a dominant realist aesthetic (1996: 5–6). By quoting some authors and avoiding others, Cook seems to me to overstate her case, ignoring a sea-change that has taken place since 1983. While within official British film culture generally there may still be a yearning for British cinema to offer a unified national identity, in feminist film theory and in the teaching of British cinema the emphasis has swung very much the other way. The work of Cook herself, along with that of Aspinall, Harper, Landy and Thumim, has not only put Gainsborough on the map but has come close to constructing a new critical orthodoxy in which Gainsborough women's films, with their costumes, contradictions and narrative excesses, are deemed (to varying degrees) to be the films of the period that best speak of and to women, who constituted the main audience during and immediately after the Second World War. In this criticism, Ealing operates as the opposite pole, the patriarchally run studio making films committed to realism and social order.

This re-evaluation of Gainsborough has broadly been conducted by a methodological approach that tends to explain Ealing films through narrative analysis, while Gainsborough's are understood through a broader range of factors, including visual expression, audience response and star image. The effect of this is to set up Ealing and Gainsborough as exemplary opposites. Sue Aspinall's chapter in Curran and Porter's 1983 collection, *British Cinema History*, offers an early example of this approach. In looking at the role of women in British films from 1943 to 1953, she finds that 'a particular style of realism was in fact closely allied to a traditional, conservative attitude to women and marriage, while the unrealistic costume dramas and melodramas ... were more unstable in their attitudes to women's sexuality and role in life' (273). The melodramas, she argues, offer the possibility of some images escaping from the restrictions of narrative. Thus, in *The Wicked Lady*, Margaret Lockwood's star image, 'her bitchiness and bravado', is translated into 'a positive celebration', and 'the images of the film that persist are those of Lockwood as a defiant wife, an energetic highway robber, an enthusiastic lover, an instigator of action. These images are more powerful than the pat ending' (276). By contrast, Ealing's realist *Dance Hall* is dismissed on the basis of its plot. The film 'assumes that, once she is married a working-class girl will give up work. The heroine is also required by her husband to give up dancing ... Reconciliation is achieved when the husband overcomes his possessiveness and allows his wife her little interest' (291).

However, at certain points Aspinall suggests a need for more rather than less realism. She argues of the wartime films that 'the most painful experiences of women during these years were not represented' (282). Later work moves away from this approach and sees little potential for realism as a form. Harper's stark summary of the differences between Ealing and Gainsborough immediately after the war illustrates this. She argues that, in Ealing's post-war output, 'there is only one film which deals with female autonomy: *The Loves of Joanna Godden*' (102). After offering readings of a number of films based largely on narrative analysis and quotations from scripts, she sums up: 'so many Ealing films offered a horrid set of alternatives to the female audience. The only ratified conditions were virginity or respectable conjugality. Any departures from these norms met with severe punishment' (103). By contrast, Gainsborough films are understood, at least in part, through their visual expression of female autonomy; they 'were visually flamboyant, and deployed a cheap but effective form of expressionism; they contained heroines who engaged actively in their own destinies' (104). Gainsborough, until 1947, was a studio that 'celebrated female desire' (105), and the fact that the heroines ultimately failed and frequently died did not compromise Gainsborough's satisfactions for women viewers. In *Celluloid Sisters* (1992: 167–8), Janet Thumim drew on women's memories of seeing Gainsborough's *The Seventh Veil* and *The Wicked Lady* to suggest that costume, imagery and star personae could form the basis for audience readings that might oppose or get around such punishing endings. In contrast, Thumim, in a later article, argues that although 'popular cinema of the later 1940s ... is notable for its thematic concentration on female experience, it is the punishment of the transgressive female, or the repositioning of the mistaken woman, that forms the basis of most such narratives.' She cites Ealing's *It Always Rains on Sunday* as one example of post-war films that demonstrate that 'women *cannot* be permitted to act autonomously but must be secured in the heterosexual couple, the prelude to the nuclear familial unit, for their own protection' (1996: 253).

The endorsement of Gainsborough costume melodramas is based on a number of shifts in feminist writing on film and television in the late 1970s and 1980s. Feminists moved away from telling film makers and audiences what women *should* want to see on the screen – real women, positive heroines – and turned to examining the genres that women actually did watch and enjoy. Particularly important to note here is the development of work on melodrama and the woman's film, which contributed to the theoretical reassessment of Gainsborough and drew on such films as *The Wicked Lady* and *Madonna of the Seven Moons* for examples. Thus work on Gainsborough was fed by a more general interest in issues of female identification and desire, which had emerged from film theory's preoccupation with psychoanalysis in the 1970s. Cook's own work is particularly significant here. Her contribution to the BFI's 1983 monograph was an essay that sought to position Gainsborough films in the context of theoretical re-evaluations of melodrama and the women's film. She both uses the British films to contribute to an ongoing debate about the relationship between melodrama and the woman's picture and draws on these debates to understand the Gainsborough films. She begins with an account of the theoretical debates, through which she provides a generic description of the women's picture that emphasises its appeal to women and the dangers of its doing so:

> it has to stimulate desire, then channel it through identification into the required paths. It negotiates this contradiction between female desire and its containment with difficulty often producing an excess which threatens to deviate from the intended route.
>
> (1983: 21)

She then draws on this work and on the historical context of 1940s Britain to suggest that there are positive aspects to the 'lack of realism' in Gainsborough films (36) and to argue that the 'costume cycle broke the silence and at least spoke of sexual desire' (38). In *Fashioning the Nation*, this emphasis on contradiction, desire and the excess generated by the difficulty of containment is continued in a discussion that is more specifically related to the construction of national identities. Cook describes 'identity formation' as a 'fluctuating, fractured affair which militates against any final settlement' (1996: 2). She therefore relishes the masquerades and cross-dressing of the costume dramas, the narratives of schizophrenia, amnesia and transgression, the expression of female desire through visual display, the willingness to put 'identity itself in crisis' (6). Fantasy is crucial to this, because 'in the realist films, ... British characters remain first and foremost British', but the costume dramas 'deal in fantasies of loss of identity. They suggest that identity itself is fluid and unstable, like the costume genre itself, a hybrid state or form' (96). Once again, Ealing acts as a polar opposite, dismissed for its 'cosy, parochial Englishness ... and its attendant realist aesthetic' (5).

It is no accident that realism is consistently posed in opposition to melodrama because feminist work in this area clearly drew on debates in film theory more generally that had identified realism as a bourgeois and restrictive approach. In the pages of *Screen*, Colin McCabe's argument that the 'classic realist text cannot deal with the real in its contradiction' (12) won out over Raymond Williams' more sympathetic and historically nuanced account of realism's possibilities in a later *Screen* article (1977). *Cahiers du Cinema* editors Commolli and Narbonni also critiqued realism and, as we saw in Chapter 2, crucially provided a method that looked for moments of contradiction, excess and incoherence as the symptomatic evidence of a film working against its overt ideological position. The idea that realism could not speak to women's contra-dictory position was widely adopted and the practice of reading for 'cracks and fissures' offered feminists a way of looking again at films and genres that, at first sight, seemed to offer only unrealistic stories and stereotyped heroines. The excesses, coincidences and over-dramatic elements of melodramas and women's films could be read as evidence of the trouble that women created in the text. As Cook put it, 'feminists … look for excess as a sign of the system threatening to break down' (1983: 21), and melodrama seemed to offer fruitful ground for such symptomatic work.

Feminist writing on melodrama in general and on the post-war Gainsborough melodramas in particular has been extremely productive and has demanded that attention be paid to films that are clearly crucial to any consider-ation of British cinema. Indeed, one of my contentions is that its methods of reading against the grain of the text and paying attention to visual and symbolic disruptions to the narrative could be applied more widely and is illuminating in relation to the Ealing films I want to discuss. Nevertheless, in its efforts to redeem what had been derided, it has run a double risk. First, it has, as we have seen, tended to create a bad object, which is then barely examined but is used rather crudely as the contrast to Gainsborough's virtues; second, the assump-tion is sometimes made that the presence of excess is enough to challenge patriarchal positions, so that the corollary follows – that lack of excess means meekly giving in to them. In this connection, Alan Lovell has commented that 'contemporary scholarship has fallen into a trap by posing excess and restraint against each other' (139), while Christine Gledhill points out that 'as modes of imagination, documentary, melodrama and romance guarantee nothing in themselves' (227). Like Lovell, she suggests that the polarisation of melodra-matic and documentary modes in critical work on British cinema is unhelpful and argues that excess and restraint, melodrama and realism are sustained in 'tense relationship' (218) in British cinema. I want to follow Lovell's and Gledhill's suggestions and to examine more closely a number of post-war Ealing films in the light of the issues raised in these debates.

'The housewife's job'

Aspinall, Harper and Cook have all stressed the importance of looking at the historical context in order to understand why the position of women offered a particularly fruitful source of stories in post-war cinema. An important legacy of the war was that the role of women was seen as a potential source of difficulty in the post-war reconstruction. It was recognised that the demands made of women during the war had affected their traditional pre-war roles in the family and the labour market. At the end of the war, it was unclear what demands the state should make of women, how they might contribute to post-war reconstruction and how far women wanted to return to more traditional roles. The war had opened up economic and sexual possibilities for a significant number of women and there was anxiety about how far home life could be reconstructed. The Women's Voluntary Service gave advice about the difficulties of reunion between women, who had had to become more independent during the war, and men, who had become used to the all-male hierarchies and companionships of the services (Turner and Rennell: 125–6); a predicted decline in the birth-rate was blamed in part on women's 'selfishness' (Wilson 1980: 27); there was concern about how disrupted family life had affected children and about the divorce rate, which reached a peak in 1946 (Smart: 93). And while the general emphasis was on women returning to the family and making marriage their career, there were contradictory emphases in, for example, the Ministry of Labour's appeal in 1947 for women to rejoin the workforce. Ironically, by late 1946, more women were rejoining the women's services than were leaving, partly, the Soldiers', Sailors' and Airmen's Families Association conjectured, because of 'the disappointments of civilian life' (Turner and Rennell: 112). Women's magazines carried advertisements encouraging women into the forces. The ambivalence that might be felt by those women who did return to the home was sometimes recognised by those trying to work out policy: 'many [women] will also feel that they are going back to a prison', advised one leaflet baldly, 'unless they have some life away from sinks and brooms and washtubs' (quoted in Haste: 141).

The emphasis on the restoration of home life was paralleled by a new recognition of the importance of mutual care. The Labour government dramatically voted into office in 1945 introduced a series of social changes that, among other things, gave the state a feminine role in supporting and caring for its citizens at times of crisis, a role later derided in the tag phrase 'the nanny state'. The late 1940s was a period of social reform, when new institutions for health, welfare and education were being established. Of these, the most dramatic and arguably the most effective was the establishment of the National Health Service in 1948 on the basis of free treatment regardless of the ability to pay, but reforms also covered the provision of national insurance schemes to cover unemployment and sickness benefits, the state pension and the extension of universal secondary education. Welfare clinics, which provided orange juice and cod liver oil for children and advice for their mothers, were a down-to-earth example of the state's intervention in childcare and nurturing, even in very poor districts (J. Klein: 6).

The quality of family life thus underpinned the Labour government's greatest achievements but it was also at the heart of the discontent with the government that took hold with the currency crises and relentlessly hard winter of 1946–47. The government's determination to deal with the country's

economic problems by saving on domestic expenditure had serious consequences for women. Rationing of food and clothing, which had begun during
the war, continued into peacetime and, in some respects, got worse; potatoes
and bread were both rationed between 1946 and 1948. Alongside rationing ran
a black market of spivs offering meat under the counter and stockings on the
side. The fuel crisis of 1947 led to frequent power failures and bans on the use
of electricity for cooking. Even without this, living conditions were often poor.
Houses that had been of slum quality in the 1930s had been destroyed and
undermined by the Blitz and, although the Labour government had promised a
massive increase in house building ('a separate dwelling for every family desiring
to have one'), the economic situation and the shortage of manpower and materials led to a serious crisis (Hennessy: 173). 'Austerity meant that improvements
in housing, education and health care were less than had been hoped for in
1945' (Tomlinson: 87), and while historians of the period, such as Addison and
Hennessy, warn against painting too grim a view of day-to-day life in post-war
Britain, the practical burden of the economic difficulties of the period would
have been felt most vividly by women, who were responsible for bringing up
children and maintaining the physical fabric of home.

Certainly, post-war debates focused on women and how they were
managing. How was the family to be reconstructed? Would women be satisfied
to return to the home and to their husbands? How could the newly developing
welfare systems support women without taking over their role at the heart of
the family? Should women count as part of the workforce? Would the state
continue to need women's labour outside the home? The Beveridge Report, the
inspiration for the welfare reforms, had been clear about the important role of
women in the post-war world: 'in the next thirty years housewives as mothers
have vital work to do in ensuring the adequate continuance of the British race
and of British ideals in the world' (Beveridge: 52). But anxieties were expressed
about how willing or able women were to undertake this task, and there was
some concern in official circles as to the burden being placed on married
women. Beveridge had asserted that 'the housewife's job with a large family is
frankly impossible' (quoted in Wilson 1980: 19). The Denning Committee's
Report on Procedure in Matrimonial Causes in February 1947 was clear about
the burdens on married women: 'the mere mechanics of everyday life have
become so exhausting for women as to have an immeasurable effect, through
sheer weariness, on married happiness' (quoted in Turner and Rennell: 146). A
Mass Observation report in June of the same year observed that women were
finding marriage and domestic chores restrictive; they particularly resented 'the
wife being tied to the house, loss of freedom of movement and an inability to
take part in the outside pleasures and amusements of single life' (quoted in
Summerfield 1993: 77).

The immediate post-war period was thus one in which the role of women in
marriage and their attitudes to domesticity were under scrutiny. The post-war
settlement depended on them in a number of ways: it was based on a reform in
the welfare system in which they were positioned as the main providers of

domestic care; the regrouping of the family depended on their willingness to maintain the home, but the continuing rigours of rationing and material deprivation hit them the hardest. The theme of women being in a position of choice and decision and the underlying anxiety about how far women would undertake the social responsibilities placed on them have been identified as key factors in the success of the Gainsborough films produced at the end of the war. Cook commented that such films 'present their heroines' lives as in transition, undergoing radical changes as the result of choices wisely or unwisely made. Women are presented as active, able to affect the progress of history, but the choices they make must be the right ones if a healthy British society is to be built' (1983: 22). This emphasis on choice can be seen in many Gainsborough films in which the heroine's role is split across a number of characters (*Love Story*, *The Wicked Lady*, *They Were Sisters*), or the heroine herself suffers a split personality (*Madonna of the Seven Moons*). But this structure is not confined to Gainsborough. *Brief Encounter* offers an example of the 'quality film' posing similar questions for Laura, and Powell and Pressburger offered highly romantic accounts of women's dilemmas in *The Red Shoes* and *Black Narcissus*. Ealing also focuses on these post-war choices and addresses, sometimes obliquely, the problematic split between women's social role and their individual needs. In analysing three Ealing films, the 1947 film *It Always Rains on Sunday* and two from 1950, *Cage of Gold* and *Dance Hall*, we shall see how women in films of this period stand for the nation. In all three films, they are put in the position of choice: are they willing to continue to make sacrifices for the community and the nation? Are they willing to reject excitement and sensation in the interests of the national good? Do their longings for luxury, sexual excitement and entertainment indicate a genuine need for self-expression and fulfilment that the government and the state ignore at their peril? I want to suggest that these films do not fit readily into the polarisations of current debate and that, in analysing them, we need a rather more nuanced approach to understanding how women's choices could be represented and understood in this period.

Melodramatic choices

It is worth noting that these films have proved hard to categorise beyond the general Ealing label. Barr does focus on the central roles for women in his discussions of *It Always Rains on Sunday* and *Cage of Gold* but does not use generic categorisations such as 'the woman's film'. Murphy places *It Always Rains on Sunday* firmly within a realist tradition but also discusses it as Ealing's 'own spiv film' (1992: 156). Hill states that *Cage of Gold* is 'not a social problem film itself' but suggests, in the context of Dearden's work, that it provides an 'explication of the attitudes and assumptions which come to form the bedrock of nearly all the social problem films that follow' (71). Landy (1991) puts the Gainsborough melodramas into her chapter on 'The Woman's Film', but *Cage of Gold* and *Dance Hall* are both discussed as social problem films rather than women's films or family melodramas. I think it is worth looking at these films as women's films and as melodramas to see how certain generic patterns are set against or work with the broad commitment to realism that is also at work in them.

All three films have a woman in the central role, although there are some differences in terms of class position and domestic milieu. *It Always Rains on Sunday* focuses on a working-class woman, Rose, played by Googie Withers, who lives with her husband George, her two teenage step-daughters and Alfie, her own son by George. Rose's story is placed within a number of more mundane sub-plots, including two dealing with the romances of her step-daughters, which serve to point up the drama of Rose's story. *Dance Hall* also portrays working-class life; its interweaving format follows the lives of four girls who work together in a factory and dance at the local Palais. In this chapter, I am going to concentrate on the story of Eve, played by a young newcomer, Natasha Parry; the film deals with the events before and after her marriage to a young aircraft engineer. *Cage of Gold* is set in an upper middle-class milieu in which Jean Simmons plays Judith, a young painter whose well-to-do family have fallen on hard times and who marries into a professional family in which both father and son are doctors.

The films not only make women their central character but also give them the narrative viewpoint. The audience follows the story from their point of view and is given access to their thoughts and feelings. It is worth noting that this handling of the heroines' viewpoint is in contrast to the treatment given to the post-war film noir heroines of Hollywood cinema, whose enigmatic desirability depends on the distance maintained between them and the audience. The women characters of these British films may sometimes behave badly or fool-ishly (Rose, in particular, is viciously acerbic on occasion), but the audience is positioned with them; we know why they do what they do. Access to the women's viewpoint is important because the dramatic problems at the heart of the film are organised around narrative structures that specifically set individual desires and needs against those of the common good. The films are thus all structured around a polarised choice, characteristic of melodrama, in which different men stand for different lifestyles and responsibilities.

In *It Always Rains on Sunday*, Rose has to choose between her ex-lover, Tommy, now a criminal on the run, and her husband George, who is stolid and insensitive but is, as Rose says, 'decent'. Her step-daughters exemplify a similar choice for the next generation of women, as the film follows the ups and downs of the relationship between the brown-haired Doris and her respectable boyfriend and the blonde Vi's entanglement with a married man.[1] In *Cage of Gold*, the choice to be made by Judy is between two men who represent different lifestyles: Alan is responsible, caring and kind, a doctor who decides to work in the new NHS; Bill is an ex-RAF pilot who is exciting, glamorous, irre-sponsible and out to give her a good time. In *Dance Hall*, Eve has to choose between her steady boyfriend, the clumsy non-dancer Phil, and the American, Alec, with his smart suits, fast lifestyle and fleet-footed dancing skills. In each film, it is the woman who moves between fixed male positions and the audience is given access to their motives and desires. The women's strength lies in their capacity to change, to reflect on choices, to change their minds. Such a structure reinforces the sense that, during a time of social upheaval, the stability of post-war society depends on women's choices; men are what they are but women can change, and their choices both reflect and contribute to the post-war national settlement.

If we look at these choices in terms of narrative it is evident that the films try to load the choices and make it clear what the women must do to make socially responsible decisions. In particular, the character of the man who represents the more glamorous choice is severely compromised. Rose's lover in *It Always Rains on Sundays* is a criminal on the run who comes to Rose out of desperation rather than love. He does not share her intense memories of their affair and fails to recognise the engagement ring he gave her ten years before. In *Cage of Gold*, Bill marries Judy for her money and disappears the next day when he discovers that she has none, leaving her pregnant with only Alan to turn to. Alec, Eve's lover in *Dance Hall*, is a smooth American dabbling in the black market; after she has slept with him, he drops her rapidly for fear of getting over-committed but he later deliberately stirs up trouble between Eve and her husband. The good choices, on the other hand, are associated with the community and the future, particularly Alan in *Cage of Gold* with the communal values of the new National Health Service and Phil in *Dance Hall* with the modernity of aviation.

However, as in the Gainsborough melodramas, the allure of individual desire is expressed through *mise en scène* rather than narrative. In all three films, the visual expression of the women's dilemma contrasts the naturalist emphasis on the rhythms of day-to-day life with the special effects needed to represent the more glamorous alternatives. The films thus represent women's work in the home in a naturalist manner – we see Rose in her apron, peeling the potatoes and making pastry, Eve doing the ironing, even Judy has to look after her invalid father-in-law – but other devices are needed to express the excitement of less mundane possibilities. The sensuality and glamour that the heroines seek are represented most convincingly through visual style.

In all three films, this choice between men is expressed visually through the appearance of the women themselves. When Rose first meets Tommy, she is a flirtatious blonde barmaid; married, she is dark-haired, harassed and tired. Eve on the dance floor wears swirling skirts and low necklines; married, she appears in high-neck jumpers and dresses even at the Palais (Kirkham 1995). Even the middle-class Judy is subject to such transformations: the shoulderless, full-skirted evening dresses of her affair with Bill change after her marriage to high necklines and long sleeves. In addition, dissolves, camera work and editing are used to create transformations and to give visual expression to the desirability of the less worthy choice. A dissolve takes us from dark-haired Rose, looking in the bedroom mirror in her East End home, to a flashback sequence in which she is a young blonde barmaid. A further flashback is used to show Rose and Tommy in a highly stylised countryside setting for a love-making scene. In *Cage*

Figure 5.1 Googie Withers in *It Always Rains on Sunday* (Ealing Studios, 1947).
Courtesy of the Kobal Collection.

of Gold, the montage sequence of dancing, fairground rides, aeroplane displays and boxing matches represents the good time Bill appears to offer to Judy; she paints him in his RAF uniform, and when Alan comes to her flat to criticise her for falling for what Bill appears to offer – pink roses, champagne and 'a wonderful time' – the camera moves to position the confident and handsome portrait between the unhappy pair. The dance hall sequences in *Dance Hall* are characterised by quick editing, montage sequences, striking close-ups and, in the end, dissembling costumes and grotesque masks. In all three films, the *mise en scène* thus offers a way of imagining certain feelings, emotions and ideas that cannot be expressed in the more documentary style that characterises the domestic scenes of marriage.

If the films are read by posing an opposition between the polarised narratives and the more openly expressive visual elements, it is difficult to disagree with Thumim's identification of post-war films such as *It Always Rains on Sunday* with 'the punishment of the transgressive female', films in which it is demonstrated that women 'must be secured in the heterosexual couple ... for their own protection' (1996: 253). Nevertheless, the films have to work hard to get to this conclusion, and the difficulties of rejecting 'a wonderful time' are clear in the devices that are used to render the good choice the only alternative. Seduced by the visually expressed sensuality, all three heroines initially make the wrong choice by sleeping with the wrong man outside marriage. This is explicit in *Cage of Gold* and *Dance Hall* and heavily signalled in *It Always Rains on Sunday*. The films condemn not so much the act itself but the choice that it represents and in order for the woman to revise that choice the men associated with the expression of sexual need and desire are, in the manner of melodrama, heavily marked as evil. Tommy punches Rose and refuses her pleas to give himself up to the police; Bill callously leaves Judy, returns to blackmail her and is shot by his French mistress in a manner that places both Judy and Alan under suspicion; in *Dance Hall*, after a quarrel caused by Alec's maliciousness and Phil's jealousy, Eve is reconciled with her husband in a dramatic thunderstorm with the kind of romantic clinch that we have already seen fail to resolve the pair's problems earlier in the film.

In many ways, then, these Ealing films share some of the melodramatic elements of Gainsborough's women's films. They have female protagonists whose emotional choices form the basis of the narrative; they use the device of doubling male and female characters to stand for that choice and they express feelings visually through dress and *mise en scène*. The difference is that these melodramatic elements are set within a realist context, which, as we have seen, has been read as a betrayal of any aspirations to express women's autonomy. In turning now to the realist elements of these films, I want to argue that, although Ealing's drive for realism certainly makes these films different from Gainsborough's costume dramas, it does not necessarily mean that they fail to acknowledge the concerns of women in the late 1940s or to deny the emotional cost of the decisions they make.

Marriage and isolation

The bleakness of the women's position is underlined by the fact that in none of the films does the audience enjoy the marriage ceremony, in which the heroine confirms the good choice that will bind her into post-war society. The films leave us in no doubt that the correct choice has been made but they do not celebrate it. In their realist mode, the films force their narratives on beyond the point of marriage (the conventional ending of most romances and the point at which the choice might be deemed to have been made) to explore the consequences, the experience of marriage to the right man. The view of marriage that emerges from these films hardly conforms to the 'respectable conjugality' that Harper claims Ealing promotes (103).

The films' emphasis on realism serves to underline a number of features. It underlines the isolation of the women who are making these decisions and the material bleakness of the situations they are in. In making their choices, the women are placed outside the social structures that might offer some support.

The younger Rose appears to have no friends or family, and she makes her home in the pub where she works; Judy's family went to Canada after the war, and her romance with Bill isolates her not only from Alec but also from the family servant, Waddy, who, although initially delighted to see Bill again, is deeply suspicious of his motives; Eve's mother is unsympathetic, and Eve does not tell her friends about her feelings for Alec or her anxieties about Phil. The wedding in these films marks the further isolation of the woman and her confinement to the home. Once married, Rose and Eve give up their jobs, and although Judy is referred to as a successful painter we never see her working as an artist after her marriage. This social isolation is compounded by the fact that the men whom they marry lack either the glamorous villainy or the tender understanding of melodrama's heroes. In the Ealing films, the heroes are ordinary, presented as typical men whose main fault is that they lack any intuitive understanding of the women's positions. Even the good ones are weak and lack sympathetic understanding: 'you're thick-headed and smug,' Eve's friend Mary tells Phil in *Dance Hall*, in words that might apply to George and even Alan. The weakness of the men lies in the stubborn way they occupy the fixed positions determined by the narratives; they cannot accommodate change, or the point of the stories would be lost. Since the films share the viewpoint of the heroines, any understanding offered by their husbands can only occur retrospectively, as it does in *It Always Rains on Sunday* and *Cage of Gold*, making the men appear, for the bulk of the films, to be obstinate or unseeing.

Stuck in the home, the women are also lacking in one of Ealing's traditional sources of support – community. In wartime films and in the post-war comedies, the security of communal feeling is a reward for sacrifice and restraint. But the pleasures of community do not seem to be an option for the women here. The emphasis on women in the home, rather than the working women of some realist films of the war, underlines the lack of community as a factor in the heroines' lives. Rose's angry denunciation of her step-daughters and her wariness with her neighbours leaves her with no allies, and we do not see her leave the house to join in the communal scenes in the pub or the market; a policeman and a nosy journalist are her only visitors and both presage disaster. Judy too, as Barr indicates, appears to be trapped in 'a large, enveloping dark house' (1977: 151), and the one social occasion we see, the party for her son, increases her sense of danger and isolation. In *Dance Hall*, the newly married Eve misses her friends and the social pleasures of the dance hall but her return to the Palais is unsuccessful; the music stops as she finally gets back on to the dance floor.

The isolation of married women from the community is backed up by the films' more general refusal to offer the traditionally cosy view of community and hence of nation with which Ealing is often associated. Closely bound up with the choice in favour of the community that the women have to make is an unease about what the communal now represents. In contrast to some of the Ealing comedies, these social melodramas seem to indicate that wartime versions of the nation pulling together no longer provide a rationale for communal support. The war is hardly referred to and, interestingly, when it is in

Cage of Gold the wartime experience invoked is not the traditional one of the community pulling together but of the unleashing of forces associated with masculine aggression, which are a threat in peacetime. Post-war modes of community, particularly around the social spheres of health and education, find little expression in these films. Alan, Judy's good choice in *Cage of Gold*, decides to work in the NHS rather than go into private practice but even here there is little sense of reward or thanks from the community: one of his patients harks back to Alan's father as 'the doctor' and insists that 'you can't beat the old ones'. It is significant that the social spaces of the films – markets, dance halls, clubs – are places of exploitation as well as pleasure, where middlemen and racketeers conspire to make women want something. In *It Always Rains on Sunday*, the bustling street market hides spivs, con men, liars and criminals offering goods that are desirable and dubious, 'guaranteed stolen goods' as a woman stallholder points out ironically to a policeman. *Cage of Gold* lacks communal spaces, except the crowded venues that Judy visits briefly with Bill; the London streets are shrouded in fog towards the end of the film and exemplify the risks that Judy is taking in trying to get rid of Bill. Even the dance hall, the most benign of these social spaces, is run by a con man (played significantly by Sydney Tafler, who was Vi's untrustworthy married man in *It Always Rains on Sunday*), and the film works to expose the way in which the fun and glamour is a façade, depending on people pretending to be something they are not; the glamorous continental dance team, Chiquita and Juan, turn out to have London accents and the masks at the new year dance take on a cruel aspect as the revellers ignore Eve's distress.

This bleak view of marriage, in which the woman is isolated in the home and lacks any communal resources, is a consequence of the realist approach adopted in these films. This is reinforced by the use of realist detail which grounds the women's position in a specific social context and offers the women in the audience the possibility of recognition of their own situation. The audience's access to the woman's viewpoint encourages identification with her in the manner of the woman's film, but it also constitutes part of the claim to realism: the heroines' plausibility makes them both ordinary and representative. This is particularly the case in *It Always Rains on Sunday* and *Dance Hall*, both of which depict the mundane drudgery of women's work in the home and use it as a point of reference to the post-war social world outside the film. Rose's kitchen is draughty and bleak, the broken window panes ineffectually stopped up with old blackout material; the rhythms of her Sunday are so typical and predictable – cooking the Sunday joint, the family meal, George's nap on the sofa, 'never in the bedroom', a trip to the pub in the evening – that Rose can feed and hide Tommy within its interstices. In *Dance Hall*, Phil is seen to get used to the married man's role quickly, expecting Eve to take all the domestic responsibility. His jealousy and sulkiness, his assumption that Eve's interests should be governed by his needs, are expressed through his heedless disregard for the difficulties of rationing and shopping and could hardly be represented in a bleaker or more direct fashion. When Eve reads from the labels on the tins that

Phil has so wastefully opened in protest at having to make his own meal, there is a despairing accuracy in her complaint that he has 'eaten enough for four persons and the meat was on points'. Commentators such as Aspinall and Mash have commented on the banality of Eve's cry to Phil that she is 'bored, bored, bored', but the complaint is taken seriously in the film because it acknowledges a common fear that female dissatisfaction with the drudgery and boredom of housework would create rebellion.[2] Although Hill argues that *It Always Rains on Sunday* and *Cage of Gold* work towards 'the construction of a new stability in which the woman will accept her proper place' (71), I would suggest that the films' representation of marriage calls this 'proper place' into question and makes the home feel more like the 'prison' warned against in the post-war pamphlet quoted earlier (Haste: 141).

The expression of feeling

I place an emphasis on feeling because I want to argue that the films offer not only a description of women's lives in the late 1940s, the apparently objective account associated with McCabe's classic realist text, but also a sense of what such a life might feel like. I have argued that these three Ealing films work with both melodramatic and realist approaches. When this has been recognised, there has been a tendency to argue that it is the melodramatic elements that reflect the contradictions being experienced by women in this period and allow for the expression of feelings of desire or fear. An early example of this is Sheila Whittaker's account of the way in which the 'melodramatic narrative discourse' of *It Always Rains on Sunday* must 'subvert, if not destroy' the realist tradition at work in Ealing (25). Landy's discussion of the social problem film emphasises the eclectic nature of the genre, 'fusing melodrama, docudrama and social realism' (1991: 432), but she offers readings that explore the tensions between 'the quest for realism' (436) and the melodramatic expression of the problem of female sexuality, which is at the heart of so many of the films (including *Dance Hall* and *Cage of Gold*). I have much sympathy with these approaches, to which my discussions of the films are indebted. However, I would also suggest that the expression of feeling in these films is made possible by the way in which the realist and melodramatic elements work together rather than against each other and that realism plays an important part in generating this emotional affectivity. An example of this can be found in an examination of acting and performance.

Alan Lovell has argued that 'British cinema is often at its most exciting when restraint and excess work together' (239), and he cites Googie Withers' acting as an example of this. In fact, I think it is possible to see a similar mode of performance in all three films, a mode based on extreme restraint that neverthe-less gives expression to the frustration and anger experienced by the heroines. In all three films, the central performance depends on the way in which ordinary behaviour can be disrupted by deep emotion, which has then to be reined back again. Withers' performance in *It Always Rains on Sunday* is based on a deliberately blank face, a rigid body and a highly controlled use of gesture. In the first scene, her excitement and fear at hearing of Tommy's escape is marked only by a brief pause and a clenching of the comb as she continues to curl up her hair. On a number of occasions, although her face is held blank, swift movements of the eyes indicate fear and calculation. Sometimes, we are denied even this and Rose's extreme anxiety is expressed through her rigid back, as when the camera is placed behind her as she watches through the kitchen window to see whether George will discover Tommy hidden in the air raid shelter. This restraint gives way for a moment in the scene in which Rose attacks Vi for trying to get into the bedroom where Tommy is hiding. Withers breaches the distance that she usually puts between herself and the other characters as she seizes Vi's shoulder and pulls her hair. At the end of the scene, though, Withers physically resumes her normal composure as she shifts her shoulders and walks straight-backed down the stairs, her face blank again. Rose's extreme despair at the end of the film, when she tries to gas herself, is again handled with restraint; she walks around the kitchen, touching each door as if measuring out a cell and locks herself into her own kitchen. The face is blank but the small gestures express the feeling of entrapment in her own home.

Withers' performance has been widely acknowledged but its refusal of facial expression and its use of limited but expressive gestures are also features of the performances of Natasha Parry and Jean Simmons. For instance, in a key scene in *Cage of Gold* in which Judy talks first to Alan and then to Bill about 'the wonderful life' she is enjoying, Simmons' expression is frequently hidden as she is positioned with her back to the camera and to the two men. At the end of the scene, when Bill realises 'You're going to have a baby,' her face remains still, and when he announces 'We're going to get married,' nothing moves in her face to show her relief and pleasure except a sideways movement of the eyes. Parry's work in *Dance Hall* is similarly marked by the restrained play of emotions across a calm demeanour, occasionally switching to moments of extreme emotional expressiveness. Eve's decision to 'go with' Alec occurs in a wordless scene and is registered through Parry's blank face and averted gaze; a movement in the throat and a parting of the lips indicates desire, until finally she turns her head towards him to indicate acceptance. Later on, however, in a row with Phil, she expresses emotion more fully, both verbally and physically through clenching her fists, a gesture that she repeats in frustration at the end when she is locked out of the Palais.

Another example of the way in which melodramatic and realist modes come together to represent the women's position can be found in the *mise en scène*, which, at key points, transforms the home from a mundane and ordinary domestic space into a trap or prison. The realist emphasis of the films means that we build up knowledge of the domestic space by following the heroines through their domestic tasks. The routines of everyday life are lived out in rooms that are familiar in their ordinariness and are recognisably representative of difficult but not unusual housing conditions. At points in the narrative, this realist focus is allied with a melodramatic reordering of the domestic space to express the heroine's feeling of entrapment. Again, I would argue that realism is not being 'transcended' but is an essential component of the way in which restraint and excess are working together to express emotions rooted in a material context that focuses tightly on what home and marriage actually have to offer. Thus, in *It Always Rains on Sunday*, the *mise en scène* stresses the cramped house which makes it difficult for Rose to keep her lover out of the communal household areas such as the kitchen and stairs. At key moments, Rose is isolated in watchful close-up as she tries to work out how the different family members are moving behind and above her and hence how near they are to discovering the hidden Tommy. In the more spacious home of Judy and Alan, Judy's isolation is also expressed through the geography of the house through the use of the central stairway and hall. She is on the stairs when she first hears Bill's voice at the front door when he visits her on his return from Paris, and she moves out of the Christmas party into the isolation of the hall when the full implication of his return hits her; it is in the hall that she takes the phone call from Bill that leads her to go and meet him, and later she walks down the stairs through the hall, ignoring the phone call from Alan that might have held her back. *Dance Hall* is organised between the cramped spaces of domestic life and the wide spaces of the Palais. One striking example of how this is used to express feeling occurs when we cut from Eve leaving for her honeymoon with Phil (the car drives past the closed Palais) to a scene that is clearly representative of their married life. There is no period of grace within this marriage, for Eve is trapped in their small flat, doing the ironing and waiting for Phil's late return from work. The rented flat is dark and cramped; Eve trips over and is clumsy in dealing with the housework, lacking the physical grace she shows on the dance floor. Eve's despair is compounded by the fact that she feels herself that the home should offer her more. She tries to convince Alec that married life is satisfactory – 'it's silly really to keep going out when you've got a nice home of your own' – but her frustration is clear in her stumbling run down the stairs when the communal telephone rings and offers the possibility of release.

I have argued that the films of the post-war period in Britain continued the wartime emphasis on women as representatives of national choices and, in their realist emphasis, provide an account that was grimmer and less hopeful than official versions. If they can be criticised for the limited choices they offered their heroines, the failure is surely not to be ascribed to the limitations of realism but to the difficulties that the post-war settlement had both in reassessing women's roles and in providing the material circumstances that might have made women's lives easier. One historian comments that 'after 1947 the government never regained the confidence and verve it had shown in the early months of power' (Tomlinson: 89). Ealing's realism captures not only the physical circumstances of this moment but also what it felt like to be a woman trapped within it. Far from being unsympathetic to the heroines' dilemmas, these films offer a recognition of the bleakness of their position in post-war society; their realist and melodramatic elements work together to offer an account that is both emotional and analytical. The concentration on the viewpoint of married women is achieved through a realist emphasis on the minutiae of their day-to-day lives in post-war Britain. But the reworking of the experience of rationing and harsh economic restraint into an acknowledgement of what the hard work of domestic life and the lack of warmth in marriage felt like results in an account of contemporary life that surely has its place alongside Gainsborough's more expansive modes.

6   European relations

Sex, politics and the European woman

This chapter brings together two rather different concepts that at first sight seem to have significance in different spheres: the British state's political relationship with Europe in the post-war period and British cinema's attempts to deal with representations of sexuality in the 1950s. In the films of the period, however, these two problematics are brought together, and we can understand the emergence of one of the most familiar clichés of fifties British cinema – the beautiful, free and sexy foreign woman – if we consider it in terms not only of sexuality but also of post-war politics. In this chapter, I suggest that, in the early part of the period, the European woman is used as a key figure to express British ambivalence about Europe, that this political ambivalence finds expression and a limited form of resolution through an emphasis on sexuality, and that this complex sexual aura continues to be a key feature of the representation of such women even when its political resonances have fallen away.

The European woman is one of the most familiar features of British cinema of the 1950s. She crosses genres and appears, sometimes unexpectedly, in a wide range of films. Understandably, she features in war films throughout the period from *Against the Wind* to *The Password is Courage*, and in specifically post-war thrillers such as Carol Reed's *The Third Man* and *The Man Between*. She helps the British hero in thrillers such as *The Golden Salamander* and *The Man from Tangier*, or hinders him in *The Venetian Bird*. But she also features in romances such as *The Glass Mountain* and *The Young Lovers*, and she pops up in comedies, as, for instance, the foreign girlfriend for the resolutely British Kenneth More in *Doctor in the House* and the *au pair* who wreaks havoc in *Upstairs and Downstairs*. When the New Wave looked north, she passionately seduces Joe Lampton in *Room at the Top*, and she is an elegant social problem in *The L-Shaped Room*.

At one level, this link between the foreign woman and sexuality can be understood as another example of the ubiquitous 'other' who, as psychoanalytic accounts tell us, is a troublesome construction that both repels and fascinates the dominant order. But it is important to place this ahistorical 'other' into a historical context, and I will argue that the figure of the European women can be read not just through accounts of sexual difference but through the hints of political difference that the emphasis on sexuality hides. The figure of the

European woman draws on well-established notions in British culture of the Continent as a place of sexual freedom, exemplified, for instance, by the image of *fin de siècle* Paris or decadent Berlin in the 1920s. After the Second World War, this emphasis on sexuality is underpinned by a particular post-war understanding of European politics. I will argue that it is the British attitude to the politics of Europe that is suppressed or hidden in these films and the emphasis on foreign sexuality is the mechanism for that suppression.

This essay focuses initially on four films from the earlier part of the period, all of which in different ways make conscious reference to post-war Europe. *Snowbound* (1948) is a conventional thriller involving a hunt for Nazi gold, which allows spectacular shots of mountains and skiing; *The Third Man* (1949) and *The Man Between* (1953) are more prestigious productions, both directed by Carol Reed and set on the borders between East and West; Hamer's *The Long Memory* (1953) has an entirely English setting but draws on references to wartime Europe for its symbolic meanings. The figure of the European woman is crucial to these films, as a link between the wartime past and the Cold War present, between stability and confusion, war and peace, evil and innocence, knowledge and ignorance. As time passes, however, the political connotations of the figure begin to drop away, but I suggest that her sexuality is still marked by traces of her original role. This helps to explain the use made in the late 1950s of two European stars, Hildegarde Knef and Simone Signoret, whom I discuss at the end of this chapter.

'Thank God for the English Channel'

Before we study the European woman in cinema more closely, we need to look briefly at British attitudes to the post-war political situation. As we have seen, the period after the war was marked as a time of reconstruction on the domestic and the international fronts. The 'post-war settlement' was, as Hennessy describes it for both Labour and Conservative politicians, 'built around an understanding that Britain would remain a great power abroad' (2). It was assumed that Britain had a key role to play in restoring stability in international relations but remaining a great power, in the light of Britain's parlous economic position, was a daunting task. Internationally, the post-war settlement in Europe involved addressing the problems of both Germany and the USSR and maintaining the USA as a source of support.

Anne Deighton argues that British foreign policy as the war ended was 'to sustain American interest in Europe and to forge an anti-Soviet coalition.' As she notes, this was not a policy 'immediately acceptable to British public opinion', since it involved reassessing relationships with former allies and enemies (6). It involved long-term plans for German economic recovery in the Western zones in the belief that, as Foreign Secretary Ernest Bevin put it to his Cabinet colleagues in May 1946, 'the danger of Russia has become certainly as great as, and possibly even greater than, that of a revived Germany' (quoted in *ibid.*: 62). At the same time, this policy meant identifying the Russians as enemies against whom the Allies (now including West Germany) had to unite. Such changes in attitude were by no means straightforward, either to members of the government and the civil service or to the British, who had endured six years of war. As the war ended, Germany was still in the minds of many a threat,[1] while Hennessy comments that the reaction of the public and the press to Churchill's Iron Curtain speech in 1946 showed that many were 'far from ready to substitute for the image of the brave, defiant Russian ally at Stalingrad in 1942 the threat of a predatory Soviet Union armed to the teeth and ready to swoop in western Europe' (261). It was not until January 1948 that Bevin made his foreign policy in Europe public: 'given the climate of public opinion in Britain, the true direction of Britain's interests in Europe could not be disclosed publicly at home until memories of wartime Soviet heroism had begun to fade' (Deighton: 226). The redrawing of boundaries, which turned the Russians from allies into enemies and the Germans (or at least some of them) from foes into friends, had to go on in people's heads as well as on the ground.

Even those wartime alliances that persisted into the peace could still be a problem, since there was fear of the withdrawal of US interest, and France was seen as an 'unreliable' (40). Although involved in Europe, British politicians were reluctant to see British interests as being served by more formal ties. Churchill, out of office, might call for a 'kind of United States of Europe' (quoted in Lane: 226), but in 1950 Britain refused to join France and Germany in the European Coal and Steel Community, the precursor of the European Common Market. Hennessy quotes Jean Monnet's assessment that the reasons for Britain's unwillingness to join can be found in the different experiences of war ('Britain had not been conquered or invaded. She felt no need to exorcise history' (364)) and Britain's fear of another continental invasion ('Britain has no confidence that France and the other countries of Europe have the ability or even the will effectively to resist a possible Russian invasion' (402)). This link between wartime experience and attitudes to post-war Europe is crucial. As Churchill put it, when he took over government after the Conservative victory in October 1951:

> We help, we dedicate, we play a part, but we are not merged and do not forfeit our insular or Commonwealth character. I should resist any American pressure to treat Britain on the same footing as the European states, none of whom have the advantages of the Channel and who were consequently conquered.
>
> (quoted in *ibid.*: 401)

Or, as a character put it rather more succinctly in *The Colditz Story*, when reminded of the suffering of occupied Europe, 'Thank God for the English Channel.'

Europe in the period immediately after the war was envisaged as a place of possible danger and entanglement. Involvement with Europe was necessary but it was also important to maintain a distance. The changing allegiances that led to the fixed blocs of the Cold War took time to negotiate, and during that time Europe is associated with unstable and shifting national positions. In addition, Britain's different experience of the war meant that national identity was tied up with an insular image of standing firm, while the compromises, collaborations and betrayals of occupation and defeat were associated with Europe. But it is worth noting that Britain was not immune to the movements of people that occurred during and after the war. Sheila Patterson's study of West Indian immigration in the 1950s comments that migration was not an uncommon phenomenon and points out that post-war labour shortages meant that the government encouraged migrant labour from Europe, including official schemes such as the Polish resettlement programme of 1946–51 and the European volunteer workers programme for displaced workers, as well as a number of smaller schemes for German, Austrian and Italian workers (62). Post-war interaction with Europeans was therefore possible for many British people and, in the context of this chapter, a comment tucked away in Gorer's account of the English character is intriguing: from responses to his newspaper questionnaire, he noted the 'frequent appearance of foreigners as partners in ... non-marital sexual relationships' (93).

And perhaps, to adapt Monnet's phrase, the British did have something to exorcise – not the experience of defeat but their deeply ambivalent attitude to their post-war European allies. If the war films present the myth of British superiority in its most untroubled form, British doubts and uncertainties find their expression in those films that feature the European woman. Here, the nature of the war itself becomes more problematic. It is no longer a question of two sides, of right and wrong and of deserved victory; questions are raised about what was being fought for and how sides were chosen. The clarity of the fifties version of the Second World War depended on the construction of abstract ideals being fought for in the past; setting a film in the European present had the effect of making the wartime past ambiguous and hard to understand. As we trace the figure of the European woman from films of the late 1940s to the late 1950s, we can see how this process is managed through narratives in which sexual knowledge and submission can be seen to stand for problematic political relationships. In their discussion of *Frieda*, a 1947 film that takes the question of revised Anglo-German relations head-on, Charlotte Brunsdon and Rachel Moseley suggest that 'ideas of femininity ... are used ... to negotiate a new peacetime idea of national identity' (129), and Frieda's transformation into a good wife to her English husband can act as a metaphor for the wished-for relations between the two countries. I want to extend this analogy and suggest that, in a variety of films, gender relations (not always within marriage) act as a metonym for national relations. In these films, the figure of the European woman emerges, presenting a particular configuration of sexuality and politics that not only tells us something about how the European woman became a site of fantasy about sexual possibilities but also provides a metaphor for Britain's relationship with Europe at the point when Cold War attitudes and boundaries were being fixed into place.

Wartime experiences and post-war memories

The heroine of *Snowbound* is the Italian Countess Forelli, known in a previous life as Carla, played by Mila Parely, who like many of the foreign actresses in such roles appeared in only one or two British films. *Snowbound* tells the story of a guileless script writer, Blair (Dennis Price), who is sent by an ex-intelligence agent to find out why a collection of dubious Europeans are congregating at a remote ski hut in the Alps. The answer turns out to be a race to find Nazi gold buried in a ski lift at the end of the war. The main villain is Kellerman (Herbert Lom), an unrepentant Nazi who wants the gold to establish another Reich, but others in the group searching for the treasure include the very British Mayne, who has stolen the identity of another soldier. The more Blair finds out the more his life is at risk but, in the end, Kellerman and Mayne die and the gold remains unfound. As the contessa embraces Blair, she reveals that she knows where the gold is, but 'already too many people died trying to find it. I will never say.'

The contessa's position is deeply ambiguous. Like the men in the group, she disguises her true identity and tries to hide her past but it becomes clear that she was also deeply implicated with the Germans. However, she tries to ensure that Blair is not hurt by the others and indeed saves his life by calling out a search party when Mayne leaves him injured and lost during a skiing expedition in the mountains. She thus tries to shield Blair from danger and stand between him and the men who want to kill him. This urge to protect Blair is linked to her knowledge of the ruthless nature of Nazism and of the lengths to which greed and ambition will take them. While Blair seems unaware of the dangers of investigating the past, the contessa's wartime experiences mean that she understands the current dangers posed by Kellerman and Mayne.

But this knowledge is translated into something more than the secrets of her own past because she links it to an understanding of how Europe has suffered and the contrast between the European and English experiences of war. This is made explicit in a scene in which the contessa takes Blair skiing. The contessa's greater knowledge is at first demonstrated in terms of her superior skiing ability, which, unlike Mayne, she uses to help Blair by teaching him how to stop. Blair does not take the hint and tells her that he has found out something of her past and her links with the Nazis. In response, she does not deny it but makes a comparison between herself and Europe. The speech indicates so clearly what is implicit for other European women that it is worth quoting at some length:

> Such a long time ago … what's the good of torturing oneself with memories. It's so easy for you English, you live on your island until there is a war. You come to the continent and fight and then you go back to your island but here things are different. There's always intrigue, suspicion and fear. One does things one doesn't want to do.

When Blair protests that he understands, she retorts:

> No, you don't understand. You are intrigued, fascinated. I am an adventure
> for you … You don't see that I am like any other girl, only sometimes life
> has been too difficult.

Then with a quick change of mood, she asks 'Why are you so serious?', points
to the beauty of the snow and the sky and promises 'Tonight we will dance.'
Blair once again protests: 'Carla, this isn't the real you,' and she grows serious
again. 'Do you know what is the real me? … I don't. I wish I knew but I don't.'
She skis away, leaving Blair puzzled and intrigued.

A number of points are worth making about this speech, since it is paradig-
matic in its use of certain references and elisions. First, a specifically European
experience of the war is called on, but details are vague and are expressed in
terms of broader references to 'life' as 'difficult'. There is a shift from the
personal to the universal in the shift to the impersonal pronoun: 'One does
things ….' The continent is different from England because 'things' are more
complicated there and people are suspicious and fearful in the face of what
cannot be understood. There is the quick change of mood, which makes the
contessa seem brittle and flirtatious, but we have learned that this is a façade,
hiding pain. Finally, she returns to her own personal position and the question
of identity but by now she has taken the ambiguity of Europe itself and cannot
tell him who she really is. The effect is to give a tragic dimension to the moral
compromises and betrayals of war and to make the war itself the fateful determi-
nant for actions that cannot be judged by the ignorant English hero.

Throughout the whole exchange there is a sexual undertow, which is created
by the contessa's oscillation between genuine intimacy with Blair and flirtatious
play. The complications and mysteries of the contessa's politics are indeed inter-
twined with her sexual activities. As the story unfolds, revelations about her
politics are revelations about her lovers and it is sexual power that brings her
political knowledge. Blair's investigation of the mystery of the group at the hut
starts with a photograph of the contessa and turns into an investigation of her
sexual history. It was her German lover, Stellman, who originally buried the
gold; in a flashback, we see how 'she got out of him' the plans for moving the
gold and persuaded him to bury it in the Alps; he 'couldn't resist the temptation,' says Kellerman contemptuously. In addition, she passed on information
about the treasure to her subsequent lover Mayne, which explains why he has
also turned up at the hut to find it. Her sexuality is thus associated with wrong-
doing but is also, it would seem, what drives her to help Blair. Although she is
accused of using love cynically, of 'playing with' Blair as she did with Mayne,
she retains her belief in romantic love: 'he loved me always,' she says of
Stellman. Her sexual appeal for Blair is not fully developed, perhaps because she
is too compromised by her Nazi connections, but the ending hints at redemption through suffering and love. Although she still has knowledge of the gold,
she renounces its use.

The contessa's survival indicates that she is in a different position from the
men in the group, who are harshly condemned for their wartime activities. It is

through the European woman, rather than the men, that forgiveness and under-standing of the European experience of war might be achieved. *Snowbound* begins to show how political activity during the war can be fictionally trans-formed into sexual experience and be forgiven.

The Man Between also has, as one of its central characters, a woman who is a former enemy but one who is more sympathetic in her attempts to ally herself with the new post-war boundaries. In this film, an innocent young British woman, Susanne (Claire Bloom), visits post-war Berlin to meet her sister-in-law for the first time. Her brother, who is a doctor in the army, has married a German woman, Bettina, played by German actress Hildegarde Knef. As the plot unfolds, Susanne learns that Bettina is actually still married to Ivo (James Mason), an East German with an extremely dubious past whom she has assumed was dead but who has reappeared and is desperate to get over to the West. Bettina dominates the first half of the film, but in the second half the narrative is driven by the love affair between Ivo and Susanne, which ends when Ivo is killed helping Susanne to escape from East Berlin.

An explicit contrast is set up between Susanne and Bettina. The film opens with Susanne flying into Berlin, taking the detached aerial viewpoint of the British outsider. The film contrasts Susanne's youth and her ignorance of the ruined city and its complex politics with Bettina's maturity and knowledge. She both protects and explains, at one point pulling Susanne back from the path of a speeding car, at another explaining that a group of poor people at the airport are 'refugees from the East'. She knows that spies can be small boys on bicycles and labourers who are working too hard. Her knowledge is not just political but also sexual. She is sexually experienced and mature, her appearance is admired, and she has an air of authority and control. But she is also associated with a sense of loss, and throughout the film her appearance and behaviour imply strong sexual possibilities which go unexpressed. Her husband is at work all the time, so Bettina is isolated both in her home, which is among the ruins, and in her journeys around the city and across the border.

Such is Bettina's sexual aura that Susanne misreads her anxiety about Ivo and assumes that Bettina is having an affair with him. The audience is invited to share this suspicion. She notes Bettina's anxiety in Ivo's presence, the furtive phone calls and her apparent jealousy when Ivo starts to take Susanne herself out. As the narrative unfolds, we learn that at face value Bettina is hiding the fact that the return of this previous husband renders her marriage to the British soldier/doctor invalid. But what is being hidden is not just a sexual past but a political one, although as is typical that remains much more shadowy. Ivo, Bettina finally admits, has 'appeared out of the ruins of Berlin', and it becomes clear that he acts as a reminder of her nationality as well as her sexuality. The title of the film refers to Ivo as the man between, but Bettina is equally divided, structurally positioned between West and East. She lives in the West but crosses the border between East and West confidently and easily. She talks to Susanne in English but returns to German when it is politic as they cross the border. Through her British 'husband' she is working for the Allies but she is married to a German, and she knows that crime in East Berlin is also a form of national politics, a rejection of Allied hegemony. Ivo claims her not directly as his wife but as a fellow national: 'You're a Berliner still, aren't you if only in name?' Later it is assumed by one of the East German villains that she will be loyal: 'She is a German woman no matter who she has married since.'

Bettina's knowledge of the politics of East and West, her understanding of the compromises and evasions that are part of her life, is based on her own history. She warns Susanne about getting too fond of Berlin (and Ivo) and suggests that Susanne's ignorance is tied up with her different past and experience of the war: 'There's a hundred years difference between the way we've lived.' Bettina wants to live in the present, the new Europe, but the past claims her. She has more knowledge than either her husband or her sister-in-law, not just of sexuality but also of what went on in the war and what goes on in the East. Explaining why she hid her knowledge of Ivo's return, she broadens the issue: she was hiding more than a marriage – 'I wanted to protect you from all this dirt.' Her husband and Susanne can never know the full truth, but Bettina's self-abnegation – 'You are free,' she tells Martin – offers her hope of a truer reconciliation. Unlike Ivo, who is killed as he tries to cross the border, Bettina is offered a new beginning when her British husband asks her to marry him again, this time with a fuller understanding of her past.

Figure 6.1 Hildegarde Knef in *The Man Between* (United Artists, 1953).
Courtesy of the Kobal Collection.

Both *Snowbound* and *The Man Between* present heroines who have enemy nationality. The remaining two films deal with those who can be more readily presented as victims of the war. In *The Third Man*, the European woman, Anna Schmidt, is played by the Italian actress Alida Valli but is given a Czech identity in the story. The film tells the story of American writer Holly Martins (Joseph Cotten), who arrives in post-war Vienna, a city controlled by the Allies and divided into four sectors run by the USA, Britain, France and Russia. Holly gets involved in the search for his friend Harry Lime (Orson Welles) and, in the process, discovers that Harry is evil and corrupt. Anna was Harry's lover and initially at least helps Holly in his search. In the end though, she allies with Harry and tries to save him from capture. Unlike *Snowbound*, the initial emphasis is not on the politics of the wartime past but on personal friendship and love. Anna is an actress, and Holly's first conversation with her takes place as she removes wig, eyelashes and makeup in her theatre dressing room. This stripping away of the surface helps to associate Anna with a kind of candour, a willingness to reveal herself and her feelings. She has a frankness that surprises and attracts Holly, an openness about her feelings for Harry and a commitment to a kind of clear-sighted love. Holly becomes disillusioned about Harry as he learns more about his evil activities but Anna protests that further knowledge should not change what one feels. Holly started with an image that he finds is not true; Anna starts with feelings to which she is faithful. 'A person doesn't change,' she tells Holly, 'because you found out more.'

However, this discourse about love carries other connotations which make it problematic and which ensure that once again politics and sexuality intertwine. Anna is a Czech and thus can be understood as a victim of Hitler's invasion. But now she is an Eastern European who is in the wrong zone, she has forged papers and knows that 'the Russians would claim' her. Nothing is said about what she did in the war; instead, Anna's descriptions of her feelings for Harry and her actions to save him come to stand for her untold experiences of war. The way she speaks about love has strong resonances of collaboration and complicity. She tries to recognise Harry's guilt and to reject him but knows that she is emotionally caught up in it. 'I don't want to see him, hear him,' she tells Holly, 'but he's still part of me, that's a fact.' In the end, she collaborates by protecting Harry and tries to cover herself by accusing Holly of betrayal: 'Look at yourself. They have a name for people like you'.and 'You must be very proud to be a police informer.' Such language serves to raise the unexpressed question: what did Anna herself do in the war?

The figure of Anna stands as an intermediary between the innocent Holly and the evil Harry. She has knowledge of the past, she is committed to loving without illusion but in the end she proves unable to detach herself from that past knowledge and is trapped in a love focused on Harry but which also seems to carry with it ambiguities about her own role and loyalties in the war. The national positions of the other characters are confirmed by their attitudes towards this ambiguous European figure. The American Holly is naive and trusting; he has to learn not just about love but also about politics, and he has to come to terms with the constantly shifting positions of the Europeans he encounters. The tilting camera work and shadowy *mise-en-scène* emphasise that Holly cannot trust what he sees. The Russians are the heavies who threaten Anna. If she is taken by them she will disappear into the darkness of Eastern Europe and be beyond the help of the Allies. Callaway, the British officer in charge of security in Vienna, played by Trevor Howard, is wary of Anna but is willing to use her. Unlike the American hero, he has gone through the learning process and refuses to be drawn to her charms. While he supports Anna in her desire to avoid being handed over to the Russians, he does so with a weary cynicism about her ability to detach herself from old allegiances. In the end he is proved right; in this case, the European woman's capacity for love cannot be transferred to the West. Anna cannot reject the past or seek forgiveness. As she walks past Harry, at the end of *The Third Man*, she retains her independence but seems to be walking back into the complex politics of Eastern Europe.

The Long Memory is also concerned with the complexity of the European experience of war but makes use of it in a rather different way. In this film, it becomes a symbolic event that goes beyond politics. This film, unlike the others, is set in Britain, partly in London and partly on the flat landscape of the Kent coast. The plot apparently has nothing to do with the war, although the hero, Davidson, is played by John Mills, who constantly appeared in war films in the 1940s and 1950s. His star image as an average man who will not give in to injustice is drawn on in this role as a man who years before was betrayed by a woman, Faye (Elizabeth Sellars), and was imprisoned for a murder he did not commit. Coming out of prison, he is determined on revenge and pursues Faye, who during his time in prison has married a high-ranking police officer, Arthur Lowther (John McCallum). However, in the end, Davidson is reconciled to his past with the help of a woman, Elsa, played by Eva Bergh, whom he meets in a rundown beach cafe.

Elsa is a 'foreigner', 'one of those refugees, come off the ship'. When we first see her serving in a rundown cafe she is mute, watching Davidson with wild, staring eyes. She is clearly a victim of the war, but the experience she recounts is pared of detail and has the universal quality of a folk tale. 'They came when I was 12,' she tells Davidson. 'Our village was burned. What happened to my mother and father I never knew. Since then I've never had a place to be where I was happy.' Davidson was betrayed by the woman he thought he loved, but Elsa's experiences both during the war and afterwards as a refugee go beyond his individual story to something more universal. It is this experience that Elsa draws on, not for political knowledge but for her understanding of human nature and her belief in the power of love. Her experience of the war has been more brutal than that of the British and she brings that knowledge to her personal judgements: 'You are not a cruel man,' she tells Davidson. 'I have seen too much cruelty not to know.' She also knows that it is possible to survive 'bad things' without being warped or twisted by them, as Davidson has been. 'I knew that you were not bad,' she tells Davidson. 'Bad things have happened to me but I'm not bad.' Her capacity to forgive is based not on ignorance but on knowledge: 'perhaps it is not worth it, to hurt people back.' She sees through the surface of things because she has seen so much: when Davidson rejects revenge and returns to Elsa, she accepts his embrace with the words 'You are suddenly the person I always knew you were.'

Elsa is younger than the other women we have looked at and appears to have no romantic past. Nevertheless, her appearance is charged with sexuality; her hair is untamed, her face slightly sweaty, her skimpy blouse is tight under the bust to reveal her figure. Like the other women, she has a quality of intimacy; she makes direct eye contact with Davidson and focuses her entire attention on him. The contrast with the repressed, middle-class, English Faye is marked, particularly in the sequence that cuts between bedroom conversations of Elsa and Davidson and Faye and her husband. The contrast is both visual and verbal. Although Elsa and Davidson are sleeping apart in a wrecked barge, their heads are connected by the angles of the bunks, and close-ups show us Elsa's face, slightly sweaty, her hair pushed back, as she speaks openly to Davidson. By contrast, Faye and Arthur are physically unconnected as they lie sleepless in chaste single beds; Faye hides her face as her husband presses her clipped evasions to discover that, throughout their marriage, she has hidden the fact that she lied during the murder trial.

For Elsa, love is linked to loss and knowledge of the cruelty of war. The portrayal of Elsa pushes to the limits the capacity for the abnegation of self in sexual surrender that both Anna and Bettina hint at. Her candour and frankness in love turn into a self-surrender, an abasement in which she takes nothing for herself. She is twice filmed on her knees, scrubbing the floor, and she offers to 'keep things clean for you, cook for you.' When Davidson demands 'Why should you think I want you here?' she replies: 'I did not think you would want but I thought perhaps you would not mind.' On her first night at the shack, with Davidson mute and angry by her side, she nevertheless declares 'Tonight ... I've been happier than I ever remember.' In *The Long Memory*, this self-abnegation is presented as a psychological justification for her character precisely because it is linked to her experience of the war. For her, loving is enough: 'I know my love is not matched but love is love.' Her surrender of herself is thus linked to a broader model of redemption through abnegation, which Davidson learns from her.

In these films of the late 1940s and early 1950s, the European woman was a complex figure through which we can see British attitudes to Europe represented. She combines sexual experience with a tragic knowledge of the war, which enables her to understand emotionally the post-war realities, which generally escape the Anglo-Saxon protagonist. Although the European woman is not the central figure, the films are structured around her, so her ambiguities and dilemmas come to represent those of Europe itself and the relationship between her and the protagonist parallels Britain's relations with Europe. In each of the films, the central character goes through a process of growing up, learning about loss and betrayal and coming to terms with the complexity of European culture, whose difference is represented through the figure of the woman. She has knowledge not only of the war and her own past but also of the evil of which mankind is capable, which gives her a tragic dimension and a sense of being driven by forces that are beyond her control. Her own identity is fractured; she tries to negotiate across national boundaries, is a refugee who does not live in her own country. She sometimes has to put up a façade, to take on a different name like the contessa, or to struggle to lose a past identity, as Bettina does. If her identity is ambiguous, so also is her morality. The evil she has seen is literally unspeakable and can only be described in banal terms as 'difficult' or 'bad'. Her possible involvement in such matters is thus disguised and her own past activities treated as a mystery.

In each case, sexuality is used as a metaphor for politics. The women's experience of the war endows her with a capacity for feeling that gives her sexuality a tragic dimension. She is marked as sexually available but generally not culpably so, since her frankness in love, her willingness to give herself up to the experience, are signs of an emotional surrender that may be understood as a plea for forgiveness and a political surrender. Her belief that powerful forces cannot be resisted is expressed through her readiness to believe in the power of love and her willingness to surrender to it. The mystery of her political past becomes a mystery about her previous sexual experiences and the fact that she knows more about suffering and evil is transposed into an understanding of sexuality which is greater than that of the protagonist. But her ambiguous politics and her unknown past also render the European woman suspect, so in her representation there is always the potential for betrayal, for complicity, for secrets. Doubts about European allies and concerns about their behaviour in the war are here transformed into a more familiar sexual metaphor in which the woman's sexual history stands for or hides her political past.

It is this combination of politics and sexuality that gives a particular intensity to the figure of the European woman. None of the heroines I have discussed become good wives, as Brunsdon and Moseley argue that Frieda does though, towards the end of *The Long Memory*, Elsa appears to be moving in that direction when she adopts the headscarf and bulky woollen suit of the respectable British housewife. But they do, I think, offer a vision of 'a more pliable post-war femininity' (131), a woman who is sexually available and knowledgeable but willing to love unreservedly and sacrifice her own interests for the male hero. And if we take into account the political dimensions of this figure, we can see that what is being explored here is not just a more pliable set of relationships between men and women but also a more pliable set of relationships between Britain and Europe. In the films, though, as in Europe, this was not easy to achieve; even sexual merging requires complex negotiations and may not lead to a happy ending.

The European woman in the war film

As the 1950s went on, the uncertainties and ambiguities about Europe began to be resolved through the development of new European institutions and the fixed hostilities of the Cold War. The cinema saw the conventions of the war film become firmly established as a largely male preserve and the success of the French actress Brigitte Bardot, whose star image emphasised a natural sexuality and a free spirit that had nothing to do with the war. Two later examples of the war film, *Seven Thunders* (1957) and *Operation Amsterdam* (1959), show how the figure of the European woman became somewhat schematic, drawing on wartime references that had now become familiar.

Seven Thunders is a highly international British film directed by the Argentinian Hugo Ferengese and starring the American Stephen Boyd. Boyd plays Dave, who with his friend Jimmy escapes from a POW camp and, with the help of the Resistance, hides in Marseilles in 1943. The pair survive various scares and searches, and Dave falls in love with Lise (Anna Gaylor), a blonde French girl who lives in the same house. Finally, the Nazis decide to clean out the old quarter, and the film ends with Jimmy, Dave and Lise escaping once again on a fishing boat organised by the Resistance. It is a somewhat unusual fifties war film since it takes place largely in the domestic space of the (makeshift) home and perhaps for this reason can deal with love affairs and comedy.

Seven Thunders offers a good example of a European woman who retains some aspects of the immediate post-war figure but who is also influenced by Bardot. She is blonde, and we first see her dressed in a striped top and full, tightly waisted skirt. She is childish and quick to express her needs, selfish in demanding what she wants, whether it be a pair of high-heeled shoes or a trip to England. She is impulsive in her speech, and Dave tells her that she would be 'like a fish out of water' in England: 'you say whatever comes into your mind.' She is physical in her expression of emotion. At their first meeting, she bites Dave's hand when he tries to hold her and they first make love after Dave has saved her from attack by a German soldier. 'I am grateful, very, very grateful,' she tells him as she kisses him. Dave describes her as 'a little animal'.

Dave initially deeply distrusts Lise. After their first night together, he discovers that both Lise and his money are missing, but he is reassured when Lise returns with food, milk and coffee. He continues to be wary of her, particularly when he discovers that her previous boyfriend was a German soldier who has been sent to Russia. Dave begins to be more sympathetic when he learns that she is totally alone, although typically her history is rather vague in that her father ran off before she was born and her mother was 'sent away' when the Germans came:

Lise:	Perhaps she is dead by now.
Dave:	You mean there's no one looking after you?
Lise:	You now.
Dave:	And after me, someone else I suppose?

Finally, though, Lise proves that she can be trustworthy and put her love for Dave before her own interests. She persuades the Resistance to wait for Jimmy and Dave, and she goes back into the quarter as it is being blown apart by the Germans to get a message to them. This act of redemption is rewarded, and she escapes on the fishing boat. However, the film cannot quite imagine their life together and it closes with a shot of the carefree Lise, soaking wet with her hair ruffled in the sea breeze, passionately kissing Dave.

The second war film, *Operation Amsterdam*, stars Peter Finch as Jan Smith and Eva Bartok as Anna. It is set in May 1940 and is more typical of the action-based war film, which normally has little room for women. It deals with a secret mission launched from Britain to get industrial diamonds out of Amsterdam. The three men land on the coast amid chaotic scenes as refugees struggle to escape. They meet Anna on the quay when Jan stops her driving her car off the pier into the water. She agrees to drive them into Amsterdam, where it tran-spires that her father is a major diamond merchant, who eventually persuades the other dealers to give up their diamonds. The Nazis are taking over the city, and Anna helps the trio to evade capture and successfully collect all the diamonds, and she drives them back to their pick-up point on the coast.

The group has been warned about fifth columnists and at first their leader, Major Dillon, suspects that her suicide attempt was faked. He observes her talking to German soldiers and is angry when rather than waiting outside with the car as instructed she disappears. On her return, he orders her upstairs: 'If you don't get out, I'll shoot you.' Anna, on being questioned by him, sits smoking and replies coolly 'I don't like being threatened.' However, it gradu-ally emerges that Anna is working with the Dutch who are resisting the invasion and that she can be of crucial help to the British mission. Major Dillon is convinced and apologises: 'I was wrong about you Anna. I'm sorry.' Anna is proved to be entirely honourable, and her initial promise to them – 'I keep my word' – is entirely vindicated.

Anna's mature dignity and the sense of tragic loss that surrounds her is based on her personal position and her national identity. At a personal level, it emerges that her fiancé Josef is half Jewish and is fighting in the army; he is missing and Anna believes him to be dead. In addition, his parents have been killed trying to escape; watching from the quay, Anna saw their boat being blown up, hence her distress at the beginning of the film. Anna's commitment to Joseph is such that, although it is clear that Jan has fallen in love with her, he makes no sexual move towards her and indeed expresses his love by referring to the three of them: 'you know that we all love you,' he tells her as they prepare to depart and gives her a diamond 'from all of us'. In addition, Anna as a char-acter is depersonalised so that she becomes a symbol of Dutch resistance. She refuses to accept their offer to take her to Britain, deciding that 'Holland will need all the help she can get'. At the end of the film, both Anna and Holland are symbolised by the orange rose that Jan has brought away with him. Major Dillon pays his tribute to Anna – 'she's a brave woman' – but the film closes with a tribute to Holland: 'There'll be many Annas in Holland before it's all over.'

Depoliticising the European woman

These films set during the Second World War continue to use the war to underpin their characterisations. On the one hand, the upheaval of the war, the loss of her family and the German occupation provide a rationale for Lise's earthy sense of survival; on the other, Anna's involvement in the Resistance and the loss of her fiancé turn her into an icon of sacrifice. In other genres, though, as the experience of the war began to fade, the political aspects of the European woman began to fall away so that she came to be positioned in terms of her sexual knowledge and availability alone, without that sense of political history that so clearly marked her in the immediate post-war films. In the final part of this chapter, I will trace the change but suggest that some of that intensity, that surrender to passion and capacity for self abnegation, still marks such women even when the war has ceased to be available as an explanation for such complexity. Broadly, the women now fall into two types, which we have seen in *Seven Thunders* and *Operation Amsterdam*: the young women, who are marked by a self-confident and assured sexuality; and the mature women, who offer a more complex persona that still seems to be characterised by a sense of loss.

The young women are found particularly in comedies, where their pragmatic understanding of sexual behaviour contrasts with the more fearful approach of the British male. The first two *Doctor* films offer examples of this. In *Doctor in the House*, Stella is Grimsdyke's foreign fiancée; he describes her as 'ravishingly beautiful, adores me, a splendid thing to have about the house,' but she is very much in charge of their relationship. Although technically she lives in the flat below, she is clearly at home with the male students who share with Grimsdyke and combines a sexual presence with that of a friendly flatmate. She alarms Simon initially when, at their first meeting, she appears from the bathroom in her petticoat and asks him to bring her tea in the bath, but she also darns socks and reminds them of their revision programme. Stella's pragmatic attitude is neatly summed up when she allows her body to be used for the students to practise using a stethoscope or finding an eardrum, laughing when Grimsdyke intervenes with a mild protest. *Doctor at Sea* uses a variant of this, with Brigitte Bardot as the blonde Helene, who disrupts the whole ship with her good looks and innocently refuses to acknowledge the disruption she causes. This figure reappears in, for instance, Ingrid the *au pair* in *Upstairs and Downstairs* and Madelaine in *The French Mistress*, who arrives in England to teach at a boys' boarding school. Although the expectation is that these attractive young women will be sexually available, they are actually rather moral, and the emphasis is on their knowledge of how to handle and control sexuality. As Madelaine says, when told that the boys have been advised to behave like gentlemen, 'Don't worry … In France, we learn to deal with gentlemen also.' Frankness and candour remain key components in this representation of the young European woman but the scope of her knowledge is now restricted to quite practical questions of sexual behaviour.

However, the mature woman continues into the late 1950s to be associated with the loss and self-abnegation of the earlier European heroines, even though the specific reasons for this tragic dimension are not referred to. Hildegarde Knef and Simone Signoret offer good examples of this, since they appear in films that span the period. Knef's star image emphasised not only her sexual presence but also her German nationality; the *Daily Herald* (3 November 1952) pointed out that she was 'the first enemy alien since the war to capture the interest and admiration of the democratic countries.' We have seen how as Bettina in *The Man Between* she is committed to the West but haunted by her past and by a sense of loss. Her two later British films have something of the same quality, even though the specific references to post-war politics have disappeared. In *Svengali* (1954), Knef plays Trilby, a bright, lively artist's model in Paris who lives a bohemian life with a group of artists, whom she looks after in a companionable way. Despite her nude modelling, she is innocent and romantic ('I'm not really wicked') and falls in love with a British artist from a wealthy background. But it is clear that Trilby has a capacity for passionate self-sacrifice; when her fiancé's mother protests that the marriage will wreck his career, Trilby immediately announces 'I won't marry your son ... I will never see him again.' It is this side of the actress's persona that is used in the later part of the film, when Svengali uses hypnosis to impose his will on her. Trilby loses her natural air of independence when she is put in a trance; she sings to his instructions, endures his anger and pleads for him to be kind. The film suffers from an over-theatrical performance from Donald Wolfit as Svengali but Knef's performance combines both aspects of the European woman in her split personality: the young woman at ease with men and her own feelings; and the woman who gives herself up to the experience of extreme emotions and denies her own self-interests.

Knef's third British film of the decade returns her to post-war Europe in a 1959 Muriel Box thriller, *Subway in the Sky*. Knef plays Lilli, a German night-club singer who hides Baxter Grant, a US soldier falsely accused of drug dealing and murder. The film is set largely in Lilli's flat, and in a complicated set of manoeuvrings ends with Baxter's exoneration through the discovery of his step-son's guilt. In the process, Lilli and Baxter fall in love and, when Baxter is finally able to leave the flat, they drive off into the future together. Knef's performance has a depth and understanding that go well beyond the plot-driven twists of the film, and again her character calls on features of the European woman from an earlier period. Lilli's past is mysterious – there are 'lots of things you don't know about me' she tells Baxter – but what little detail emerges associates her with loss and pain: she has been married before and been badly hurt. This may explain why she likes being isolated, 'cut off from the world, alone' in the high-rise apartment. But when Baxter appears in the flat, Lilli instinctively stands between the authorities and their pursuit of an individual on the run. When Baxter asks why she does not give him up to the German police, she uses a vocabulary that draws on the experience of occupation: 'I'm not an informer ... I don't like policemen forcing their way into my home.' The post-war implications of this for her, as a German woman, are underlined when the American Army in the person of Captain Carsons picks up the search. Lilli rather than Baxter is the one questioned by the American and she has to resist his persistent interrogation and sexual innuendo. It is one of the oddities of the film that although she spends much of her time lying, Knef as Lilli always gives the impression of speaking the truth. She places a premium on frankness, advising Baxter initially that he should face the authorities and tell the truth, and later telling her old friend Karl the truth about her feelings for Baxter 'even if it hurts you'. She invests even less serious matters with this intensity: 'I don't want that on my conscience,' she says of a late appointment, and she responds to a joke with a heartfelt 'don't, if you love me.' When she realises that she loves Baxter, she gives herself without reservation. She demands the truth from him and, when the evidence piles up against him, she reassures him with 'I want you to know that I believe you.' Thus, the character of Lilli draws on the European woman's experience of past suffering, her capacity for emotional surrender and her frankness in love to give weight to a fairly lightweight thriller.

These characteristics are drawn on by another European actress in a much better British film of the same year, Simone Signoret in *Room at the Top* (1959). Signoret had appeared in a 1948 Ealing war film, *Against the Wind*, in which she played a Belgian woman working with British saboteurs not only to fight for her country but to atone for her past love for a man who became a quisling. She wanted the job of killing him, 'to wipe out the past, both pasts together'. Michelle is thus strongly associated with loss and pain in terms both of the war and of her personal emotions and, although this is little spoken of, scenes in the film often end on a close-up of Michelle's face as if to seek understanding of her experience. In *Room at the Top*, Signoret plays Alice, the older lover of Joe Lampton (Lawrence Harvey). After an explicitly sexual affair, he abandons her to marry the wealthy Susan, and she dies a horrible death in a self-induced car crash. Alice is French, although her background is vague, and indeed her marriage to George and her presence in Warnley are not explained convincingly. Nevertheless, Signoret's presence and performance are highly significant. The *Films and Filming* reviewer used what are now familiar terms in describing her performance as 'overwhelmingly tragic, honest and acute' and commented that 'the emotional truth she brings to her relationship with Harvey is so much more intense than his' (February 1959: 21).

Such a review indicates that the tropes being worked with in *Room at the Top*, one of the first films of the British New Wave, are familiar from the post-war films we have looked at in this chapter. Signoret is marked by the sexual availability, candour in love and sense of fate that is characteristic of the European woman. The dialogue consistently emphasises her honesty. 'I don't tell lies, you know that,' she tells Joe, and he falls in love with her directness. 'You're such an honest person,' Joe tells her, 'Why the hell do you have to so honest ... I love you for it.' She offers Joe the opportunity to be similarly honest: 'You don't ever have to pretend, you just have to be yourself.' When Joe finally tells her that he is to marry Susan, she links his lack of honesty with a lack of courage: 'You're a timid soul … You had it inside you to be much bigger. You only had to be yourself.' This emphasis on honesty is reflected in the way in which the scenes with Signoret are shot. Large close-ups of her face draw attention to the signs of age in her face and she is filmed apparently without make-up, with her hair wet and bedraggled. The light falls harshly across the flat planes of her face. These close-ups also give access to her feelings, and the length of the scenes between Alice and Joe give an unusual amount of time to the exploration both of their physical love making and their intimate conversation. Honesty is thus linked to her sexuality and involves the complete surrender of herself in a way that Joe, in the end, cannot match.

Alice is out of place in Warnley, marked out by her sadness as well as her foreignness. The two are linked, as an early exchange between her and Joe indicates:

Joe: It must be funny, being French in Warnley.
Alice: No, it's not funny.
Joe: Are you very unhappy, Alice?
Alice: No, not very.

Love for her is strongly associated with pain, loss and memory. Joe reminds her evocatively of 'a boy I used to know in the university in Paris' and being in love is for her painful: 'I'm alive now,' she tells Joe, 'all of me is alive. It hurts sometimes but I don't mind.' She has a strong sense of fate: 'nobody was ever meant to be as happy as I am now. It can't last,' she reflects during their holiday in Dorset. As the holiday comes to an end, she gives him a present 'to remind you of the happiness we had.' Rightly, Joe recognises that the gift indicates that she expects the affair to end: 'you talk like a requiem,' he protests as he takes the cigarette case. The intensity of the affair depends on Alice's capacity to love without regard for her own interests or indeed her own existence. When Joe finally ends the affair, she reminds him 'I believed in our love. What else have I got?' In her death, she is sacrificed for his social success.

Alice's Frenchness is used to explain her sexuality, not her politics. Since *Room at the Top* is often presented as a film that challenged the complacency of the 1950s, it is worth noting that both the book and the film are set, not in the late 1950s but in the immediate post-war period. The book's first-person narration has a successful Joe Lampton looking back to 1946. The film lacks that retrospective voice-over and rather confusingly, in her first scene, Susan is presented as a typical mid-fifties teenager with her record player and pedal pushers.[2] Nevertheless, the film's references to the war and scenes like Joe's return to the bombed house in which his parents were killed provide an indication of when it is set, and it retains from the book a fairly consistent account of Joe's wartime experiences, including his time in the RAF and as a POW. Alice accuses him of using the war for his own ends, of not knowing what it was like to be hungry, even in the POW camp; Joe responds angrily that he had to use the time in the camp to study, not in heroic attempts to escape. Alice's own past is rather vague, but it is made clear that by 1937 she was in England and about to marry her husband, George. Her behaviour during the war years, which she presumably spent in Warnley, is not an issue, although significantly Joe makes an oblique reference to it when he taunts her about her age: 'What did you do, fifty years ago, back in the Great War?' Alice lacks the political complicities and compromises that marked earlier heroines, and her past is significant for its sexual rather than its political history. Joe gets angry when he discovers that she modelled nude for a painting, but Alice refuses to be criticised by him, asserting that 'I'm not ashamed of anything I've ever done.'

In some senses, *Room at the Top* is a transitional film that provides the first version of the figure of the young working-class man who looks forward to the future and threatens to transform British cinema. But the character of Alice is based on past memories of women characters whose sexual availability is beyond criticism because it is so strongly associated with the sense of fate engendered by European experiences of the war. In narrative terms, Alice could have been a banal character who over-invests in a love affair and worries about growing old. But as a European woman, played by Signoret, her mature sexuality still has a tragic dimension even though the political explanation for that dimension has slipped away. The complexity associated with the European woman's wartime experiences and her politics is here entirely transferred to her sexuality, giving it a depth, a capacity to surrender and a sense of loss that Joe cannot match. 'You don't know about these things,' she tells him, in a statement typical of the European woman. 'They are not as simple as that.'

7   The Commonwealth film and
the liberal dilemma

The new Elizabethan Age began in Kenya when, in February 1952, the new queen received news of her father's death while she was on an official visit to Kenya. The setting for the story of the accession seemed both exotic and familiar. Princess Elizabeth and her husband were taking a break from the tour, watching for big game in a reserve, but the notion of a royal tour with the accompanying newsreel footage of the rituals and celebrations that welcomed them was a familiar one. The post-war Commonwealth was similarly strange and familiar, built out of the British Empire but with a new and more modern emphasis on self-government and multi-racial co-operation. Ironically, in 1952, when Elizabeth became head of the Commonwealth as well as queen, Kenya's bloody experience of decolonisation had yet to be completed.

The debates about Europe, discussed in the previous chapter, had, as their counter, debates about the Commonwealth. For many, closer ties with Europe meant abandoning the Commonwealth, an institution that was emerging from the massive bulk of the British Empire and that seemed to offer Britain more stable possibilities than the uncertainties of Europe. But relations within the Commonwealth were themselves problematic, and as immigration, from the West Indies in particular, became a major issue in the 1950s, questions about race and culture became a major factor in domestic as well as foreign politics. This chapter will examine how the Commonwealth was used as a setting for a number of films in the period and, in particular, look in detail at how questions of racial difference and the liberal position on race are approached in two films that deal with the dismantling of the empire, *Simba* (1955) and *Windom's Way* (1957).

Of the two films, *Simba* has been the subject of some critical debate, largely focusing on questions of racism. By concentrating on the deaths of white settlers, the film largely ignores the fact that very few such settlers were killed in the 1952–56 conflict, while over 14,000 Kikuyu died (Boxer: 81). Jimmy Vaughn included *Simba* in a list of films that he condemned for their representation of Africa as a source of either 'violence and bloodshed or lurid glamour' (31). Lola Young argues that the film 'may be seen as representing the terror of the imminent end of Empire and the assumption of white supremacy' (81), while Dyer suggests that it is 'in the broadest sense racist' (1988: 51) in the way it sets up a binary opposition between white modernity and black backwardness and in its evolutionary belief that to become civilised black people must adopt white values. Kenneth Cameron points out that *Simba* largely focuses on the moral struggles of the white characters while ignoring those of the main black character.

Simba, in which the murder of a white settler by a black man occurs even before the credits, is certainly a deeply problematic film in its handling of race but in the context of British cinema of the time, it is hardly surprising that *Simba*, and indeed *Windom's Way*, are vulnerable to charges of racism. Of the two popular genres of the 1950s, the war films consistently omitted any reference to black Commonwealth participation in the war and comedies like *Doctor in the House* quite unselfconsciously used skin colour and accent as a source of humour. The alternatives of exclusion or rigid stereotyping are characteristic of films of the period. What is perhaps more striking about *Simba* and *Windom's Way* is that they actually try so hard to endorse the official, liberal view. In a cinema that consistently guyed official ideas and praised practical common sense rather than airy-fairy ideals, it is this outbreak of liberalism rather than the racism that seems surprising. In looking at these films, then, I want to set them in the context of changing discourses about the Commonwealth and, in the light of this, to examine more closely how the films struggle to represent a liberal position.

The Commonwealth

In the immediate post-war period, the Commonwealth presented itself as what Harry Hopkins called 'a more satisfactory arena than Europe' (63) for a number of reasons. Britain's claim to be a major power obviously rested on its role during the war but could be reinforced by reference to its pre-war Empire and its post-war role as head of the newly emerging Commonwealth. As the Cold War began to divide the world between two great powers, there appeared to be some possibility of 'a third force' as a bulwark and mediator between them; 'if the curtain had fallen on the Empire, had it not risen again almost immediately to reveal the multi-racial Commonwealth – as striking evidence as could be wished of Britain's continuing political genius?' (63) The Commonwealth then appeared to offer Britain a moral and political role that would maintain its status as a world power better than fighting for position in the competitive cockpit of Europe. In addition, given the desperate position of the economy, the Commonwealth was important as an economic resource. Countries within the Commonwealth provided both a market for British goods and a supply of raw materials – Malayan rubber, Rhodesian copper, Indian tea, New Zealand lamb (Judd: 329). The African colonies continued to be seen as a source of unexploited resources well into the 1950s (Hennessy: 221–4).

In addition, the Commonwealth offered Britain a symbolic role in which the metaphor of the family is consistently used. Britain could continue to be the mother country for a family that, although it now contained some independent members, continued, so British politicians insisted, to look to the centre for

guidance and support. The role of the monarchy and the new queen in particular was hugely important in maintaining this symbolic structure. Some of the
Queen's most publicly significant moments were associated with the
Commonwealth. Princess Elizabeth's first official tour abroad had been a family
tour of southern Africa in 1947, when, in a radio broadcast from South Africa
on her twenty-first birthday, she looked forward to working 'to make of this
ancient Commonwealth which we all love so dearly an even grander thing –
more free, more prosperous, more happy and a more powerful influence for
good in the world' (Dimbleby: 11). The news of her accession to the throne
brought her back from a planned five-month tour of the Commonwealth, and
the way in which Elizabeth was proclaimed queen in Commonwealth countries
was the subject of much newsreel coverage. Her coronation provided the spectacle of innumerable exotic Commonwealth dignitaries, including most
famously the queen of Tonga, parading on television in a display of unity.

The association of the Commonwealth and the Queen was firmly established
during the 1950s, partly because, as Prime Minister Harold Macmillan observed
to his press secretary in 1961, 'she took very seriously her Commonwealth
duties' (quoted in Pimlott: 307). The fact of her being a white woman also
affected the way in which the symbolic family relationship between Britain and
the Commonwealth was understood and could provide some odd or disturbing
disjunctures. The president of Ghana, Kwame Nkrumah, was reported to have
been deeply upset in 1959 when the Queen had to cancel a visit there because
of pregnancy and told the representative who brought the news 'had you told
me my mother had just died you could not have given me a greater shock'
(quoted in *ibid.*: 305). In 1961, outrage was expressed in South Africa, by then
no longer in the Commonwealth, over news photographs of the Queen dancing
with the president when she did visit Ghana, with the press complaining that
she was in the arms of 'black natives of pagan Africa' (quoted in *ibid.*: 308).

The image of the Queen and the president dancing embodied the multi-
cultural rhetoric of the new Commonwealth, which offered independence to
black as well as white nations. 'In 1939,' Harry Hopkins asserted, 'it had still
been possible to think in terms of Empire' (59) even though Australia, Canada,
South Africa and New Zealand had been granted dominion status within the
Commonwealth in 1931. After the war, though, it was evident that the British
Empire could not continue and the device of the Commonwealth became an
'immensely useful instrument' (Hennessy: 220) in the process of transforming it
into a new Commonwealth based on an equality between self-governing and
independent nations. Although Burma chose not to join, India, Pakistan and
Ceylon became members in 1947. The independence achieved in India,
although deeply scarred by the process of partition, was deemed historic in that
it transformed the Commonwealth into a multi-racial institution. Leaders of
Commonwealth countries entered into a different relationship with Britain in
which they could not be required to follow automatically the British line. As the
Queen reflected, in a speech in 1961, a 'wide degree of disagreement and intelligent discussion' (quoted in Pimlott: 308) had to be expected. This notion that

Britain was subject to the Commonwealth's much praised democratic and modern structures put new limits on Britain's imperial powers, which became clearer as the African colonies moved towards independence at the end of the decade. In official discourses at least, Britain was giving up power and acknowledging new dignities and rights in its former colonies.

This emphasis on a rational move to a new Commonwealth was further complicated by the fact that at times the changes appeared to be neither rational nor peaceful. Hobsbawm comments that after the Second World War, the British, 'by and large, did not resist decolonisation' (211) and, with hindsight, it is sometimes assumed that the 1950s saw a rapid and dignified move to independence in the British colonies in Africa, Asia and the West Indies. But economic, political and cultural factors meant that Britain resisted independence movements that were deemed to be precipitate. As late as 1959, for instance, a conference of governors of East African colonies did not envisage independence for Kenya until 1975 (Boxer: 81) and a puzzling pattern emerged in which leaders of independence movements were initially imprisoned by the British but released after years of agitation and violence to participate in elections and become respected Commonwealth leaders. Different factors were at work in different colonies. Malaya, for instance, was affected more directly by the politics of the Cold War and, in the early 1950s, the British promise of Malayan independence within the Commonwealth was meant to win over those who might otherwise join the Communist-supported independence campaign. A state of emergency was declared in 1948 and 250,000 British and Gurkha troops were engaged in full-scale conflict there (Howarth: 200). Constitutional changes in 1955 prepared the way for independence for Malaya in August 1957. In Kenya, one of the richest of the African colonies with a powerful group of white settlers, the British brutally put down the Mau Mau rebellion of 1952–56, triggered by white expropriation of Kikuyu ancestral land. The Kikuyu leader, Jomo Kenyatta, was imprisoned in 1953, and there was strong reaction in Britain to some of the methods used against the Kikuyu. The second wave of decolonisation after Suez took place from 1957 to 1964, led by Ghana in 1957, where the process, despite the imprisonment early on of the independence leader, Kwame Nkrumah, was deemed by the British to be 'almost a model of ordered withdrawal' (Boxer: 79). The appointment of Ian Macleod as Colonial Secretary in 1959 underlined Macmillan's determination to move swiftly in Africa, although Kenyatta was not released until 1961 and Kenya gained independence relatively late in the process, in 1963. All in all, the official discourse about what a Labour MP, Patrick Gordon-Walker, extolled in 1948 as 'the nobility of the conception and practice of the Commonwealth' (quoted in Howarth: 160) was somewhat contradicted by the processes of its evolution. Mike Phillips recalls seeing the guerrilla war in Malaya, the Mau Mau in Kenya and the independence of Ghana on newsreels and experiencing them as 'images that made you tense up... terrors ... about to burst through the screen into your world' (Phillips and Phillips: 144).

Official views on the multi-racial Commonwealth were further undermined by the growing clamour about immigration from the new (i.e. black or 'coloured') Commonwealth. The arrival of migrants from the West Indies from 1948 onwards was entirely in accord with the imperial tradition of rights of entry, which the 1948 Nationality Act extended to people from the newly independent Commonwealth countries. As Prime Minister Clement Attlee wrote to MPs concerned about the arrival of the first group of migrants from the West Indies:

> it is traditional that British subjects, whether of Dominion or Colonial origin (and of whatever race or colour) should be freely admissible to the United Kingdom. That tradition is not, in my view, to be lightly discarded, particularly at a time when we are importing foreign labour in large numbers.
>
> (document in Phillips and Phillips: 70)

Attlee's emphasis on tradition combined with a pragmatic view of the need for labour continued to mark government policy into the 1950s. The minutes of a Cabinet discussion of the Conservative government in 1955 noted both 'the traditional policy that British subjects should have the right of free entry into the Mother country of the Commonwealth' and that 'immigration, including Commonwealth immigration, was a welcome means of augmenting our labour resources' (document in Boxer: 106). However, resentment against the West Indian migrants was fuelled by politicians and the press in a hostile rhetoric of influx that was explicitly opposed to the official emphasis on multi-racial harmony. 'Multi-racial countries have a colour problem,' said the MP for North Devon in a House of Commons debate in March 1958. 'We see it in countries like South Africa and America and the mixed colonies; and a very deplorable and sad thing it is' (quoted in Miles and Phizacklea: 10). The notorious 'riots' four months later, caused by white attacks on black people, were used as further evidence of the 'colour problem' and the need to control immigration from the new Commonwealth. The 1962 Commonwealth Immigrants Act did exactly that, restricting entry to those with employment vouchers, students and dependants. The discourse of immigration, with its emphasis on race, colour, number and controls, had won.

The Commonwealth as film spectacle

The post-war British film industry also had an interest in the Commonwealth that was similarly a mix of economics, symbolic stories and spectacle. In the drive to build on the wartime success of the industry, the Commonwealth was envisaged by J. Arthur Rank as an important exhibition area. Murphy records how Rank established a worldwide organisation, based on the Commonwealth, taking over cinema chains in Canada and Australia in 1945, in New Zealand in 1946 and in South Africa and the West Indies in 1947 (1989: 76). In 1948, in a speech to the Cinematographic Exhibitors Association, Rank stressed the importance of box office success in the (white) Commonwealth. Despite the failure of his attempts to get into the US market, this overseas emphasis had some success. Films set in the Commonwealth proved successful at the box office, and two of Rank's biggest box office successes in the early 1950s were *Where No Vultures Fly* (1951) and *The Planter's Wife* (1952), which were set in Kenya and Malaya, respectively. In 1953, 'half the company's film revenues came from overseas', and 1954 saw a particularly successful year in Canada and 'demand in the Eastern hemisphere remained high' (Porter: 129).

The Commonwealth offered more than exhibition possibilities; it provided plots, settings and spectacle as well. An Australian letter writer to *Picturegoer*, complaining that British films were 'too shut in', suggested that British producers use 'the vast landscapes that the Commonwealth provides' (23 November 1957). Films set in the Commonwealth offered the possibility of epic spectacle, which was becoming increasingly important in cinema's battle with television in the 1950s. Colour was crucial, somewhat unusually in British cinema, which made popular black and white films well into the 1960s, and could be used with sweeping camera work to display the landscape, the crowds, the rituals of the natives and the patterns of action in battles and uprisings. There was a tradition of successful empire films in the 1930s, exemplified by Korda films such as *The Four Feathers* (1939), which provided a repertoire of images and characters that could be drawn on. Marcia Landy sees in these films of empire the British counterpart to the American western. She identifies a narrative pattern in which the British hero, soldier or administrator, works within (colonial) law to bring civilisation to more primitive lands. The indigenous people are judged by how they relate to British rule and divided into categories: the childlike natives, who are 'easily misled'; those who remain loyal to the British; and the 'unscrupulous native leaders' (1991: 98) who seek to establish power for their own selfish ends. As Young and Dyer have pointed out, a wealth of images was available that associated those subject to British rule with what was primitive, violent and threatening, although they could also be sensuous and natural. Such narratives thus offered moral and symbolic frameworks that sustained a confident vision of white superiority. But if there were possibilities in this well-established genre of empire, there were difficulties in simply transforming it into narratives that would work in the 1950s.

Films of the new Commonwealth could not simply take on the traditions of those set in the pre-war empire. They were faced with an official liberal discourse that emphasised equality and independence for the colonies but the move to independence was accompanied by violence and struggle in which British invincibility was by no means the norm, while debates about immigration at home had made respectable behaviour about race that was marked by a 'deep current of racial resentment and hostility' (Phillips and Phillips: 164). There were ways of avoiding the uncomfortable issues that arose in contemporary debates, of keeping the epic sweep, the emphasis on adventure and the colourful locations without the politics. One approach was to set the story in the old dominions – Canada, New Zealand, Australia – where the concerns of the indigenous populations seemed less pressing, and to draw on the traditions of the American western for story lines and set pieces.

The Overlanders (1946) was an early example of a Commonwealth film that did this very successfully. Set during the Second World War, it tells the story of an epic cattle trek across the Northern Territory, combining a documentary emphasis on the details of droving with a spectacular emphasis on movement and landscape that must have been exhilarating to audiences more used to the cramped spaces of many British films. The leader, Dan, acknowledges the 'black fellas' in one scene in which Aborigines watch the convoy passing through the valley beneath them and, in the progressive spirit of wartime films, the group of drovers includes a young woman, Mary, and an Aborigine, Jacky, both of whom prove to be brave and competent. Generally, however, this is an adventure story that eschews politics, although it finds a little room for a romantic sub-plot. A decade later, *Campbell's Kingdom* (1957) follows a similar pattern, setting a story from a western involving land rights, oil and defiance of big corporations in the Canadian Rockies. Since the film stars Dirk Bogarde as Campbell, the element of romance is stronger than in *The Overlanders* but the film's other source of pleasure is the spectacular setting, with its snow-topped mountains, pine trees and ravines. In neither film do questions of colonial power or British political responsibilities arise.

When such questions did occur, it was helpful to set them in the past. The date of the setting of *The Beachcomber* (1954), for instance, is uncertain, but everything about the story, perhaps because it was a remake of the 1938 *Vessel of Wrath*, points to the past certainties of British rule. The Welcome Islands are administered wisely by the Resident, who arrives in full dress uniform, and the plot deals almost entirely with the other white characters, two missionaries and an exiled, semi-aristocratic drunk. The natives conform to Landy's categories, with loyal servants, childlike tribespeople and an evil witch doctor, who tries to incite his people against the British. In the end, British reason and medicine help to defeat a cholera epidemic but in some senses the plot matters less than the location, filmed in Technicolor, which, on the one hand, emphasises the beauties of nature in the white, empty beaches, palm trees and sunsets and, on the other, the exotic rituals, dances and costumes of the islanders.

However, some films did take their locations and their stories from the political upheavals of the new Commonwealth and in analysing two of them, *Simba* and *Windom's Way*, I want to look at how debates about independence were handled in popular films of the period. *Simba* was released in 1955, when the future of Kenya had yet to be resolved, and the British public's knowledge of the situation was largely determined by sensationalist reporting of the Mau Mau rebellion. The film takes as its subject the different responses to the situation created by the threat to white rule. Mary (Virginia McKenna) is a white woman born in Africa but deeply committed to a liberal view that education and humanity are the only answer and that black and white must learn to live together. She is romantically involved with Allan Howard (Dirk Bogarde), newly arrived from London, whose brother is killed by the Kikuyu at the beginning of the film, and she works with Peter Karanja, the son of the head man, who has been educated as a doctor and runs a practice for the Africans. As the rebellion erupts into the white community, Mary's parents are killed and Allan defends his farm against attack. Peter names his own father as Simba, the leader of the rebellion, and when he tries to use persuasion rather than force to stop the attack he is killed by his own people. *Simba* tries to combine action and adventure, with a romance and with education; *Picturegoer* described it as 'a film for those who like to think while they are being entertained' (19 February 1955).

Windom's Way came two years later and had a script by Jill Craigie, a left-wing film maker largely associated with documentary film making during and after the war. It is set in an unnamed Far Eastern country, apparently after colonial rule has been replaced by a repressive post-colonial regime, but it is clearly based on British experience in Malaya. The story centres on an idealistic doctor, Alec Windom (Peter Finch), who works in a small settlement in the jungle with his nurse, Anna, who is clearly in love with him although he does not recognise it. His personal life is disrupted by the arrival of his estranged wife, the glamorous Lee, and political disturbances are triggered by a rebellion against the repressive regime of the British-owned rubber plantation, led by Anna's brother, Jan. Windom tries to protect the villagers and act as their mediator with the plantation manager and the government. In the end, Anna is killed by government forces trying to control the village, while her brother and his supporters unhappily join the Communist-led resistance. Windom thus fails in his attempts at mediation but, with Lee's encouragement, stays on to continue his work for the village. *Picturegoer* (25 January 1958) found the script 'guilty of over-stating and over-simplifying its case' but praised the acting and found 'the atmosphere of this troubled outpost of the British Commonwealth … remarkably convincing.'

Both films have the characteristic emphasis on landscape as a source of spectacle. The credits of *Simba* are accompanied by aerial shots from the aeroplane that, we later learn, is bringing Allan to Kenya, emphasising the vast terrain with its lakes, trees, roaming herds of wild animals and small huts. The opening shots of *Windom's Way* are more intimate but still serve to emphasise the strangeness of the setting. Behind the credits, a camera moves up to a barred window and is then picked up again, sliding across the backs of the crowd and around the hanging cages and draped curtains of what is revealed to be the village hospital, where Windom is attending to the birth of a baby. In both cases, the audience is positioned initially outside the setting and knowledge is gradually revealed, in *Simba* by a series of edited shots that conclude with the plane landing at the airport, in *Windom's Way* by the sensuous movement of the camera, which explores the exotic locale. In addition, the natural setting is dwelt on in both films, particularly in scenes of romance when Allan and Mary climb to the top of a mountain to look down on the plain or when Windom and Lee escape to a deserted beach for a swim. But it is also used as a continual reminder that the landscape can determine the characters' possibilities for action. The African landscape provides a continuous backdrop for discussion in *Simba*, the reddish-brown tones of the land dominating the outdoor scenes in the film. The white characters try to control the land but the black characters are shown to be at home in it. The white characters have cars and jeeps to drive across the land, seeing on it the lines and boundaries of colonial settlement, which Mary explains to Allan, but the final scenes show rebel Africans swiftly moving on foot through the rough countryside and communicating easily despite its distances. In *Windom's Way*, a long final sequence shows the perilous journey that Windom has to make through the jungle and mountains and emphasises his difficulty with the terrain. The audience is thus offered the possibility of understanding this new terrain but is also continually reminded of its intractability for the white characters.[1]

Simba and the liberal position

Both films try to combine what we might call a political plot with a romantic one, adopting the typical mode of the popular fiction film, in which public debates are expressed and understood through personal relationships. Both these plots are worked out through triangular relationships, but the different ways in which these triangles operate is instructive in looking at how the films deal with race. In *Simba*, the key arguments in the political plot are put forward by Mary Crawford's father, by Mary herself and by Peter Karanja. Crawford forcibly expresses the hard-line views of the white settler and represents the irrational side of white thinking. He insults the Kikuyu by calling them 'Kukes', asserts that they are all untrustworthy, childish and unfathomable and, gesturing with his gun at his own house boy, remarks that 'he'd probably slit all our throats at the first opportunity.' He believes that the move to more freedom has been disastrous and that 'we've given the African the wrong sort of toys, ideas of self-government, nationalism.' He argues that the only answer is forceful repression. A number of characters support this position, including Inspector Drummond, the colonial police officer, and, more tentatively, Allan Howard, who is shocked by the killing of his idealistic brother, whom he feels may have been 'hiding weakness with a whole lot of ideals'. Against this, Mary argues the liberal position on humanist grounds: 'You can't lump five million people together and tie a label on them,' she tells her father. She suggests that, far from being mindless, the Mau Mau are rational in their plan to kill those whites who treat their 'boys' well in order to remove any examples of good relations between white settlers and their black servants and workers. She passionately insists on the need for trust, otherwise 'there's no end to this horror', and she argues that judgements about people should be made on the basis of behaviour rather than race. She is worried that Allan is unwilling to do that: 'You're beginning to hate the Africans?' she asks him, and gets no reply. Mary's main ally is Doctor Hughes, who pleads for the white settlers to act humanely, since 'otherwise you'll force them over to the enemy,' and he argues that all must 'learn to live together, side by side, black and white.' The third element in this political triangle is Peter Karanja, the educated black man who speaks for his people but criticises the Mau Mau. 'My people are simple,' he tells Mary, 'and they have their grievances.' It is these grievances that the Mau Mau can use to stir up anger, and he condemns their violence: 'I condemn any man who preaches violence and intolerance.' But although he appears to distance himself from the Kikuyu, Peter does identify with as well as represent them. He has the scars that the army uses to identify the Kikuyu and, in the end, he walks into the violence because 'these are my brothers'. Unlike the others, Peter has no one to share his position, despite Mary's sympathetic support.

These three characters offer passionately held views, through which the political debate is expressed. Allan, newly arrived in Africa and shocked by the death of his brother, has separate conversations with each of the three in his attempt to sort out his own position. Two points are worth making about the way in which this political debate is represented. First, although Dyer comments that the liberal position is weakened because the people putting it forward are 'socially subordinate; a woman and an Irish doctor'(1988: 51), the film appears, initially at least, to support Mary's position by making her a sympathetic character who is able to refute the more extreme charges made by her father. However, despite Dyer's argument that the white position is associated with reason and rationality, it is important to note that Mary's liberal position is based largely on emotion and she cannot articulate a clear political way forward. Second, the representation of Peter skews the argument in a particular way. Young has condemned *Simba* as one of a number of films in which 'only the quiescent or Europeanised Africans are allowed the privilege of individual subjectivity' (80). Hobsbawm has pointed to the significant role in independence movements of an educated minority whose ideologies and programme had often been formed in Europe and were based on modern European ideas which were 'Western: liberal; socialist; communist and/or nationalist; secularist' (202). Europeanised in this sense does not necessarily mean quiescent, and Peter could therefore represent a significant position in the film. However, what is striking is that his Europeanisation is linked to a humanist caring – 'I studied for six years, six long weary years,' he tells Allan angrily. 'I became a doctor to save life' – rather than the oppositional politics exemplified by the Western-educated African leaders whom the British were locking up at the time the film was made.

The triangle of the political plot therefore emphasises the ideals of the new Commonwealth – black and white, living together in multi-racial harmony – but lacks any coherent expression of anti-colonial ideas by a black character. This gap is filled in a powerful way at the visual level, particularly by the use of colour. The call for balance and harmony is not reflected in the film's palette, which, in its 'rigid binarism' (Dyer 1988: 49) makes strong use of contrasts between light and dark, brightness and gloom, blonde and black. While the political debate makes links between Mary and Peter, the visual organisation works to separate them. The lighting, following the conventions analysed in Dyer's *White* (1997), highlights Virginia McKenna's fair hair and complexion: at key moments, as for example in the first debate with her father, her face is luminous against a dark, blurred background. She herself is the source of light in the image on such occasions, an effect reinforced by the fact that she consistently wears light-coloured or pastel clothing except, significantly, for the scarlet dress she wears at the end, almost as a sign of the blood that is to be shed. Lighting, dress and *mise-en-scène* work together to emphasise Mary's whiteness and to give her 'the glow of white women' (122), which Dyer argues is strongly associated with purity and moral idealism. Mary's presentation of the liberal position is thus strongly reinforced by her visual representation.

By contrast, Earl Cameron in the role of Peter Karanja appears to have been 'blacked up' for the part. He too is often lit from above, but in his case the light does not appear to be shining through him but bounces off the surface, emphasising the darkness of his skin and making him look shiny and uncomfortable. His skin colour is specifically drawn attention to in two incidents that would have had resonances in contemporary Britain: the first when Allan refuses to shake his proffered hand; and the second when Mrs Crawford refuses his medical help because 'I don't want him to touch me.' Looking at his own hands, Peter associates his skin with her terror: 'even to look at me filled her with horror.'[2] His father and the other African figures are also very dark-skinned and the two key scenes of the rebellion take place at night. In the first, the initiation ceremony[3] is filmed in velvety blackness in which the limited light sources fall sideways across the shadowy, watching faces. The white paint and feathers of the witch doctor throw his face into dark contrast and the orange ritual dress provides lurid splashes of colour. In the second scene, in the attack on Allan's house at the end, the rebels appear out of the darkness. The fires that they start throw reddish light into the besieged house and, while Allan and Mary are by the window in this light, Peter is harder to see, positioned as he is against a much darker background. Thus, although in the dialogue Karanja is associated with the white liberal position ('he's a white man' is his father's accusation), the use of colour consistently associates him with blackness. The political position of black rebellion, which cannot be actually spoken in the dialogue, is articulated through the visual organisation of the film and is strongly associated with darkness and threat.

I will discuss further the way in which the political plot reaches a conclusion, but first we need to look at the parallel workings of the romantic plot. The romantic triangle appears to be more clear-cut but is, I would argue, also problematic. Initially, Mary and Allan seem to the key figures here. Following the credits, the film gives indications that it will be following the conventions of the romance genre.[4] Mary meets Allan at the airport, and the attraction and tension between them is clear. In the classic manner of a romance, however, there are impediments to their relationship. On the drive back from the airport, Mary reminds him of their earlier meeting in London, when she criticised him for being irresponsible. More important though are the differences of opinion between them about attitudes to the Kikuyu and the political situation. This is elaborated in a series of discussions in which Allan is unable to share her point of view, a fact underlined in a love scene set on the top of a hill from which they can look down on their farms and land. In this scene, they acknowledge the sense of fate that overtook them at the airport ('I felt like running away,' says Mary, to which Allan responds with 'I saw my independence slipping away. I felt trapped'). Allan asks her to marry him, and Mary expresses her love with a passionate kiss but says she cannot give him a reply, since 'we're at war here, at war with each other ... I'm afraid of what you might become.' Large close-ups on her face emphasise her strength of feeling and her longing for peace with him as well as in Kenya. After this scene, however, with the murder of Mary's parents, plot events rather than political differences begin to drive the narrative more strongly, and when Allan's farm is threatened she goes to help him, taking the gun he offers. When he protests at the danger – 'I wish to hell you hadn't come' – she declares her place is at his side: 'Too late for wishing, darling, I'm here, that's all I care about.' And the film ends with Peter's death and the couple being rescued by the army.

The narrative, which thus works to bring together the romantic couple, is underpinned by other non-narrative factors. One is the star system, which had by this stage of his career typecast Dirk Bogarde as a romantic hero whose handsome good looks and tentative, tender, gentle manner was hugely appealing to women in a cinema otherwise dominated by rugged, silent types. The appearance of Bogarde in a film indicated that there would be a strong emphasis on romance and that emotion would be valued as an important

Figure 7.1 Virginia McKenna and Dirk Bogarde in *Simba* (J. Arthur Rank, 1955).
Courtesy of the Kobal Collection.

element in making judgements about appropriate actions. A further factor underpinning the romantic plot is the visual organisation, which emphasises the equal way in which the two stars are filmed. Throughout the film, Bogarde is lit as McKenna is, with a flattering light falling on his face, emphasising his eyes and cheek bones in a manner appropriate to a romantic male lead. The visual organisation also expresses the romantic movement of the two characters coming together from equal but different positions. An early shot at the airport shows them looking straight into each other's eyes, their faces positioned at each edge of the frame in a relationship of equality that expresses both antagonism and attraction. This framing is repeated during the discussion after the meeting of white settlers, when Allan expresses his doubts about his brother's ideals. In the love scene on the mountain, when Mary and Allan embrace, McKenna is positioned below Bogarde, who looks down on her, but in the *dénouement* of the attack on the farm, a different kind of equality is reached as the *mise-en-scène* places the two together within the frame, looking out towards the common enemy.

However, just as there are gaps and absences in the political plot, so too are there are awkwardness and improbabilities in the romantic plot. In narrative terms, Mary's relationship with Peter seems to indicate different kinds of possibilities for her. A romantic triangle, in which Peter is the third party, is implicit in the film but cannot be acknowledged directly. The narrative hints at but continually blocks off the possibility that Mary and Peter could have a romantic relationship which 'fitted' better than that between her and Allan. Peter embodies the qualities and ideals that Mary respects and that give meaning to her life. She works with him in the dispensary and, when her mother comments on possible danger, Mary asserts: 'It's the only useful thing I do.' She shares Peter's commitment to non-violence, and even after her parents' deaths she expresses her intention of continuing to work with him. The equality between them is expressed in the similarity of their positions within their communities. When Peter comments that her working with him is 'a sign to my own people', she responds 'and to mine, perhaps.' This emphasis on their shared trust and mutual respect is particularly important because of the narrative's failure to resolve the political differences between Allan and Mary in a way that would give conviction to the romance. The conventional romantic plot places emphasis on the man changing to accommodate the woman's needs and to learn respect for her position. But in *Simba*, despite the weight given to Mary's views and her initial refusal to commit herself to Allan because of their political differences, it is evident that, when Mary joins his defence of the farm, he has made no move towards her, and he even mocks Peter for his proposal to talk to 'a bunch of howling savages'. The narrative thus shows Mary giving in to Allan's ideas rather than reaching the mutual accommodations typical of the romance.

This narrative awkwardness is accompanied by aesthetic problems, which seem to centre on performance. Andy Medhurst has suggested that, during the 1950s, Bogarde was at odds with the 'existing norms of masculinity' as expressed by stars like Kenneth More and Richard Todd (1986: 347). However, the role of Allan Howard in *Simba* seems to require a much more conventional approach, and Bogarde seems to be cast against type, a romantic hero in an action film that required none of the more tender, nurturing qualities he brought to other roles in the mid-1950s. What is interesting though is that performance is also a problem in the scenes in the film that involve romance rather than action, particularly the key romantic scene on the mountain top, when McKenna, who is entirely confident in her 'political' scenes, is also ill at ease. Landy comments that the scene is 'poorly acted' and that the love making is 'characterized by the couple's awkward grasping' (1991: 116), while a glimpse of the audience response can be caught in a letter to *Picturegoer* in which a reader comments that 'I've seen *Simba* four times and, when Virginia McKenna said in an ultra-Mayfair drawl: "My God, darling, but I do love you," there were shrieks of laughter on every occasion' (3 September 1955). Certainly, the studio-bound setting, the embrace, which seems to pin McKenna under Bogarde with her neck cricked and her elbow stuck up at a right angle, the stiff acting and the script, which reaches for romantic heights that it has not earned, all have the untoward effect of making the romance entirely unconvincing.

I have emphasised in some detail the rather clumsy and contradictory ways in which narrative, *mise-en-scène* and performance are handled in *Simba*. I do so not because I think it is an exceptionally bad film but because I want to argue that, by analysing the points where the narrative becomes problematic, the performances clumsy or the visual representation of the Kikuyu runs counter to the heroine's plea for humanity, we can see the trouble being caused in the text. The trouble is caused not only by the attempt to contain and control the black voice by representing it as Other, as Young suggests, but also by the attempt to accommodate the liberal discourse of the new Commonwealth within generic conventions that are strongly linked to the films of empire. The film provides us with a model of black virtue, educated in Western sensibilities, and then not only denies him the woman who is his white equivalent but has him die at the behest of his own father. The position of the white liberal is privileged through being personified in the heroine, a white woman who literally glows with moral virtue and for whom political beliefs appear to be more important than romance. But in the end, the liberal emphasis on humanity and tolerance offers no solution in the face of extremism and violence. Instead, the brutal position of white settlers such as Mr Cartwright, which has been criticised as inhumane and doomed to failure, appears to be adopted by the romantic hero and Inspector Drummond, who has consistently been wrong in his suspicion of Peter and his understanding of what the rebels might do, comes to the rescue in a flurry of gunfire.

The stress of the work being done to hold these different ways of thinking together is revealed in the final frames of the film, which reach towards the melodrama often associated with Comolli's and Narboni's emphasis on the cracks caused by internal ideological tensions. Peter, whose words of peace held the crowd momentarily until his father challenged him, lies dying from the wounds inflicted by 'his people'. Allan and Mary run to him and hold him up. They are united in their concern for him but separated by his body, which lies between them. Mary's red dress stands out dramatically against the darkness and the white faces are framed in close-ups that emphasise their strong emotions as characters and remind us of their status as stars. Peter despairs that 'they didn't listen', but Allan, who had previously insisted that a gun was 'a better weapon than words', now reassures him with 'I listened' and looks significantly at Mary. Peter, as he dies, looks towards a young black child, Joshua, who had sought refuge on the Howard farm and pleads: 'Perhaps we don't deserve peace but he has done nothing wrong.' The conventional ending of a romantic film demands a final embrace of Mary and Allan, but this is blocked by Peter's body, and the film ends with the child walking towards the camera and a close-up of his face. This focus on the child as the symbol of the uncertain future provides a highly emotional ending, particularly given the emphasis in the 1950s on children as the future, but it makes little sense in terms of either the political plot or the romantic narrative. Its significance lies in the last-minute attempt, through Allan's conversion and the symbol of the child, to restore a liberal position that had been thoroughly defeated. It is as though the film, having been overtaken by the pessimistic logic of those bewailing the loss of empire, tries in a final throw to reinstate liberal humanism as the dominant discourse. But, as a final twist, in its creation of a new and symbolic family with the African represented as a helpless child, *Simba* unconsciously exposes the paternalism of the liberal view.

Windom's Way and post-colonial politics

In turning to *Windom's Way*, we can see how some of these ideas and images are reworked in a different situation. *Windom's Way* is more sophisticated in its mapping out of the political situation and the Malayan setting offers a different repertoire of images based on stereotypes of the Far East. Nevertheless, the similarities and differences between the two films help to fill out some of the discourses that underpinned attitudes to the Commonwealth. The film's political plot involves a Cold War struggle in which the nationalist government of the province, represented by the urbane and untrustworthy Commissioner Belhedron, is at war with the rebel Communists. Within the village of Selim, though, the arguments of the political plot are given a specifically British and colonial dimension through the characters of Windom and Patterson, which, as the *Films and Filming* review (February 1958) observed, 'brings the problem nearer home.' The initial debate is conducted between three figures: Windom himself; the rubber plantation manager, Patterson; and Jan Vidal, a villager who works on the rubber plantation. Patterson, played with neurotic fussiness by Michael Hordern, is presented as an ex-colonial who is concerned only with profit. He wears the shorts and long socks of the colonial administrator, refuses to listen to what the men have to say and seeks to repress opposition rather than to understand it. He refuses to understand or accommodate the traditions of the villagers, branding their wise man, Father Amyan, an agitator and rejecting their request to grow their own rice. 'It's rubber that's made this country what it is,' he argues and, for that reason, the needs of the plantation must be paramount. This position is similar to that of the white settlers in *Simba* but, as the plot develops, Patterson becomes less significant as a figure, and his arguments for harsh retribution against those who challenge business interests is taken over, with more skill and subtlety, by Belhedron. *Windom's Way* thus suggests that the colonial attitudes of the British have now been passed on to the nationalist rulers taking over from them.

Windom himself is positioned outside the formal structures of employment or government, and his political philosophy is based on compassion and humanity. He rejects the official advice of the British consul that 'we mustn't forget that we're visitors here' and when Lee, his wife, argues that he is getting over-involved he responds that he is doing 'what any human being would do'. He is convinced that his work as a doctor means that he has to be 'part of people's lives' and involved in the life of the village. Windom emphasises that it is natural that the villagers should want 'freedom and dignity and independence' and that helping them to fulfil these needs is not only right but also politically sensible: 'They want to stand up,' he tells Belhedron, 'help them and they'll thank you.' He refuses to attach himself to any particular political position, defending himself against accusations of Communist sympathy but arguing with Patterson that Jan, Father Amyan and others who rebel must be seen as individuals and not just labelled as agitators. Windom emphasises the importance of personal relationships and trust. He persuades the villagers to rely on their personal faith in him rather than any belief in a more abstract political philosophy. As Jan leads his supporters out of the village to escape from the incoming nationalist troops, he tells Windom, 'We are leaving our village to you, our homes, our families, our futures ... We would leave them to no-one else.'

Jan, who acts as spokesman and leader of the villagers, is positioned between Paterson and Windom. Like Peter Karanja, Jan has, albeit to a lesser extent, been Westernised in that he speaks English, often wears Western dress, and his surname 'Vidal' indicates that he may have a non-Asian background. His arguments combine a recourse to tradition with a more modern discourse of, for instance, meetings, strikes and resistance when attacked. Like Peter, he acts as a representative and spokesman for his people, whom he presents as powerless and simple. Explaining to Windom that the villagers wish to grow rice for cultural as well as economic reasons, Jan emphasises the modesty of their ambitions: 'rice is a part of our life, a part of us ... to us the important things in life are very small, very simple – our village, our rice.' While Jan values this simplicity and works with rather than for his people, as Peter does, nevertheless the implication is that he can see and judge his culture from outside, through Western eyes. The powerlessness of the villagers' position is emphasised at the end, when, as Windom had predicted, the government's use of force pushes Jan and his followers into the Communist-supported rebel camp.

We can compare the way in which this political debate is set up with that in *Simba*. First, as in *Simba*, the liberal position is treated sympathetically and given the endorsement of being both emotionally appealing and proposed by the star of the film. Like Mary, Windom is a caring professional whose political views come from his emotional attachment to his work and his desire to help. Both characters are given some political justification for their arguments, but their rationale is trust and humanity rather than the recognition of political rights. However, having a man take on this liberal position means that Windom does have more public as well as moral authority and he acts forcefully, for instance, when he refuses to allow the chief of police to arrest Jan at his hospital. Mary argues with her father, but Windom's debates are with those in public authority such as Patterson and Belhedron, and Peter Finch's star persona as a tough personality with an Australian background gives a particular force to such exchanges. Nevertheless, the weakness of the liberal position based on trust is exposed here as in *Simba*. Windom attempts to reach a deal to protect the villagers from government retribution, but his mission ends in failure when he discovers that the government has no intention of keeping its word or of allowing the villagers a peaceful return. 'I made a bodge of the whole thing,' he tells Lee, although she tries to reassure him that the fault lies with those, including herself, who 'didn't want to understand'.

There are also differences from *Simba* in the way in which the anti-colonialist position is expressed. Jan is allowed a much more articulate expression of the links between the 'simple' need to grow rice and the political desire for independence and self-respect: 'we are not going back to the old ways,' he tells Windom from the rice field, when the doctor suggests that the villagers repair the rubber plantation as a sign of good will. The violence and agitation associated with the anti-colonialist position is presented as being an understandable response to unreasonable behaviour rather than a recourse to tribal practices and primitive rites. Thus the initial attack on the plantation is triggered by the death of Father Amyan at the hands of the police chief, while Jan turns to guns when the villagers' attempts to restore the rubber plantation are misread as sabotage and one of his men is killed in an air attack by a government aeroplane. However, two factors are at play that work to tone down support for what might otherwise be deemed legitimate violence on the part of the villagers. First, although Windom consistently supports the villagers' grievances and seeks to work with Jan, his endorsement is withdrawn at key points when Jan appears to be moving towards violence. At such points, Jan either denies his involvement, as, for example, with the decision to strike and the burning of the rubber plantation, or, in the face of Windom's protestations, decides against confrontation with the authorities. Second, the film suggests that the traditions of the villagers themselves are opposed to violence. In its representation of the Malayan villagers, the film does not draw on the repertoire of violent and primitive images so readily used in *Simba*. Instead of the witch doctor and the violent chief, *Windom's Way* offers the saintly figure of Father Amyan, who personifies Eastern pacifism. Thus, although the film offers a more sympathetic account of civil unrest that anything attempted in *Simba*, Windom, as he articulates the dilemmas of the liberal position to Jan – 'Are you quite certain you're willing to take responsibility for human lives?' – is able to use Jan's own culture against him.

As in *Simba*, this political story runs alongside a narrative that centres on romance. Windom is once again the central figure in this story, but the other characters involved are his wife Mary and the head nurse, Jan's sister Anna. The romantic story is set up as a possibility when Lee's telegram giving the time of her arrival ends with a joke: 'at least you have time to get rid of the dancing girls.' The British consul who accompanies Lee on her journey jokes along the same lines when he meets Anna, telling Lee 'you didn't come a moment too soon.' But, although it is clear from her glances and demeanour that Anna is in love with Windom, the possibility that he might reciprocate is never expressed. Instead, the romantic narrative centres on Lee and Windom and the question of Anna's feelings never becomes an issue between them. The film carefully traces the old fault lines in the marriage, with Windom refusing to believe that Lee is willing to give up her glittering social life and successful career to become a doctor's wife, while Lee not only tries and fails to behave like a good nurse but continues to question what she sees as her husband's over-involvement with the village people. By the end, with Windom's attempts at mediation a failure, their positions have been reversed: in a mutual change of position typical of a romance, Windom wants to leave, while Lee insists that he must stay and continue his work. He agrees and, as he walks away to the hospital, it is also clear that the marriage will continue.

The effect of the romantic plot, then, is not so much to provide space for the expression of the women's feelings but to reinforce the film's focus on Windom and his beliefs. Far from being rivals, the two women come together in their love for Windom and try to save him and the village from the consequences of his failure at mediation. It is Anna who overhears Commissioner Belhedron's orders to bring the troops back into the village and, having warned Lee, she tries to escape to head off Windom and Jan. Following her, Lee inadvertently alerts the government troops to Anna's fleeing figure and she is shot as she tries to escape into the night. The scene ends with Lee holding Anna's body to her, the barriers between them having been removed by Anna's sacrifice.

The romantic plot is thus relatively low-key, partly because of a mismatch between Anna and Lee as rivals for Windom and the way in which the two women come together to support him. Nevertheless, the film's political meanings are underscored by images and motivations that stem from this romantic narrative. Unlike *Simba*, *Windom's Way* does not raise the question of race as a specific issue: Jan's people are defined by their allegiance to their village and their culture rather than to their race. Nevertheless, as in *Simba*, skin tone and colour do carry symbolic significance. Although the film makes hardly any use of the connotations of blackness, whiteness remains a key signifier even for judging the Asian characters. Thus the chief of police and his henchmen are much swarthier and darker than Jan, and the virtue of the dark-skinned Father

Amyan is signified by his white beard and robe. Jan and Anna are played by white actors,[5] and at times the light on their faces appear to bleach out the colour of their skin. Anna is always seen in her white uniform, with her dark hair covered by her nurse's white veil.

But if Anna is 'white' in comparison with her fellow countrymen, she is dark in comparison with Lee. Jan reveals the racial divide that makes Anna's love impossible when, in a moment of anger, he mocks the way Anna worships Windom, despite it being clear that she 'cannot belong to him'.[6] The implication is that Lee can belong because she is white, but her whiteness is initially a problem. The figure of Lee, as played by Mary Ure, draws on complex connotations of whiteness, and her conversion to Windom's way is signalled by a shift from one form of whiteness to another. With her blonde hair swept up and her white dress, Lee is, from the moment she steps down from the plane, a figure of film star glamour. In the early part of the film, her pearls and white suitcases, high heels and make-up indicate that this is a glamour that is highly constructed and fragile, that relies on the work and the acclamation of others to maintain its beauty. The artificiality of this persona is emphasised by Ure's performance, in which she almost seems to be holding herself at a distance from the character's glamour and drawing attention to the way it is constructed through smiles, hairstyle and walk. The work of the film is to transform this figure so that her whiteness becomes not a sign of artificiality but of internal moral strength, turning Lee from a superficial blonde into an archetypal good woman.

In this connection, one key scene indicates how Lee's transformation has resonances with the political narrative of the film. When, at Patterson's initiative, Commissioner Belhedron arrives in the village, he questions Windom about his involvement in the riots. Lee, anxious for Windom's safety and fearful that he will say too much, goes to the hospital and politely insists that the interview be continued over dinner in the bungalow. The dinner scene starts with the camera moving through the jungle of plants around the verandah, making the contrast with the civilised dinner table over which Lee presides. She is wearing a strapless white dress, with her bare neck and shoulders set off by a gold necklace and her blonde hair smoothly curved under so that the light gleams off it. Interestingly, Belhedron here is in ethnic dress, wearing a traditional high-collared jacket and sarong. The conversation is far removed from the interrogation at the hospital: Windom gets the chance to express his idealistic position, and Belhedron agrees to the arrangements he proposes, while Patterson storms off in disgust. Belhedron thanks Lee for being such a skilful hostess and conjuring up 'so much elegance out of Selim'. At first sight, this would appear to be Lee's triumph, bringing her own skills at presentation and performance to the service of her husband and transforming, at her table, the Westernised commissioner into a sympathetic representative of the East. Instead, this dinner party is the scene of Windom's betrayal, when his willingness to trust is taken advantage of by the politicians, who are interested in power rather than justice. Thus Lee cannot simply turn her sophisticated elegance to good ends. She has to be transformed.

She reaches towards this possibility at various points in the narrative by declaring her willingness to change. When, for instance, she tries to help in the hospital, her make-up is discarded, her hair hidden by the nurse's white veil; in the reconciliation scene on the beach, she looks more natural with her hair wet and tangled from swimming. In the final scene, the transformation is complete; when Windom hesitates on being called to the hospital, a close-up shows Lee's face, pale with no make-up, but glowing from within against a dark, blurred background. Windom, now supported by Lee, decides to go on with his work. This ending, although much less fractured than that of *Simba*, shares some of the earlier film's difficulties. Through Lee, the film accepts the flaws and problems of the liberal way but endorses it as the only way forward. But this is achieved by the eradication of those who represented the Malays: Father Amyan has died in prison; Jan's ideals have been perverted by the repressive Communist ideology; Anna has been killed trying to put right Windom's mistake. As in *Simba*, the future of the indigenous people is represented by a child in the care of a white couple. Kosti is a small boy who has popped in and out of the film as Windom's staunch helper. He explained early on to Lee that his parents were dead and 'the doctor my father now'. 'You be my mother,' he asked Lee, but she gently turned the question away. At the end, though, sitting on the verandah, she holds the sleeping Kosti in her arms as she watches Windom walk back to the hospital, called, as he had been at the beginning, to the delivery of a baby.

Lola Young describes *Simba* as 'a late entry to the colonial adventure canon' (81), but in conclusion I would argue that both *Simba* and *Windom's Way* are best seen as films that try to imagine what political and personal relationships might be like in the post-imperial situation that the new Commonwealth was meant to create. Thus, despite their differences, and certainly *Windom's Way* shows a political awareness that *Simba* entirely lacks, the films share certain characteristics that mark them as Commonwealth texts. In the contemporary context of messy wars in Malaya and Kenya, the films suggest that military imperialism and British invincibility could no longer be offered effortlessly, even as a symbolic answer. The 'white settler' position cannot be relied on as the position of patriotic common sense in contemporary dramas. Indeed, the liberal position comes to the fore in these films because the easy assumption of white political power is no longer possible. Hence the official, colonial figures of Crawford, Drummond and Patterson are replaced by Mary and Windom, who operate outside those structures and indeed find themselves in opposition to those who want to behave as if Britain still ran its empire. This liberal position is marked not just by an emphasis on reason, order and debate, which Dyer (1988) associates with the whites in *Simba*, but by an extreme emphasis on empathy, care and healing. It as if the good white characters must prove their right to take part in Commonwealth affairs by demonstrating their capacity for sacrifice, their unselfish goodness and their capacity to win, through goodness, the respect that had previously been demanded by the assertion of power. The lack of a political dimension to the liberal position turns the question of political rights into one of humanitarian largesse. The multi-racial ideal of the Commonwealth, of black and white living side by side, of children growing into independence, then becomes not a political decision in which the colonised might have some say but a choice that (some) white characters make out of their humanity. And just as the Queen as a young white woman presiding as head of the Commonwealth used the rhetoric of sacrifice, so the films make of the white woman a key image of moral goodness and shining virtue.

Given the highly rhetorical nature of this version of the white liberal position, it is perhaps not surprising that the films fall into confusion and, in trying to organise the narrative around these tropes, reveal the kinds of contradiction that have been explored in this chapter. In general, the espousal of the liberal position founders on two key issues. First, the repression of sexual relationships between the white liberal and their black or Asian counterparts indicates that the multi-racial family of Commonwealth rhetoric was precisely that. The films cannot imagine how a narrative based on such a possibility can be worked through. Second, the emphasis on the caring unselfishness of the white liberal is premised on power being given up rather than it being taken away. Mary and Windom argue not for giving in to violence but for making the changes that humanity demands. But the effect is the same, for in emphasising this abnegation of power, the narratives of both films show the repeated failure of the liberal project. The inability of the central character to control the narrative underlines their failure at the political level, leaving an overwhelming impression of 'white helplessness' (Dyer 1988: 53). These two problems – of sexual denial and liberal powerlessness – are gestured at in the films' endings. In the final images, the liberal, multi-racial family, which the narrative cannot deliver, is created symbolically but the contradictions are too great for the gesture to be convincing. The liberal failure cannot be assigned directly to the white characters, although the twists that the narratives have to make to render them blameless demonstrate that there is a problem here. The vacuum created remains to be filled and the final irony is that in seeking to emphasise the moral virtue and lack of culpability of the liberal protagonists, the films draw on their most extreme examples of stereotyping. *Simba*, set in Africa, deploys the familiar images of black primitivism, while the Cold War provides the scapegoat for the more liberal *Windom's Way* in the shape of the Communists, who promise Jan and the villagers victories won with 'cold steel'. In the end, the films become examples of the kind of liberal failure they have described, apparently helpless victims of ways of thinking about race and ideologies that they thought they had escaped.

8 Reconstituting the family

'It's for the children that I'm worried'

Children are everywhere in post-war British cinema. They play on the bomb sites and the empty streets; they get lost, make unsuitable friends, go to school and are attended to in hospitals and children's homes. In 1959, *Room at the Top* was calling on a familiar image when Joe Lampton discussed life and death with a small girl playing with her dolls in the ruin of his bombed out home. But if children literally run through the films, there are also changes in how they are treated and in the explanations of childhood that are offered. This chapter explores those changes and will focus, in particular, on the position of the young child in the family. Writing on British cinema of the period has tended in its discussion of the representation of youth to focus on juvenile delinquency and the rise of the teenager. Writers such as Hill (1986) and Landy (1991) have pointed to the ambivalent use of the teenager in social problem films to represent the attractions and dangers of affluence, sexuality and the influence of the mass media. In this chapter, I hope to complement such work by focusing on the discourses of care and responsibility that surround the younger children and that provide explanations for their behaviour and plans for their well-being. 'Family's an awful responsibility,' Lucy tells her husband William at the end of the 1945 film *They Were Sisters*, 'a responsibility, yes, but don't let's make [it] an *awful* responsibility,' William responds reassuringly. In looking at how some of the films of the period handled the issues of childcare and the family, we will test whether Lucy's anxiety or William's optimism was the more justified.

A concern about children and the family can be traced across the period. This chapter begins with an analysis of the representation of the family in two rather different kinds of film in the post-war 1940s and concentrates in particular on the way in which the family is narratively reconstituted. It moves on to the mid-1950s to look at a number of films in which a small boy is the protagonist and identifies the vulnerable child as an important sign that dominant ideas about childcare are being reworked in cinema and transforming the way in which fatherhood in particular is represented. The chapter concludes by looking at the role of the expert in the family and at the tentative way in which educational and psychological understandings of the child are acknowledged in fifties British cinema.

Restoring the family

In some ways, the presence of children in films reflected the increased numbers of children in the population. Despite fears about a decline in the birth rate, the first three post-war years produced a marked increase in the number of births, 33 percent compared with the last three years of peace (Hennessy: 169). These were the children who were to grow up, go to school and find jobs in the 1950s and 1960s. But the war had had other effects as well. The children of the post-war bulge were joining those who had been children during the war and whose lives had been disrupted by conscription, bombing and evacuation. The reconstitution of the family at the end of the war could be very difficult. Children whose knowledge of their fathers had been restricted to letters and a photograph found his physical presence hard to accept, particularly when he claimed rights to their mother's bed or tried to impose a military discipline on his family (Turner and Rennell: chapter 4). Father's return from the Services could, as the oral histories recount, 'cut right across established routines and disrupt intimate relationships' (89). There were other cases where families had been destroyed altogether, and it is significant that Bowlby's influential work began as a report, commissioned in 1948 by the UN, on 'children who are orphaned or separated from their families'. As if in compensation for all this separation and loss, Winnicott's advice to parents movingly stressed the basic importance of human presence; 'one of the things that father does for his children is to be alive and stay alive during the children's early years' (116), he writes, and 'the mother is needed as a live presence. Her baby must be able to feel the warmth of her skin and breath' (89). Rebuilding the family and re-establishing emotional relationships in it was thus deemed a crucial post-war task.

As we have seen, despite British cinema's reputation for realism, it often deals with social issues rather indirectly. Its handling of this problem of restoring the family is no exception. I want therefore to comment on two different approaches, which, although they do not deal overtly with the aftermath of the war, seem, in their narratives and characterisation, to be organised around a regrouping of the family and a reassertion of its proper hierarchy. The first study is of a popular Gainsborough melodrama, *They Were Sisters*, and the second of a series of domestic comedies produced, scripted or directed by Sidney and/or Muriel Box.

They Were Sisters was made as the war was coming to a close. It opens in 1919 and much of the action appears to takes place in the 1930s; however, the end makes a clear reference to the rhetoric used during the war in a final speech in which William tells Lucy that there are 'millions like you … muddling through'. The film thus combines escapism with a clear indication that it is dealing with issues that might be encountered in ordinary homes all over the country. The film, which follows the different marital histories of three sisters, Lucy, Vera and Charlotte, has been analysed, by Landy (1994), for instance, in terms of its exploration of women's position within and outside the family at the end of the war, but it is also extremely interesting for the way in which it uses children's desires and wishes as the mainspring of its narrative. It has to be confessed that the generally upper middle-class tone of the film is probably most hard to stomach in the accents and behaviour of its child actors, but these highly conventional children actually assert their rights to be heard in a rather unusual way. The narrative interweaves the stories of the three families that the sisters establish: Lucy marries William but has no children of her own since their daughter died at a young age; the worldly Vera marries the boring Brian and has Sarah, probably conceived, as William points out, by mistake; Charlotte has three children – Margaret, 18, Stephen, 13 and Judith, who, like Sarah, is around 10 – but her role as a protective and caring mother is severely compromised by her inability to defend herself against the cruelty of her husband, Geoffrey. All these natural families are in some way dysfunctional, and the narrative works to remake them into a single family in which the ideal parents, Lucy and William, are claimed by the children whom they love, Sarah, Judith and Stephen.

For this narrative resolution is not achieved by fate or even by the activity of the most effective adult, Lucy. Crucial decisions are taken by the children and are based on their rather matter-of-fact insight into the situation. Judith, in particular, is the key to sorting out the wrong families and helping the right one to get together. Early on, she shows an understanding of her mother's situation, commenting on how badly her father treats her and how he then pretends to be ill so as to win her round again. It is Judith who telephones Lucy for help when Charlotte is made ill by Geoffrey's harsh treatment, and she also tries to help Sarah to improve her relationship with her father, advising her that 'it must be jolly nice to have a daddy who bothers'. She and Sarah form a sisterly alliance early on, which is paralleled by Judith's close relationship with her older brother, and the three young children thus form a group with Judith at the centre. It is Judith, Stephen and Sarah who make the interventions that lead to the re-establishment of the new family at the end. Stephen decides to run away from home and his father because otherwise 'I'd kill him'. Judith suggests that he might turn to Uncle William for help and thus starts the process of realignment whereby both children are taken in by Lucy and William. Sarah completes the process when she overhears her mother planning a new future without her; she telephones a message to Judith to say that she is coming because 'I'm not wanted here anymore' and marches off with her overcoat over her arm. The film's representation of these children, making their own plans and leaving home on cycles and on foot, is strongly reminiscent of the evacuation stories in which children took their own decision about whether they would go or made extraordinary journeys to get back home from unhappy billets.[1]

A further indication of the unusual centrality of children to *They Were Sisters* is that adult characters are judged by how far their own actions are motivated by the children's needs. Lucy pays attention to the small things – Judith's fears of sleeping in a strange house – as well as to the large; William, in an extraordinary way, devotes his time to playing with the children (he is never seen to work) and takes their conversations entirely seriously. As Judith says, 'You can't help enjoying yourself' with William and Lucy. But even weaker characters can be redeemed by their understanding of childcare: Charlotte knows that her children need consistent love ('There is no justice in giving something only to take it away,' she tells Geoffrey) and Brian offers his daughter time for reading and play, in contrast to Vera, who is making herself beautiful for a dinner party. And, while Geoffrey's sadistic behaviour towards his wife is psychologically more complexly motivated, it is his melodramatic threat to kill his son's dog that finally condemns him in the eyes of Lucy and Charlotte.

The family that features in the blatantly happy ending of *They Were Sisters* appears to be a natural example of the model nuclear family. But it is not. It is, as William reminds us, an 'adopted family', one put together by death, coincidences and conscious decisions. At one level, its makeshift character looks back to the dislocations and disruptions of the war; at another, in its emphasis on the importance of children being with people who put their needs first, *They Were Sisters* was looking forward to debates that were to take place in the 1950s. By contrast, the Box comedies offer a more conservative vision in which order is restored by paternal action rather than childish determination. Here the Huggett family is the model. Appearing first in *Holiday Camp* (1947) and then in a successful series, Jack Warner established himself as the quintessential father figure with his loving but scatterbrained wife (Kathleen Harrison) and three daughters. Other films provide variants on the model: in *29 Acacia Avenue* (1945) and *Easy Money* (1948), Warner also took the paternal role, while in the later *The Happy Family* (1952) Stanley Holloway replaces Warner, although Harrison continues to play the wife and mother.

The Box films share a number of characteristics in their representation of the family. Unlike the Ealing comedies of the same period, such as *Hue and Cry* (1946) and *Passport to Pimlico* (1949), which emphasised the power and support of the community, these films present the individual family as the cornerstone of society. The family may, as in much of *Holiday Camp*, join in communal pleasures but at difficult points it is up to the family to defend itself against the world, for, as Landy points out in her discussion of *Holiday Camp*, it is 'familial relations' rather than communal solidarity that are 'the antidote to [the] frightening world' (1991: 317). In its most extreme form, the enemy becomes almost everything outside the family, and the films express deep suspicion of the post-war consensus, exemplified in *Passport to Pimlico*, in which the nation and community are deemed to be united. The threat to the family comes not just from the spivs and shysters who feature in *Easy Money* and *Holiday Camp* but also from the state and the community. The Huggetts sleep out with the crowds in the Mall for the royal wedding but miss seeing the parade because Joe gets into a fight with others in the crowd. In *The Happy Family*, the Lord's family shop and home is scheduled for demolition because it is on the site of the Festival of Britain. This sets the family in opposition to the state, since, as the young daughter puts it, 'Some government chap's trying to pinch the house'; the government official is indeed shocked when the Lords refuse to move: 'you'll be refusing to help your country, you must oblige.' Henry and Lillian explain what the house means to them in terms of hardship and struggle, a dream that they maintained through the Depression, the General Strike and the war, but national and local officials refuse to help, and even the press and the BBC seek to sensationalise the story rather than to understand the family. Isolated, the family submits to a siege, with the police trying to batter down the door until the prime minister intervenes and saves the home as 'a shrine to the Englishman who dared to fight to prove that his home was, whatever the cost, his castle.'

This image of the embattled family contributes to a rather bleak sense that the family, although outwardly respectable, is not secure within the social order. This is particularly true of the father, who frequently finds his position in the public world threatened. On the surface, these male characters are entirely in tune with their suburban surroundings and are unhappy when removed from them; Joe Huggett pines for 'The Wheatsheaf' when he's crossing the desert, while Mr Robinson prefers a holiday in Bognor to a cruise in the Mediterranean. But *The Happy Family* begins just as Henry Lord is about retire and hence to retreat not only from his secure social position at work but also in the darts team and the union. In *29 Acacia Avenue*, Mr Robinson is ill at ease with his snobbish neighbours and retreats to tend his begonias. For Joe Huggett, this retreat is more enforced than voluntary. In *Here come the Huggetts* (1948), Joe's insecure position and his vulnerability to the whims of others is demonstrated when he resigns because he is demoted at work for a mistake he did not make. Similarly, the Huggetts decide to emigrate in *The Huggetts Abroad* (1949) because Joe is falsely accused of stealing at work and again resigns. In neither case does Joe have the means to fight back; he can only withdraw, and it is left to plot devices to return him to his position.

The films generally try to restore order by restoring the father to his authoritative role in the family. This can be seen particularly strongly in the frequent versions of this narrative in which the father, who for much of the film has been ineffective or ignored, in the end rescues his son from some kind of harm. Thus in *29 Acacia Avenue*, Mr Robinson, who has been absent on holiday for much of the film, returns to prevent his son Peter being involved in a divorce case: 'thank your father,' the wronged husband tells Peter, 'he persuaded me.' In *Holiday Camp*, Joe goes to the rescue of his son Harry, who has been gambling with card-sharps; he not only wins back the money with the help of an extra ace but threatens to throw their blonde accomplice into the swimming pool. In *Easy Money*, the recently demobbed son of the family gets involved in shady business dealings but when the police visit his home, his father Philip, again played by Jack Warner, insists on being at the interview – 'It's my house and I shall do as I please' – and saves his son by claiming responsibility himself. And in *The Huggetts Abroad*, it is Joe who finally makes it through the desert, when even his cheery son-in-law Jimmy has collapsed, to get help for his family when the van breaks down. These films of the post-war period thus initially portray an apparently weak or ineffectual father but work to restore him to his authoritative position, even at the expense of his adult sons who are represented as childish and dependent.

This combination of social unease and paternal power does much to explain Jack Warner's star image. His paternal qualities, most famously on display in *The Blue Lamp* and in his subsequent television role as Dixon of Dock Green, are clearly established here. He is experienced, worldly wise and kindly. But there is also a side that was exploited in his more villainous roles, such as *Hue and Cry* and *Against the Wind*, in which his egotism and the chip on his shoulder created by social insecurity is to the fore. Warner has a bulky physical presence, and even when he is acting benignly his way of restoring order implies that physical force might be in reserve. His narrow upper lip can make his mouth cruel and his flat voice often has a sardonic edge. In these comedies, this side of Warner's persona is expressed in a persistent grumbling about his family's lack of attention and respect. The opening of *Here Come the Huggetts* is typical of this: Joe grumbles over the breakfast table, wants to be able to read 'my' newspaper and generally complains that 'nobody does anything I ask them round here'. Warner's paternal figure will sort his family's difficulties but, in return, he expects to be restored to his rightful position at its head. In these family comedies, he generally is.

The vulnerable child

The disruption of the family and its regrouping after the war was not the only post-war topic of discussion so far as children were concerned, and there were other consequences of wartime experiences that were seen as more positive for children. R.M. Titmuss, in a lecture delivered in 1955, reflected that the Second World War focused attention on the psychological and physical state of civilians as well as of those fighting and argued that the welfare state that emerged from the social measures taken during the war 'was centred round the primary needs of the whole population' (82). The needs of children were seen as crucial, and it was symbolic that the family allowance payments to all mothers for their children was the 'one key building-block of the Beveridge temple' that had 'a consensus ... [that was] all but absolute' (Hennessy: 129). From child allowances to free cod liver oil dispensed through children's clinics to free secondary education based on different kinds of ability, there was an emphasis on the healthy upbringing of children for the nation's benefit.

For individual parents, children represented hope for a future, and they invested much in them. Sociologists of the period felt that the diminution of poverty gave parents more confidence so that 'when the family's subsistence problems cease to weigh so heavily, the child comes to represent the family's new hopes for the future' (J. Klein: 559). Jackson and Marsden found in their study of working-class families with children in grammar schools a large number of parents who 'kept before their children some wider vision of social possibilities' (77). The post-war parents in Roberts' study of women and family life in Lancashire 'were determined that their children should have a "better" life than they themselves had experienced' (143), and these families devoted 'more attention to their children whose needs and interests had a high priority' (157).

How to bring up children to make the best of the new future was the subject of much study, to which sociologists, psychologists and educationalists all contributed. From a huge literature, we can note certain themes that are critical to an understanding the films that deal with children in the 1950s. There is a growing emphasis on child-centredness, so that care relates to what is good for the child rather than convenient for the parent. As one mother told researchers, 'People nowadays think more about what's good for the children, from the children's point of view ... I'm thinking in advance for his comfort all the time ... most people think more of their children's good' (Newson and Newson: 258). Although such attitudes could be found across class divisions, this child-centred thinking tended to be associated with middle-class families, and researchers consistently used class as a basis for their analysis. One observer reported that, in a deprived community in Liverpool, 'children are trained by a mixture of indulgence and shouting and threats' (Kerr: 58), while in slum areas in London, 'the early period of indulgence ... is followed by more or less permanent neglect' (J. Klein: 631). In contrast, a greater child-centredness was reported in studies of middle-class homes (611). A 1954 report, for instance, found that the middle-class boy 'felt more accepted ... could discuss things with his parents ... could confide in them, and they shared his interests' (H. Himmelweit, quoted in *ibid.*: 611).

A further feature of this work, running parallel to the emphasis placed on the crucial importance of the nurturing mother, is a commentary on the changing role of the father, who, modern childcare manuals suggested, should play an active role in bringing his children knowledge of the outside world. Through his work and his hobbies, wrote Winnicott, the father 'widens the children's view of the world', and if he joins their play, 'he is bound to bring valuable new elements that can be woven into the playing' (116). Fathers themselves commented on how their role was changing. A working-class interviewee complained that 'since t'war they've played up this children job too much and t'children's taken advantage of it. I was brought up wi' t'boot and t'fist in my young day, but nowadays you can't touch 'em' (quoted in J. Klein: 591). Zweig, in his 1961 study of *The Worker in an Affluent Society*, found men who were less negative about this change – 'I suppose I am a better father than my own' – and concluded that a 'new image of a benevolent, friendly and brotherly father' was emerging which was different from that of the powerful but remote father of previous generations (quoted in *ibid.*: 565).

But sometimes this concentration on the child's needs and relationships could cause anxiety: 'Nowadays, if they don't turn out right you wonder where you've gone wrong, don't you?' one mother told researchers. 'I think we're not so happy about ourselves these days' (Newson and Newson: 258). Another mother, in a 1954 sociological study, confessed that 'It's for the children that I'm worried' (quoted in J. Klein: 559). Parents could go wrong in various ways. The absent mother was one problem, but the delinquent child could also be 'the over-indulged child' (Kerr: 124), and sociologists identified 'the dangers of possessiveness' in 'the reluctance of mothers to relinquish their hold' (V. Klein:

150). Problem fathers could also err in two ways. On the one hand, the decline in his authority may have gone too far, so that he lacked authority and status. In this situation, the child may have 'no model of confident and respected masculinity to copy'. Delinquent boys were identified as being closer than usual to their mothers and less likely to accept their fathers' discipline (J. Klein: 574–5). On the other hand, sociologists and psychologists were equally wary of the over-dominant father. Examples are given of fathers who have too much authority, and a community that is too much ruled by masculine order and the routines of his work may also fail its children; in the mining village of Ashton, sociologists noted a 'taboo on tenderness', so that 'softness, gentleness and sentimentality are discouraged and eventually crushed permanently' (J. Klein: 83, 118).

In a situation in which the theoretical and practical models of childcare were rapidly changing, the question of discipline was the subject of professional and popular debate. George Gorer's research in the early 1950s for his study of the English character found that 'the typical English view of childish nature is that the young child is inadequately human and that, unless the parents are careful and responsible, it will revert to, or stay in, a "wild" or "animal" state' (183). This conception of the child as an untrained animal led 68 percent of parents to answer 'yes' to the question as to whether 'children need more discipline' (161), but the question remained as to how that discipline should be asserted. A Metropolitan Police report of 1948 argued that juvenile crime proved the common-sense moral of 'spare the rod and spoil the child' (Turner and Rennell: 157), but the parents of Gorer's survey claimed to be more likely to use isolation or deprivation of sweets or television than corporal punishment. Other accounts stressed that bad behaviour arose from psychological needs. Winnicott, for instance, offers an account of delinquency in which the child has not developed internal modes of discipline and therefore offends because of this psychological need. The parents' behaviour as much as the child's therefore needs to be addressed. Thus the child who compulsively steals 'has lost touch with his mother in some sense or other' (163); 'in full blown delinquency ... what meets us is the child's acute need for the strict father' (229) because he has not been given the means to develop internal controls. In both cases, anti-social behaviour is 'the SOS of an ill child', and what is needed is 'a strong stable environment with personal care and love' (230), not physical punishment.

In the context of this massive post-war investment in children's upbringing, it is perhaps not surprising that the early 1950s saw a remarkably high number of films that have a child as the protagonist or take the care of children as a central motif. It is as if the film makers are keeping track of the post-war babies and following them into childhood: 1952 alone gave us *The Yellow Balloon*, *Mandy*, *Emergency Call* and *Hunted*, as well as the slightly older teenagers of *I Believe in You* and *Cosh Boy*. The films of the 1950s take the family as a central motif and explore, in a more direct way than had been usual, some of the ideas about childcare that were so widely disseminated at the time. Issues of education, discipline and children's psychological needs are addressed directly in these films. The childcare experts had created an image of a young child who was vulnerable to the ignorance of its parents, a child who could easily be damaged even in, or perhaps most particularly in, the intimacy of the family. Somewhat unusually, the liberal and child-centred approach of the literature finds its way into British cinemas.

In looking at this we need to distinguish between fifties films about teenagers and those about younger children. Films that are concerned with teenagers as a social problem tend to offer an explanation that is in accord with the sociologists' scenario of an over-indulgent mother and an absent father. *London Belongs to Me* (1948), *Cosh Boy*, and *I Believe in You* are all instances of films in which the delinquency is blamed on a mother's closeness to her son and the lack of traditional discipline. As Hill shows, the resolution through 'social control' (124) that he finds in these films is based on a particular analysis of how some kinds of gendered parental behaviour both cause and can resolve the teenage problem. But other films of the period seem to express unease about traditional discipline as a solution and in particular about the disciplinary role of the father, the role so naturally assumed by Jack Warner. We can examine this development by grouping together a number of films of the mid-1950s that take a young boy as their protagonist: *The Yellow Balloon*, *Hunted*, *The Spanish Gardener* (1956) and *The Scamp* (1957). Although the films are different in many ways,[2] they share a common plot in which a pre-teenage, slight, fair boy (Jon Whiteley in *Hunted* and *The Spanish Gardener*, Andrew Ray in *The Yellow Balloon* and Colin Petersen in *The Scamp*) is set at odds with his father and forced to fend for himself in seeking a relationship in which his needs can be met. This crisis is normally precipitated by the erratic and sometimes violent behaviour of the father. In *The Yellow Balloon*, the fear of punishment by both parents throws Frankie into the clutches of the criminal, Len, but it is his father who gives him the beating that is supposed to bring him back to order. In *Hunted*, Robbie runs away from his adoptive home and attaches himself to a young tearaway, Chris. Robbie fears his father and the marks of beatings on his back confirm that he is right to do so. In *The Spanish Gardener*, paternal cruelty is mental rather than physical when an obsessive father, recently divorced, punishes his son, Nicholas, by isolating him and withdrawing his affection. And in *The Scamp*, Tod is abandoned by his father, Dawson, who acts on his belief that there is 'only one way to deal with a hysterical kid … knock it out of him hard'.

The films, despite their different settings, have a number of common features around the figure of the child. First, the narratives have a double viewpoint whereby the viewer is positioned both with the child and outside him. Thus the audience is privy to the child's thoughts and reasoning and to the social conse-quences of actions that the child cannot see. In *The Yellow Balloon*, for instance, we understand Frankie's motives for stealing an expensive pineapple to give to his new-found friend but we know that Len will not appreciate it and that the market trader will see the act as straightforward stealing. In *The Scamp*, when Tod smashes the jam pots for, according to the housekeeper, 'no reason at all', the audience knows that it is because Tod has been accused by his friend Eddie of going 'soft'. Thus, unlike the social problem films about teenagers, where the audience is generally excluded from what is going on in their heads, in these films the narrative position involves both knowledge and understanding. The audience is put in the liberal position of the educational psychologist, which explains stealing as a cry for help.

A second feature of these films is the emphasis on the vulnerability of the children. The fears and protectiveness of the social sciences discourse – 'It's for the children that I'm worried'; 'I'm thinking in advance for his comfort all the time' – are embodied in the representation of these young boys. Even the apparently streetwise Frankie and Tod are narratively placed in positions of risk, and the emphasis is on their innocent inability to sort out the world in accordance with their needs. Looks play a strong part in creating this sense of vulnerability, and the blond hair and pale skin of the child is consistently contrasted with his surroundings. In the opening of *The Yellow Balloon*, Frankie's fair head is framed in the window as he looks down and smiles at the hectic street scene below; when he walks through the street his head bobs like the balloon he desires. Andrew Ray's fairness contrasts with the dark hair and complexion of William Sylvester, who plays Len, just as Jon Whiteley's fair curls are set against Dirk Bogarde's darkly dramatic good looks in both *Hunted* and *The Spanish Gardener*. Even the robust Tod in *The Scamp* is fair, and the lightness of his hair contrasts with the darkness of his father. The association between light and goodness, whiteness and innocence, which Dyer (1997) discusses in relation to women, is brought into play in these films to underline the vulnerability and the essential goodness of these young boys.

It is important that the boys are pre-pubertal. The oldest are probably Nicholas and Tod, who seem about to enter their teens. The age of the boys means that they are free of the overt sexual desire that is both disapproved of and punished in teenage social problem films such as *Cosh Boy* and *I Believe in You*.[3] As Hill (1986) and Landy (1991) have observed, British social problem films tend to equate criminality with sexuality, so that by 'running criminality and sexuality together', they establish a logic whereby 'the "cure" for delinquency and the price of rehabilitation into the community is ... a suppression of sexuality' (Hill: 77). The films I am discussing offer a different model. The age of the hero means that the question of sexuality is not posed and, by removing this link, the films both establish the boys' innocence (even in the case of *The Yellow Balloon* and *The Scamp*, where the question of future delinquency is an issue) and require a different form of resolution.[4] Resolutions based on punishment and discipline become less necessary when sexual repression is not involved, and instead these narratives incline towards solutions that rely on understanding and education.

In a variety of ways, then, the films set up a story in which the audience is invited to feel and identify with the vulnerability of the young hero but also to observe, from a detached liberal position, how others treat him. This mid-fifties figure lacks the resilience of the streetwise kids of Ealing's *Hue and Cry* or the confident Judith in *They Were Sisters* and he cannot sort out his own resolution. In particular, the child's welfare is seen to be crucially dependent on a father, and the task of the child is either to educate the existing father or to find a new one who will take the role of the father more responsibly.

This emphasis on what a good father might be takes time to develop. In this context, *The Yellow Balloon* is something of a transitional film. Frankie is a much-loved only child ('You want to watch him, being your only one,' advises a neighbour) being brought up in a traditional home. Frankie's father, Ted, oscillates between the two extremes of the inadequate father. Ted initially tends to give in to Frankie, to give him sixpence for a balloon and to fool around with him rather childishly, leaving domestic responsibility to the mother. Kenneth More's performance in the role emphasises a boyish exuberance and sympathy for the experience of being a child, and in that he is an early version of the more brotherly father of Zweig's model. But it is clear that Ted has little insight into his son. Like Gorer's respondents, he sees 'kids [as] proper little savages, even the best of them. I don't think that anything bothers them much.' When, under Len's instruction, Frankie is caught stealing, Ted can only attempt to impose discipline from the outside. He understands that something is wrong but he knows only the old ways of discipline and beats Frankie. The audience, with its knowledge of what is wrong with Frankie, knows that the beating is wrong; even on its own terms it does no good: 'I couldn't get a word out of him,' Ted reports to his wife. In the end, Frankie gets his reassurances from a stranger, Mary, who tells him 'If my little boy had done anything wrong … if he told me about it truthfully … I'd've got him out of it somehow.' In the final shot, the reconciliation with his parents that takes place in the empty dark streets is wordless. Although a new model of the family is being hinted at in *The Yellow Balloon*, it cannot be fully expressed.

Hunted is a more painful film about childhood that, as Landy suggests, offers 'an unusual image of male tenderness and nurturing' in a melodrama 'in which the vulnerable individual is pitted against overwhelming and oppressive odds' (1991: 274). Landy focuses on Chris, the criminal on the run played by Dirk Bogarde, who first tries to use and then to help Robbie. But the film centres on Robbie, the young Scots boy adopted into a London home whose first act in the film, as he confesses to Chris, is to 'set a house [his home] on fire'. This is one of the instances of a double viewpoint that I referred to earlier. The audience knows that Robbie has only left some curtains smouldering but understands what Robbie means by his action, particularly when he protests to Chris: 'You're taking me home, I won't go.' The narrative is driven by Robbie's rejection of his old family and his determination to make Chris into a good father. Chris is at first brusque and uncaring but he gradually takes on the responsibility for Robbie's guileless devotion. The film is quite bold in presenting the nurturing side of the new father rather than the 'brotherly' father that Kenneth More hints at in *The Yellow Balloon*. Both the narrative action and Bogarde's performance emphasise the feminine aspects of Chris's role; he is seen feeding Robbie, putting him to bed and telling him bedtime stories as the two flee from London. As the journey gets tougher, Chris has to cajole Robbie to keep him going, to carry him in his arms and to hold him, against the cold, as they sleep. The film ends with Chris's self-sacrifice; escaping on a stolen boat, he turns back to the harbour when he realises Robbie is ill. In the powerful final shots, the fishermen watch silently as the boat returns; Chris, carrying the child in his arms, walks up the steps of the quay and disappears into the male crowd. There is no family to return Robbie to, only the waiting police. Although the discourse of childcare is not directly called on in *Hunted*, the image of the vulnerable child and the caring father is powerfully represented but not yet placed in the family.

If in *Hunted* Robbie tries to create a new father, *The Spanish Gardener* focuses on how relations between the boy and his father might be re-established, and the film makes a strong and self-conscious critique of traditional patriarchal modes of discipline.[5] Medhurst argues that the film offers a complex and searching analysis about how 'men can and cannot relate to each other' (1993: 96). He suggests that the diplomat father, Harrington Brande, is associated with feminine attributes of the 1950s – he is houseproud, fussy and prone to headaches. Nevertheless, Brande's attempts at childcare are very masculine, and he wields the paternal authority associated with traditional fatherhood by preventing Nicholas seeing his mother, using isolation as a punishment and denying him the touch of physical affection. The film makes it clear that Brande lacks the selfless ability to put the child's interests first, which, as the 1950s progress, is becoming the mark of good childcare. Instead, Brande insists on his own needs taking priority; he tells Nicholas: 'it hurt me deeply that my son could be so thoughtless of my feelings,' and Nicholas knows that his father's needs are paramount – 'Father says I'm the only one he needs now.' Brande is explicitly criticised for this, particularly by the modern young couple who offer to take Nick to play with other children and by the doctor, who offers a consistently humane point of view, telling Brande directly that his form of paternal love is 'too selfish and demanding.'

Even more than in *Hunted*, José/Bogarde offers an idealised image of the new fatherhood, which is set against Brande's failures. Bogarde brings a brooding, romantic intensity to the role to provide a fantasy of caring father-hood. The character of José combines the 'brotherly' model of fatherly behaviour with a psychological understanding of Nicholas's position and of his need for unconditional love. José, like Winnicott's good father, literally leads Nicholas into the outside world, first into the garden and then into the Spanish countryside. He encourages him in the physical activity that Brande has banned for his 'delicate' son and provides him with the opportunity to develop his strength and learn appropriately masculine skills. But it is also important that José demonstrates his psychological understanding of the situation and is not afraid of the intense feelings being expressed. He talks to Nicholas, allowing him to be a small child and express his fears. He understands the psychological reasons for Brande's hostility to him and tries to explain Brande's actions in a way that his son will understand: 'he's not happy and thinks you don't love him enough.' When Nicholas runs to him in tears and frightened, José holds him, offers him reassurance – 'when you feel better we can talk about it' – and carries him to his own home for food and play. This completeness of care, which combines physical nurturing with psychological understanding, thus embodies the best practice of the childcare literature.

The Spanish Gardener offers some kind of resolution of the child's dilemma through a change in the father. Brande cannot become the ideal father, but he is dramatically reconciled with José, and in a brisk *dénouement* he agrees that Nicholas will be able to see his mother and have the company of other boys at boarding school. It is perhaps significant that the film in the group that offers, in José, the most idealised account of the new father and suggests the possibility of a change in the father (rather than a change of father figure) is set abroad, as if the changes required cannot be imagined at this point in contemporary Britain. *The Scamp* returns to a British setting and, unlike *The Spanish Gardner*, draws on some of the generic characteristics of the teenage social problem film. More specifically than the other films, *The Scamp* writes the possibility of delinquency into its scenario and tries to assess what might turn Tod away from criminal activity. The film sets up a contrast between the natural father, Dawson, and Stephen, who unofficially adopts the boy. Dawson is drawn with the melodramatic excess that Landy identifies in the social problem film. Indeed, he has the characteristics of a teenager himself in that he is working-class, rootless, aggressive and sexually active, whereas Stephen is socially secure, a middle-class teacher with a comfortable home. Dawson demonstrates the traits of the bad father of the psychological literature in that he is both violent and inconsistent. In the beginning, he bullies Tod and is literally careless in leaving him so that he can go off on his travels, but later, in an effort to win him back, he gives him expensive presents, which Tod is seduced by. Stephen, on the other hand, consistently defends Tod, tries to see his point of view even when Tod is at his least communicative and to win him over through reason.

In its treatment of the debate about childcare, *The Scamp* specifically articulates a liberal position, which the earlier *The Yellow Balloon* could not. In that film, the father tries both to befriend his son and to discipline him but fails because he has no means of articulating his paternal role. In *The Scamp*, the two aspects of fatherhood come together and make sense within the child-centred discourse that has been established in education and psychology. Richard Attenborough's youthful image and his exuberance as an actor underline Stephen's wish to understand Tod by joining in his enthusiasms. Thus, when Stephen finds Tod tapping out a beat on some oil drums he gets him a real set of drums and the pair play together; as Stephen explains to his sceptical wife, 'found something he can do. Positive way of using his energy.' Stephen is criticised by his wife for being childish with Tod but the film is careful to place his behaviour within a context of childcare that also involves psychological understanding. Stephen values talking ('Next time you get all hot and bothered, suppose you wait and talk to me first?') and giving Tod responsibility ('Is that a deal?') rather than the traditional forms of punishment. In *The Scamp*, unlike

The Yellow Balloon, corporal punishment is an issue for discussion. Stephen is forced to punish Tod with a beating by a cruel neighbour who threatens to take the boy to the police otherwise, but the use of corporal punishment fails because it forces Tod into more extreme behaviour. Far from being an example of good discipline, it is presented as a betrayal of the trust between father and son: such punishment, according to Stephen, 'makes juvenile delinquents not cures them.'

There is some tension in *The Scamp* between the strongly drawn, even melo-dramatic, posing of the choice between the two fathers and the social realist emphasis on the detail of Stephen's paternal philosophy. The film reaches its resolution by killing off Dawson (an act for which Tod initially thinks he is to blame) and allowing Tod to join his new family. The film thus endorses the impeccably liberal position that Stephen embodies, providing a didactic example of the 'new image of a benevolent, friendly and brotherly father' that Zweig was uncovering. It also inadvertently demonstrates how this new fatherhood involves a shift in power away from working-class parents (who, as Dawson demonstrates, cannot be won over to new ways of childcare) to the middle-class experts. For, unlike the fantasy father that Bogarde embodies in *Hunted* and *The Spanish Gardener*, Stephen is not only a good father but also a teacher. Although *The Scamp* focuses on the family, its emphasis on Stephen's profes-sional understanding of and involvement with children points towards an important aspect of the representation of children and families in fifties films, the role of the expert.

Children and the expert

Recourse to the expert was a feature of the new emphasis on childcare that was discussed and commented on by the experts themselves. Winnicott stressed that parents should be given 'full responsibility with regard to what is their own affair, the upbringing of their own children' (176), but official interest was inevitable given the strong sense that these children represented the new future of the nation. Popular support systems were offered by the NHS. Roberts comments that among mothers who had children in the 1950s and 1960s there was a move away from older women as traditional sources of help and 'a marked increase' (148) in references to outside helpers, which included the doctor, the health visitor and staff at the infant and child welfare clinics. A number of socio-logical studies in the 1950s found that younger mothers were 'making use of outside agencies' such as the child welfare and family planning clinics (J. Klein: 459), while a study in a Lancashire town concluded that 'the rights to have medical care under the National Health Service ... could be seen to have an important effect on the child-rearing habits of younger mothers' (quoted in *ibid.*: 459). Outside the NHS, schools and education authorities became more significant as a source of advice and admonishment as full-time secondary education became the norm. Problem parents might find themselves visited by social workers, whose brief was 'to support the family' (Wilson 1977: 89).

Figure 8.1 East Ham Minor Ailments Clinic, London, 1949.

Courtesy of Newham Archives and the Local Studies Library.

Although the initial emphasis was on the physical well-being of children, expertise was increasingly associated with help to understand the psychological development of the child. In the social work agencies, the emphasis was on working with individual families on the promotion of healthy relationships and 'a psychoanalytical approach to personal problems did gain importance after the Second World War when social work assumed a new role' (86). Roberts found that mothers were aware of 'the rapidly growing literature on childcare and believed that their job as mothers included the duty of seeing that their children developed properly, especially psychologically' (152). It was no longer enough to rely on traditional advice from older women or on parental common sense to create children's well-being. J. Klein identified 'the spread of literacy and the popularization of psychology' (549) as important factors in the move away from traditional sources of advice. In the support agencies, professionalism and training were deemed to be crucial. Bowlby was being ambitious when he declared that 'the foremost need' was for all those working in the field to be 'thoroughly familiar with the psychology of human relations, alive to unconscious motives and able to modify them' (111), but he was not alone in wanting to professionalise care. Winnicott, for instance, declared himself disturbed that the lack of training for teachers meant that 'the general mass of children are educated without first being diagnosed' (206), while, at the end of the decade, James Hemming argued that the school should be 'a therapeutic influence' for the adolescent girl, 'an auxiliary environment ... to which she may bring the undesirable attitudes acquired at home or elsewhere' (115). Thus the increased emphasis on the expert in the family was premised on a notion of intervention, which involved diagnosis and the provision of support, drawing on a psychological or psychoanalytic model.

In some senses, the intervention of the outside expert in the family (the policeman, the lawyer, the teacher) is a familiar narrative device in many films that provides the initial disruption on which many a story is based. In the 1950s, however, the expert is associated not only with the legal and moral systems that support order but also with psychological understandings, which can explain disorder. These figures represent the intervention of the modern world into the family and, given the complexity of the systems that they claim to understand, the 'authenticity of their expert knowledge' (Giddens: 28) has to be taken on trust. In this final section, I want to analyse how this 'psychologising' of the expert in relation to childcare affected the representation in British films of some traditional experts (policemen, teachers) and look at the way in which the 'new' experts, particularly psychologists, are treated. However, I will argue that British films of the period both drew on and backed away from the psychological elements of these discourses and that class as well as knowledge is a key factor in the status of the expert.

Two films from early in the period show some changes in the way in which the police are represented. *The Blue Lamp* (1950) begins with a 'traditional image of police benevolence, Dixon giving directions in the street to a passer-by, and ends with Mitchell doing the same' (Barr 1977: 83). Police work involves keeping order, dealing with criminals and finding those who are lost or have strayed, but although, as Barr has convincingly argued, the film uses the model of the family to represent both the 'close community' of the police and the 'nation as a family' (83), it is not the job of the police to work with the problem family in a direct way. Mitchell visits the hapless working-class mother to hear about her missing daughter, Diana, but, while Diana is a useful lead to the film's real villain, her boyfriend Riley, the film offers no evidence that Diana's relationship with her mother is something for the police to deal with, and they appear to make no effort to help to restore order in this specific family.

We can set this traditional approach against that offered in *Street Corner* (1953). Muriel Box's film is overtly modern in its focus on the new phenomenon of the policewoman and it is the policing of childcare that is at the centre of a number of different stories. The policewomen do not so much solve crimes as resolve family disorder, making sure that husbands, wives and children are in the right place by the end. In part, they take on this role because of their own feelings about children but, in the main, such personal engagement is deemed rather dangerous because it might lead to over-involvement. Indeed, the policewomen are poor at actual childcare, failing to stop a baby crying and being gullible about the tendency of children to get lost on purpose in order to be consoled with chocolate and buns at the police station. Instead, the model is of distanced, compassionate concern that relies on professional skills and calm common sense. In the three main stories, the policewomen remove a child from her father and step-mother and persuade her natural mother and her new husband to adopt her; sort out a bigamous relationship so that the woman can remain with the good man rather than her bad husband; and persuade a young woman who has fallen into criminal company that she should go back to her husband: 'he's a very decent fellow … settle down like a good wife and look after him and the family.' Poor Bridget, who does not have much choice, agrees that she will do 'anything, anything you say' to avoid being taken to court.

The Blue Lamp and *Street Corner* have much in common in their attitudes to policing. Their emphasis is on the importance of the communal good and the role of the police in maintaining it through common sense rather than psychology. But while *The Blue Lamp* confines its policing to the public sphere of the streets, cafes and snooker halls, *Street Corner* crosses boldly into the private sphere and shows policewomen breaking down front doors and confronting parents with their family responsibilities. While Dixon and Mitchell are policing their own community, the policewomen of *Street Corner* are middle-class professional women patrolling a working-class area. As police-women, they are not just taking on childcare cases because they are women, for they are also involved in more conventional police detective work and chases. But the fact that they are women is significant, since their intervention in the homes of working-class families is a result of modern attitudes to women in the police force (one lone Scottish policeman protests against their presence), which extends and expands the traditional notion of police work more generally. Their authority comes from the interest of the state in the welfare of children rather than from any psychological expertise. The emphasis in *Street Corner* on the highly competent middle-class expert is taken up in a number of films later in the 1950s that have a professional setting such as the police, teaching or nursing. Two later examples show both how this liberal figure developed and how it comes to be associated with a more psychological understanding of children and their needs. A somewhat stilted but nevertheless revealing film in this mode is *The Blue Peter* (1954), a Group 3 production set in the Outward Bound Sea School in Aberdovey, Wales, and directed by Wolf Rilla, who also directed *The Scamp*. The school is run on impeccably liberal lines. It provides an outdoor experience for working-class teenagers and builds up their confidence through physical activity. Its teaching ethos, expressed by the warden, is based on giving the boys 'equal chances' and treating them as individuals whose difficult behaviour has to be understood rather than simply punished. The protagonist is Mike, a Korean War hero who is sent to the school to test out the possibilities of his running a similar school in Malaya. He is sceptical about the approach and initially places a military emphasis on discipline, hard work and competitiveness. The other staff recognise that Mike is doing this for himself rather than the boys, and he is warned that this over-emphasis on strong leadership and results means that he is pushing the boys too hard and that the less able are being sidelined. Mike protests that the boys are not all equal, but the warden maintains that they all have to be given 'an equal chance to improve'. Gradually, Mike absorbs this philosophy as he begins to get to know the boys. He helps the 'dead-end kid', Sparrow, to feel himself to be the equal of the others through his talent for sport and talks to the working-class Charlie, the 'natural leader', who has to learn, like Mike himself, to be more sensitive to others.

The film then offers a therapeutic setting and an educational approach that is based on understanding. Its most explicit use of a psychological discourse is in the story of Andrew, a sensitive, middle-class boy who is frightened of heights; he is another of the fair, vulnerable pre-teenage boys discussed earlier and is being pushed by his journalist mother to follow his father into the RAF. It is significant that while the working-class boys have problems caused by their impoverished backgrounds, Andrew's problems are more psychological. The resolution of the film hinges on Mike's determination to find out why Andrew fears heights – 'if I can't get to the bottom of that boy's trouble, I wouldn't have the courage to go on.' Andrew finally tells Mike the story of his father's death in a plane crash, revealing to Mike and the audience that this is at the root of his fear. Having won the boy's trust, Mike listens to him as a teacher should (and as his mother does not) and encourages him to pursue his desire to be a doctor. Andrew resolves his fear of heights and climbs down a steep cliff to help another boy in a dramatic mountain rescue. But Mike has also learned about how to be a teacher. 'How do you feel?' Mike asks Andrew in the film's final moments. 'Sort of different,' comes the reply. 'So do I,' replies the war hero, who has now understood that in a modern civil society, wartime discipline has to be replaced by a more democratic approach to individual needs and that the caring professional has to have some understanding of psychological motivations.[6]

A similar approach can be seen in *No Time for Tears* (1957), which is set in a children's hospital and which, through a number of interweaving stories, offers an account of nursing as a profession. The matron is played majestically by Anna Neagle, and other nurses are at different stages of their careers, learning what it means to behave professionally. Here, the children are highly vulnerable, and the stories of individual children reveal a clear division between the professionals and the parents. The film distinguishes between what one of the sisters describes as different kinds of love: one is 'firm and wise and right, the other weak and foolish and wrong'. The distinction is between love that expresses the feelings of the carer, parent or nurse, and that which focuses solely on the child's need. The risk for the nurses is that they will become over-emotional about the children in their care, but they must not become too distanced, otherwise they will see the children only as patients rather than as individuals in their own right.

The nurses in the film know how easy it is for them to develop the wrong kind of love for the children in their care. Continually before them are the mothers who fail their children. The film opens with a mother who 'loses' her son and finds that he has run off to join his sick brother in the hospital.

Teenager Bridie is in hospital for an operation on her club foot, but her mother is unsympathetic to her fears and hopes. Two of the main stories offer versions of motherhood that present the opposite problems. Timmy's mother over-identifies with her son, who is blind, and wants to protect him from the world; she is advised to consider a special school for him. At the other end of the spectrum is working-class Mrs Harris, who is slatternly and dirty, with greasy hair and a slovenly dress. Her two small children have become ill because she has neglected them so badly but her real problem is that she continually puts her own needs before theirs. She blames them for her 'wicked unhappiness', and when the matron catches her hitting George, she protests that 'they drive me to it ... my nerves won't stand it'. It is the middle-class matron who can offer these children the right kind of love and the film resolves the problem of their mother's inadequate care through an ending in which their father voluntarily gives his children back to the hospital for the matron to adopt, telling her that his wife is 'past praying for' and 'I'll sign anything you want'. As in *The Scamp*, the care of the middle-class professional is deemed to be best for the working-class child.

Matron condemns Mrs Harris not as a bad woman but as a 'sick person' and by the late 1950s a psychological discourse is established as the appropriate way in which professional expertise can be expressed. Stephen in *The Scamp*, Mike in *The Blue Peter* and the consultants and nurses in *No Time for Tears* all draw on the notion that the child's problems have to be understood by looking at what is happening beneath the surface, by trying to understand what the child is expressing in its limited language and sometimes violent actions. In addition, narrative organisation and visual imagery express the underlying feeling of the vulnerability of children, which drives much of the childcare literature of the period. Films focusing on children thus reflect a greater trust in experts and their psychological explanations than we found, for instance, in the comedies. Nevertheless, there is still resistance to the full-blooded commitment to therapy that some Hollywood melodramas of the time were exemplifying, and this reluctance can be seen in the treatment of the one expert whose narrative position is regularly undermined in British films, the psychologist or psychiatrist. While popular psychology is increasingly drawn on as a source of explanation, the expert who might be considered to have most to offer in this area rarely gets the respectful treatment accorded to the police, teachers and nurses. We can see this at work in two films that span the period, *The Magnet* and *The Third Secret*. Working within different genres, the treatment of the expert in these films reveals a much more ambiguous attitude to this form of expertise.

The Magnet is a 1950 Ealing comedy that centres on a young boy very similar to the pre-teen children of the films discussed earlier. Johnny fears himself to be in trouble when he 'steals' a magnet from a small boy on the beach by tricking him into swapping it for an 'invisible watch'. Outside events conspire to make Johnny think that he is being pursued for this offence. The film uses the double narrative position characteristic of child-centred films; the audience knows more than Johnny and understands the misdeductions he is making but also shares his point of view and understand his feelings. This time, though, this double viewpoint is used to undermine rather than confirm the position of the expert who tries to help Johnny – his psychologist father. Dr Brent uses dream analysis and word association to diagnose that Johnny is frightened of growing up and imposes on his son a programme of treatment which his mother is supposed to carry out. But this treatment only disrupts the otherwise happy family life and is based in a misunderstanding of what the problem is. In the end, the psychological trappings fall away as the film reaches its *dénouement* in an action sequence from which Johnny emerges a hero; he receives a gold medal and is able to resolve his own problem by swapping it with the small boy on the beach and getting back his imaginary watch. *The Magnet* thus pokes fun at the psychologist's misreading of his own son's situation and for trying to bring unnecessary complications into an explanation for a small boy's actions. It rejects the expertise on offer in favour of Johnny's more straightforward and resilient approach; the fact that the child's viewpoint remains hidden from his parents is a happy fact of family life.

The Third Secret seems to be much more in tune with the insights of popular psychology. This thriller begins with the death of a psychoanalyst in what is understood to be a suicide but which his schoolgirl daughter, Catherine, believes is an act of murder perpetrated by one of her father's patients. She persuades one of the patients, Alex, a TV presenter, to seek the murderer among the other patients, who include a secretary, a judge and an art dealer. In the end, though, Alex himself is threatened by Catherine, who confesses to being the murderer. The film ends with her under restraint in a psychiatric hospital. In its narrative organisation and visual style, *The Third Secret* draws on understandings taken from the popular dissemination of psychology. The narrative explores the hidden lives of the doctor's patients and accepts the despair and uncertainty that lie behind their apparently successful lives; Alex's task is to listen to the stories they tell to see if they will let slip a clue to the murder. The *mise-en-scène* emphasises harsh lighting, dark shadows and unusual camera positions, which make familiar objects seem strange. The dialogue is full of obscure sayings and gnomic riddles; the title comes from a game of quotations that Catherine chalks up on the wall, waiting for completion initially by her father and then by Alex. In this sense, the film draws less on childcare tenets of the 1950s than on the idea, popularised in the 1960s through the work of R.D. Laing, that truth could be spoken most clearly through madness. But the film is also deeply sceptical about the psychoanalytic expertise of the dead doctor. His patients seem to be overly dependent on him and his decision to take on his own daughter as a patient has disastrous consequences for her as well as for him. Are Catherine's word games just childish riddles or games with meaning, encouraged by her father, which have driven her too far? Are her moments of clarity the result of childish innocence or of her father's psychoanalytic probings, which have exposed her too much? However one reads it, the ending is bleak. *The Third Secret* illustrates the limits of faith in psychological expertise. One of the psychiatrists whom Alex consults defines the killer as a psychotic who cannot be cured and, even if Catherine's tears at the end betoken some kind of release, Alex's investigation, parodying that of her father, has revealed her to be just such a killer.

The scepticism, comic in one instance, tragic in another, that these two very different films display tells us something about how far films are prepared to go in endorsing the expert. While it comes to be accepted, in the 1950s, that psychological understanding has to be acknowledged, the more explicit versions of psychology are less successful than those that are combined with the caring common sense and the middle-class confidence of the traditional professions. In the end, what the films about childhood tend to trace out is as much a maintenance of class positions as a reliance on expert knowledge.

This chapter closes with a film that handles these matters in a more complex way than the somewhat didactic manner of many of the films I have discussed so far. The 1958 film *Violent Playground* was made at a time when, as we have seen, a psychological approach is being incorporated into the notion of the professional, and the image of the vulnerable child is well established as a motif. The tough detective, Truman, resists a transfer to juvenile liaison, 'the care of the young,' as his chief defines it. 'Handling kids is not my line at all,' he protests, and the other policemen mock his pursuit of the small criminals stealing lemonade. His initial resistance is based precisely on the recognition that professional work with families is now more clearly framed within a discourse of psychology and sociology rather than policing but Truman comes to understand that juvenile crime *can* be caused by poor parenting and inadequate social conditions. Critical discussion of this film has tended to focus on the figure of the teenager Johnny Murphy and the film's ambivalent attitude to the possibilities of reforming rather than damning him.[7] In the end, Johnny is taken away in a black police van as a sign to the community that his psychopathic violence has to be contained. But it seems to me that much of the film's confusion about Johnny stems from the way in which the discourse of teenage revolt is crossed with that of the vulnerable child that we have been examining.

Truman is drawn into the family through Patrick and Mary, Johnny's twin siblings, who have been caught stealing. Although they are initially streetwise and cheeky, the vulnerability of these two is emphasised by the absence of their parents; their mother is in London with another man and their father is working on the 'China Seas'. It is with the twins that Truman has most success. He persuades their initially hostile older sister, Cathy, that he genuinely wants to help them; he takes them to a liberal children's club, where Mary is gently encouraged to paint and Patrick to channel his energies into boxing; at the end of the film the twins, sitting alone and vulnerable on the steps in the school, trust him enough to ask him to 'fetch' them home.

Johnny, as the elder brother of the twins, shares some of their vulnerability. He is slim and fair-haired like the boys in the films we looked at earlier, and, like Robbie and Frankie, his very name emphasises that he has not yet grown up. The priest to the Murphy family recalls him as 'a very brave little boy', and Johnny himself, in committing arson, is trying to return to the childhood moment when he was a good boy and rescued his family from fire. When the crisis comes and Johnny holds a class of children hostages in the school, Truman, who has learned his lessons well, keeps reminding the other police officers that Johnny is 'more frightened than the kids … he'll only shoot if he's scared'. In this context, it is possible to read Johnny's action sympathetically along the lines of the model popularised by Winnicott as a boy in search of a father, as a delinquent offending 'against society … in order to re-establish control from outside' (229) who should be treated therapeutically. But this approach is complicated by the fact that Johnny's actions are placed within the context of the harm he can do to other children.

The film makes it clear that Johnny is a danger not so much because of the arson but because his behaviour puts the twins and other small children at risk. When the teenagers, led by Johnny, confront Truman with a display of rock 'n' roll, it is not just the juvenile liaison officer who is alarmed. Close-ups show us Mary and Patrick, wide-eyed and cowering in a corner of the room: the home has become a dangerous place because of Johnny. And in the *dénouement*, when, in a long sequence, Johnny, armed with a gun, tries to use Patrick, Mary and the other children as cover, it is the risk to the children that puts Johnny beyond the liberal solutions that Truman and Evans initially try to press. The fragility of the children's safety is underlined by the head teacher, who refers to his pupils as 'babies', and by the scenes that show the crowd of mothers who gather in the playground to watch the hostage scenario unfold. As children are seen at the window, the mothers cry out and move compulsively towards the scene of danger. The feeling of high emotion is reinforced by close-ups of the tearful faces of individual women but the emphasis is on group emotion and the hysterical anxiety of mothers who cannot save their children. They watch while the experts – the police, the priest, the teacher – take the actions needed for the rescue. Even Cathy, who finally gets into the classroom to disarm Johnny, cannot control how he will be dealt with, because the police are the ones who have to act to protect small children. 'Every father and mother in Liverpool is glad,' Truman tells Cathy as Johnny is driven away. Parental anxiety is allayed, if only temporarily.

9   Femininity in the fifties

The new woman and the problem of the female star

The year 1953 saw the coronation of Queen Elizabeth II in an elaborately staged ceremony that drew on supposedly ancient traditions to consolidate the position of the monarchy. But much of the poignancy and drama of the ceremony came from the fact that it was a young woman of 27 who was now publicly declaring herself to be at the service of the people. The story of how Elizabeth came to inherit the throne was told and retold in the months before the Coronation. Princess Elizabeth, it was said, had always been close to her father, the King, because of the sense of public duty she shared with him. The news of his death was broken to her early one morning in February 1952 when she was on an official tour to Kenya and news coverage emphasised the personal tragedy of the bereaved daughter as well as the constitutional position of the queen apparent. The *Daily Mirror* reported that 'Queen Elizabeth the Second came home tonight to her mother's arms' (9 February 1952). In her person, the new queen embodied the different roles of the new woman. As well as being a daughter, she was also a wife and mother; Prince Philip as Duke of Edinburgh was the first of the Lords to swear fealty to her in the elaborate coronation ceremonial, and the four-year-old Prince Charles watched in Westminster Abbey as his mother was crowned. As a woman, the Queen was also subject to the scrutiny of the fashion writers and the cameras; what she wore was widely reported, and she was also known to be interested in fashion and society. It was this combination of roles that was the key. As Richard Dimbleby wrote at the time, in a book for children that told them about *Elizabeth Our Queen*, it was not the formal title but 'the personality of the Queen' that was important. 'What mattered in the eyes of her people was the fact that Queen Elizabeth the Second was, as Winston Churchill summed up, a fair and youthful figure, princess, wife, mother' (51).

The Coronation, with its emphasis on the act of robing and the symbolic use of dress and jewellery, took on a new resonance with a young woman at its centre. The coronation ceremony featured a passage in which the soon-to-be crowned queen was dressed in a simple white shift and then gradually loaded with the trappings of her state, what the souvenir programme described as 'the Robe Royal or Pall of the cloth of gold with the Stole Royal' along with the armills, the ring, the sceptre, the orb and eventually the crown (34). This ceremonial shift from the white simplicity of the maiden to a woman 'arrayed in her utmost splendour' (29) with the glittering regalia of power symbolised an acceptance of responsibility by the sovereign, a move to maturity and power. But the story of the accession itself was more broadly the story of a woman's growth into maturity. Here was a daughter learning of her father's death while she was thousands of miles away fulfilling her public duties; a young wife only five years into her marriage, with two young children to care for; a new queen who was committing herself to the public duty that was her work; but a young woman who still wanted to enjoy herself and who had wholeheartedly adopted the long skirts and tight waists of the fashionable New Look. In the multi-faceted demands made on her, the new Queen Elizabeth epitomised the 'new woman' who was such a feature of the 1950s. Perhaps the only thing that was unusual about the ceremony at Westminster was that it challenged, in a way more radical than the supposedly medieval trappings indicated, the idea that women should be confined to the domestic spaces of the home. As her husband and the men of the establishment knelt before her, it was clear that a woman was taking on the highest symbolic role of the state; she was that most trouble-some of creatures, a woman who went out to work.

This story of the young woman coming to the throne thus captured some-thing of the contradictory demands that women more generally experienced in the 1950s. In Chapter 2, we saw how the ideal of the new woman was constructed in four key areas – motherhood, sexuality, work and consumption – through the sociological and psychological discourses that underpinned the figure and were widely popularised in women's magazines and popular jour-nalism. In this chapter, I want to build on that account by looking further at this figure and relate it to the widely acknowledged failure of fifties British cinema to give roles to women or to nurture its female stars. I want to suggest that the discourse that constructed the new woman emphasised a movement to maturity that British cinema, with its anti-modernist tendencies, found particu-larly hard to handle. After an initial exploration of this discourse of maturity, I will look at the work of two female stars – Kay Kendall and Virginia McKenna – whose star images incorporate some aspects of the new woman, in order to see how this figure is handled in the context of British cinema.

The mature woman

The story of the Coronation was a story about growing up and the new woman could achieve the ideal only when she too had grown up. If we look at the four strands that come together in the new woman, we can see in each case that there is an emphasis on the mature achievement of womanhood. Motherhood, for instance, was, as we have seen in Chapter 2, conceived of as both a natural instinct and a set of skills and responses that had to be acquired. Education was needed to bring mothers 'to a more mature understanding of their duties', and 'the cause of family failure' began to be conceptualised in social work manuals as 'personal failure to achieve mature personalities and relationships' (Lewis:

24). Immature behaviour by their mothers had a bad effect upon children. Mothers who were inconsistent and impulsive because they gave in to their own desires were criticised for not giving their children a secure environment. Such behaviour was associated by sociologists with working-class communities, in which 'the past persists ... to a much greater extent than is generally realised' (Kerr: 189). In more modern families, the psychological relationship between mother and child was the subject of much thought. What was important, and perhaps had to be learned if it did not come naturally, was that the mother should be mature enough not to compete with the child over her own needs and interests. Motherhood was 'a time of self-sacrifice' (Winnicott: 109), but there was a reward because in the selfless acceptance of the child the woman found not only her true pleasure but her mature self. 'Even mothers,' Winnicott proposed, 'have to learn how to be motherly by experience ... By experience they grow' (49). Winnicott encouraged mothers to have confidence in their own maturity so that they can give in and adapt themselves to their child's needs without feeling that they have lost their 'newly found independence'; '*if you are sufficiently confident about yourself,*' he stresses, 'you can let each of your children dominate the scene ... inside your wider influence' (122).

This emphasis on female maturity also features in the literature on sexuality. The new woman was expected to have a satisfactory sexual relationship within marriage and again, in this discourse, there is an emphasis on maturity. As Elizabeth Wilson points out, 'in the Freud-soaked atmosphere of the time ... heterosexuality was *the* touchstone of "maturity" and femininity' (1977: 66). British psychologists and analysts followed the American adaptations of Freud in seeing female sexuality as difficult to manage. If a woman is to reach a satisfactory relationship, she has to move through different ways of sexual expression, to grow up and mature sexually. Women have to be directed to fulfilment within a male/female couple, to what the 1957 Penguin handbook *The Art of Marriage* called the 'full and natural "vaginal orgasm"' (quoted in Wilson 1980: 94). Just as a woman had to mature into motherhood, so she also had to grow into true sexuality, and sex could be pleasurable and guilt-free as long as it supported secure and well-defined male and female roles. In social work case studies, the emphasis was on 'correct gender identifications', and those who fail to become truly feminine or indeed masculine are condemned to 'neurosis and immaturity'(Wilson 1977: 87).

The debate about women working also centred on the mature woman. Paid work is seen, even by those sympathetic to women workers, as something that married women go back to in their thirties or later (V. Klein). Summerfield argues that the major effect of the encouragement for women to join the labour force in the Second World War was on the position of older women in the workforce:

> The group which the government thought most likely to want to leave work at the end of the war, older married women with children, continued to come into paid work ... the war played a major part in the transition

from the pre-war situation in which the majority of women workers were young and single to the 1950s when the typical woman worker was the older married woman with children.

(1993: 74)

Despite the emphasis on the importance of the mother at home, official thinking emphasised older women as a labour resource. In 1952, the Ministry of Labour was 'arguing that employers should open the door to people able and willing to work ... including older married women' (Lewis: 71), and just over a decade later, the 1963 Newsom Report suggested that the trend for married women to return to teaching after having children should be encouraged (104).

If work was associated with the mature married woman, so to was house-work and consumption. Consumption did indeed have its more frivolous side, which the women's magazines ('Bargain offer! Super Paris Red Lipstick': *Women's Illustrated*, 21 January 1956) offered readers alongside the recipes and knitting patterns but the general emphasis was on informed decision making and home management. The 1960 Albermarle Report on youth services stressed the role of informal education for girls to promote 'social maturity and technical competence at her job as a home-maker' (para. 57). Modern design called for women to consume 'in a disciplined and "responsible" way, exercising restraint and "good taste" by choosing well-designed ... goods' (Partington: 206). The care and discipline associated with putting together and running such a home was the product of feminine maturity. The 'tasteful and well-run home into which it is possible to invite visitors at any hour' was, according to the Newsons, the aspiration of those women who had absorbed an 'ideal self-image as a mature and sophisticated woman' (223).

In various ways, then, the new woman is associated with the mature woman who is able to hold these complex strands together within marriage. What is striking is that on the one hand these discourses emphasise moral responsibility, maturity and the ability to manage; on the other hand, they also hint at sexual possibilities or frivolous concerns with fashion, which sustain rather than subvert the image of the mature wife and mother. The frivolity and sexuality are not associated with youth, to be dropped when the woman becomes more mature. No, the wife and mother must also be sexual and smart, attentive to her husband as well as to her children. At its most extreme, we get 'the good wife' imagined by *Housekeeping Monthly* (13 May 1955: 5), who is given advice on how to welcome her husband home from work; she must be a good mother who will 'prepare the children ... they are little treasures and he would like to see them playing the part'; she is the well-organised home manager who has dinner ready and will 'eliminate all noise of the washer, dryer or vacuum'; but she is also a sexual being, who must 'touch up your make-up, put a ribbon in your hair' and be 'a little gay'.[1] If this paragon appeared only in the pages of very superior magazines, she represented the ideal that lay behind the discourse of the mature woman in both sociological literature and its popular manifesta-tions. It is in this context that the figure of the Queen at the Coronation takes on such significance. Here personified was the mature woman of the 1950s with the emphasis on glamour as well as responsibility, on youth as well as maturity, on motherhood and public duty, on being a wife as well as a mother. The resonances went deep.

One might have expected British cinema to find in the mature woman and the debates she generated a subject to explore. Wartime cinema, under pressure from the authorities, had paid some attention to the mobile woman and this interest in women as central characters continued into the late 1940s, as we saw in Chapter 5. But although the social problem film continued the tradition of making stories out of issues of public interest, the examples from the 1950s focus almost entirely on the young. In addition, the most popular genres of the period, the comedy and the war film, are male-dominated and tend to present women as childish, silly and vindictive or valorised and saintly. Women are generally relegated to the sidelines in fifties war films, and although comedies such as the *Doctor* series, films by the Boulting brothers and the *St Trinians* series certainly satirised old-fashioned attitudes, they also mocked contemporary attitudes towards, for example, marriage and women's modes of consumption. In such comedies, the sex war both dominates male/female relationships and is deemed to be rooted in human nature. Unlike Hollywood cinema, where the development of the modern melodrama in the 1950s gave some space for psychological and sociological themes, British popular cinema seemed to be locked into systems of gender that were out of line with the contemporary views about mature femininity that found a ready outlet in other forms of popular culture such as women's magazines and fiction.[2] Fifties British cinema, by contrast, provides evidence of a strong resistance to the notion of the new woman and an inability to imagine her as any kind of modern heroine.

This did not go unnoticed by filmgoers at the time. In turning to cinema, it is striking how much debate there was in the 1950s about the failure of women to make an impact on British films.[3] Male stars dominated the era but not without protests from some fans and critics. Rather pompously, *Films and Filming* ascribed the 'falling female popularity at the box office' to male superiority; 'the men give better value for money. Having been chosen, in Britain at least, more often on acting ability than physical appearance, they have more to give' (March 1955). The more popular *Picturegoer* was more sympathetic to criticisms of British cinema's failure to develop its female stars and the lack of good roles for women. One of its feature writers in the mid-1950s, Dick Richards, commented regularly on 'the crazy, criminal contempt of *women* players' by British film studios (29 January 1955) and observed that 'British films cannot rely solely on men' (1 January 1955). The common complaint was that 'British studios ... can turn out wonderful war films, first rate actors – but they don't know how to handle women' (*Daily Sketch*, 23 July 1956). Women stars were well aware of the problem and used publicity articles to complain about their poor treatment. *Picturegoer* regularly featured such comments: Glynis Johns complained that in British films 'actresses take second place to actors, ships and machines' (19 March 1955) and Kay Kendall commented that 'the rash of all-male pictures isn't exactly healthy for actresses' (29 January 1955). Phyllis Calvert, a forties star, commented on the lack of female stars in the 1950s and blamed the studio preference for promoting starlets rather than supporting mature female stars: 'bikinis don't make stars,' she asserted, and offered Kay Kendall as an example of the talent that British cinema was wasting (12 November 1955).

I want to suggest that the reason why British cinema could not produce female stars in this period was not just due to problems of discrimination in the industry or to modes of representation that affected the portrayal of women in mainstream cinema more generally, although these are important factors. What we get in the 1950s is a very particular disjuncture between the modern educational and sociological discourses in which women are thought about and placed and the regressive mode in which cinema is operating. To examine this, I present two case studies. The first is that of Kay Kendall and, in particular, her work in what we might call the comedies of the companionate marriage. The second is that of Virginia McKenna, who, despite relentless stereotyping as an 'English rose', is the closest British cinema came to a representation of the mature women. I have chosen these two, rather than the better-remembered Diana Dors, because in their work there is an attempt to represent contemporary modes in the case of Kendall and maturity in the case of McKenna. This contrasts with the way in which Dors is constructed as a much more traditional sex symbol through her appearance and in her mode of behaviour (Geraghty 1986). Dors' glamour was that of the traditional film star rather than the contemporary woman and her narrative function was nearly always to make sexual trouble. Kendall and McKenna operated differently, in ways that shed light on the difficulties that the new woman posed for fifties cinema.

Kay Kendall and the companionate marriage

If there was a star of the new look, it was surely Kay Kendall. She made comparatively few films in her short career which ended with her death from leukaemia at the age of 32 in 1959. Even before her death she had turned to Hollywood for better parts. Nevertheless, she had a distinctive film presence that was based on the glamour and elegance of a mature and sophisticated persona. Kendall's modern image was worked through in three of the four strands that I have identified as making up the mature, modern woman. In analysing Kendall, I will examine how her star image fitted within the discourses of the new woman and look at how far this image was sustained and undermined in three of her most successful comedies, *Genevieve* (1953), *The Constant Husband* (1955) and *Simon and Laura* (1955).

Kendall's stylish appearance offers the most appropriate way into a discussion of her persona as a new woman. In all her films, she dresses in a modern and fashionable manner, wearing clothes that are very much based on the new look and its fashionable permutations in the 1950s. At the same time, she develops a dashing style of her own that combines the glamour of jewellery and the extravagance of masses of textured materials with the casual air created by her turned-up collars and pushed-up sleeves. Her clothes have a swirling quality that emphasises swift movement and sudden gesture. Even in small parts in black and white films of the early 1950s it is possible to see her distinctive style emerging. In *Lady Godiva Rides Again* (1951), Kendall, who plays Sylvia, the married sister of the budding beauty queen Marge, is initially rather dowdy, appearing in a dark-coloured check blouse and then a tatty dressing gown. As the film progresses, however, she runs through a series of costumes that grow ever more glamorous: she does the ironing in a low-cut blouse with large white buttons; serves the tea in a dress with a low v-neck and full skirt; assists in the family newsagents in a striped dress with wide square collars; and goes to the rundown theatre in Derby in a short loose jacket and a white blouse that is pleated from the shoulders, with long black gloves and flowers in her hair. Here, as in her other films, she consistently wears fashionable earrings, heavy bracelets and pearl necklaces, sometime knotted and sometimes in a choker style.

When colour is used, the emphasis on contemporary fashion is even more marked. Kendall often wears clothes in unusual colours. As Rosalind in *Genevieve*, she spends much of the film in a slimline ochre-coloured suit with an unusual, asymmetrical neckline that emphasises the jade-coloured blouse underneath; in *Doctor in the House*, we first see her wearing an olive green textured suit with a turned-up, pointed collar and a slim skirt, while her dress in the restaurant scene is in burnt sienna with a low-cut square neckline. As Monica in *The Constant Husband*, she is first seen casually dressed at home in a mustard-coloured shirt with turned-up collar and pushed-up sleeves, worn with a full black and white check skirt and the usual earrings and gold bracelet. Kendall's association with the contemporary extends to decor as well as to dress, so that she is frequently positioned in a contemporary setting in which her fashionable clothes are set against modern furniture or design. In *Doctor in the House*, Isobel meets Simon Sparrow in a fashionable restaurant and sits on a contemporary sofa against the background of a screen that is covered with a modern abstract design in colours that match her dress. In *The Constant Husband*, the contemporary look of Monica's clothes is matched by the striking blue and yellow colours in her home and the examples of modern furniture such as the cocktail bar.[4] Similarly, in *Simon and Laura*, Kendall as Laura frequently appears on the modern, open-plan staircase and her living room features blue walls and modern shelving with spotlights.

Kendall's characters are thus linked to consumption by their modern clothes and contemporary settings, but they also reflect something of the new woman in that they work and are financially independent. As the Kendall persona develops, her characters are given careers appropriate to her new look style. In *Genevieve*, she is a model, in *The Constant Husband* a fashion photographer, and in *Simon and Laura* an actress. Thus the characters enter the public life of work but do so in a way that calls on the modes of display and glamour that are already operating in terms of her engagement with modern dress and fashion.

Similarly, Kendall's sexuality is very much linked to her sophisticated persona. In *The Square Ring* (1953), she plays the small part of Eve Lewis, who uses her sexual charms to get her own way with both husband and ex-lover, and she is contrasted with the frightened ingenuée Frankie (Joan Collins) and the plain Peggy. In *Doctor in the House*, the inexperienced Dr Sparrow is both attracted to and terrified by Isabel's confident manner on their date, while in *Genevieve*, it is clear that Rosalind is used to being whisked off for weekends ('that Le Touquet routine went out ages ago'), and she bats away Ambrose's suggestive proposal that they go straight to the hotel on arrival in Brighton with a nonchalant 'Steady, junior, steady'. The only aspect missing from Kendall's representation of the new woman is motherhood. That in itself perhaps underlines how difficult it was to fit all the aspects of the mature woman into a single coherent figure but also served to emphasise Kendall's freedom from responsibilities.

Kendall's star image was thus established in her films as an independent woman with a strong sense of contemporary fashion and modern behaviour. This was backed up by press reporting that emphasised her 'gay, assured manner' and referred to her as 'the queen of the fashionplate film set' (*Picturegoer*, 10 December 1955). In addition, she was presented as something of a rebel who fell out with Rank over her refusal to accept the parts offered and who protested over the lack of good female roles. This image of a strong-minded contemporary woman is strongly present in the three comedies in which she starred that are structured around the modern form of marriage, the companionate marriage, in which man and woman are, in theory at least, equal. Interestingly, the three films represent the three stages of such a relationship: the initial meeting, the honeymoon period and the long-established couple. In looking at these films, it is helpful to bear in mind the narrative model for comedy proposed by Thomas Schatz and that for romance suggested by Janice Radway.

The study of the role of women in narrative film has tended to work with the notion of women as 'trouble' which the narrative has to resolve or erase. Many films noir, thrillers and melodramas conform to this model, and Diana Dors' roles, for instance in *Here Come the Huggetts* or *Yield to the Night*, tend to fit this paradigm. Romantic comedy, however, works rather differently. Schatz suggests that in comedy the narrative centres on 'the struggle of the principal characters to bring their own views in line with one another's or ... with that of the larger community,' relying on 'a progression from romantic antagonism to eventual embrace' (29) and an 'eventual growth into social and sexual maturity' (155). This involves a greater equality between the male and female principals, since to reach equilibrium both are required to change. Radway's work on romances makes this explicit. She suggests that the appeal of romances for women lies in the narrative conventions which reach resolution (Schatz's 'eventual embrace') not just through the heroine's transformation from tomboy to mature woman but through the hero's even greater shift to a nurturing, caring and domestic husband. This model seems highly appropriate in the context of the companionate marriage and offers a way of analysing the narrative movement of these three Kendall comedies.

In *Genevieve*, it is Wendy (Dinah Sheridan) and Alan (John Gregson) who offer the model of a modern marriage which the sophisticated Rosalind and the boyish Ambrose (Kenneth More) have not yet reached. The early scenes of the film establish that the former have a marriage that is based on sharing and companionship. Wendy's equal contribution to this is emphasised throughout the film: she knows precisely how much money they have in their joint bank account, and she takes the initiative sexually with Alan, telling him 'you wouldn't want to be married to a woman of no experience whatever, would you?' In addition, she has areas of her life in which she is independent from Alan and her friendship with her old flame Ambrose is conducted with an easy camaraderie. The premise of the film is that Wendy's and Alan's balanced relationship has been upset by Wendy's irritation at Alan's passion for his veteran car, Genevieve, and the task of the narrative is to bring them back into alignment.

This well-established marital relationship is set against the initial moves being made between Rosalind and Ambrose, who, by contrast, have yet to reach this type of equilibrium. As we have seen, Rosalind is independent, stylish and sexually sophisticated, but she also has a slightly wacky, childish side, which is demonstrated by her insistence on taking her dog Suzi with them on the London to Brighton car race. The key moment in the film, which brings together both Rosalind's stylish independence and her engaging eccentricity, occurs when she plays the trumpet at the dance after the race; much as Ambrose enjoys the performance, he is sidelined by it, and Rosalind takes the stage alone while Ambrose seizes Wendy to dance. Ambrose too has an air of sophistication, but, in contrast to Rosalind, the film emphasises his boyish enthusiasms and his lack of experience. He confesses to Wendy that he has never managed to combine the London to Brighton run with what he euphemistically calls 'a really beautiful emotional experience'. He fails once again when Rosalind passes out after her trumpet playing exploits. The work of the narrative is to get this couple into a position where they might begin to be the kind of couple that Wendy and Alan are.

For much of the film, the narrative operates with a strong sense of difference between the male and female characters which hinges on attitudes to the car race. Ambrose and Alan are both enthusiastic and competitive, in love with their cars and determined to beat each other. The women, who are meant to be supporting their partners in the race, are more often united in condemning the childishness of the whole thing. 'It's all so silly,' says Wendy at the beginning. 'It's childish and a bore.' At the dance, she unites with Rosalind to demand a temporary stop to conversations about cars: 'Rosalind and I have put up with your nonsense all the way down … for a few hours, let's have some peace.' The women are consistently more sensible: throughout the race, they refuse to identify with their partners' emotions; they condemn them when they cheat; and they laugh when something goes wrong. At this level, the film can be seen as the kind of comedy that Hutchings (1993) suggests worked 'to trivialise and diminish him [the new man] through humour and ridicule' (45), while the women are justified in their more mature approach.

However, I would argue that the film works to turn this around, to endorse male enthusiasm and to suggest that it is linked to their greater feeling for tradition, which is, in the end, justified. During the race itself, the women pay for their aloofness by being made to look childish and immature. Their hair becomes windswept, their smart clothes are in disarray, coffee is poured over Wendy, while Rosalind is forced into the water to push Ambrose's car out of a ford. The *Daily Herald* critic noted that a version of this joke, in which the 'lady passenger ... has to get out and push or suffer some other indignity', was repeated, with variations, fourteen times in the film (29 May 1953). In addition, the final resolution of the narrative, which refigures the couples on the basis of heterosexual companionship rather than gender alliances, is achieved not by the men and women moving equally towards each other, as the romantic comedy model suggests, but by the women making the move into a more sympathetic position with their men. Wendy learns once again how much Genevieve means to Alan at the very point when he might lose her, and Rosalind is magically won over by Ambrose's enthusiasm for his car and the race. Both women finally find themselves caught up in the excitement of the last stages of the race back. No longer united by common sense, Rosalind and Wendy now vigorously support their respective partners and the film ends, good-humouredly, with the women allied with their men, on male terms.

The Constant Husband takes Kendall further along the marital path. In this film, she plays Monica, who, it turns out, is the latest in a line of wives that her bigamist husband Charles (Rex Harrison) has loved and left. The film opens with Charles suffering from amnesia, and when he is returned to Monica he is pleased and alarmed to discover the modern young woman who is apparently his wife. The two appear to have a balanced relationship in which Monica can be both independent and loving. She is first seen at work as a photographer, and it emerges that she not only works but also owns the house and runs her own business; she is, she says, 'a disillusioned career girl determined not to lose my independence again,' and she reminds him that they agreed before the wedding that she would continue her career. She is emotionally and sexually experienced, a divorcee who was, she confesses, swept off her feet by Charles and who frankly admits 'I love you very much'. In these early scenes, Monica comes over as the modern wife, while Kendall is presented as a star with a glamorous and forceful presence. Moreover, at this stage in the plot, it is clear that she knows more than Charles and is able to take charge of the situation. Monica, it would seem, is the modern woman who is not only capable and desirable but also carries the moral sympathy of the film; her view of marriage as one in which the woman can combine independence and desire seems to be endorsed.

The effect of the comedy is to turn this on its head. It is possible to see Charles as the main butt of the plot in *The Constant Husband*. Rex Harrison had played a similar role as the immature and irresponsible hero of *The Rake's Progress*, and as Charles explores his rakish past and discovers his complex marital history, he criticises himself for being immature, childish and selfish in his behaviour towards women. But as the film continues and as Charles discovers more wives, it becomes clear that Monica's knowledge and control were illusory, and her femininity is presented as threatening rather than desirable. In the move to farce, she loses her individuality and becomes one of the legion of women who want to possess Charles. Thus in the court scenes at the end, when Charles is put on trial for bigamy, the six wives combine to create a version of femininity that is voracious, bitchy and irrational. The official case against Charles is that he 'exploited female victims' and 'displayed an appetite for marriage ... as a method of livelihood'. But the wives refute this legal definition and compete with each other for possession of him, sending him meals in prison and swearing in court that they would take him back despite his betrayals. Even his efficient female barrister, played by Margaret Leighton, finally succumbs to female irrationality, wailing 'You beast!' as Charles insists on pleading guilty and going to prison to escape from all the women who are after him.

Although Landy argues that Harrison is presented as 'the object of desire' (1991: 283) and the subject of female gaze in this film, I would argue that by the end of the film it is his view of femininity as frightening and irrational that predominates. The court scenes are framed mainly from Charles' viewpoint as he surveys the women crowded into the courtroom, femininity on parade in bright hats, long gloves and fur stoles. The wives appear one by one in the witness box, in the order he has imposed on them, the order of their marriages to him. In swearing that they would take him back, they act for women as a group, putting on a show even as they declare undying love, preening as they are applauded by the women in the gallery. Kendall's star status is reduced as she becomes one of the line-up of beautiful women who provide what *Picturegoer* praised as a dazzling spectacle of British female glamour (23 April 1955). Although the film makes a joke out of Rex Harrison's persona and turns him into a weak and harried rake, it does so by turning the independent career woman, Monica, and the barrister in particular into temperamental and lovelorn monsters. In the end, the comedy, far from moving to a balanced equilibrium between the couple, transforms Monica into just one of a number of wives waiting outside the prison for Charles to be released. Although the final joke, in which Charles fleeing from his wives is captured by the barrister, appears to confirm the man as victim, it can be funny only because the male viewpoint of the voracious and irrational woman has been so strongly established.

The narratives of both *Genevieve* and *The Constant Husband* therefore work to undermine the modern woman. *Simon and Laura*, the final film of the trio, offers a rather different approach to the companionate marriage. *Films and Filming* praised it as 'a delightful comedy', claiming that 'the basis of its success lies in the fact that it is contemporary' (January 1956). Despite its setting in the glamorous world of show business, the film is clearly rooted in a contemporary view of modern marriage as a relationship between equals, both of whom have to fight for their position. Simon (Peter Finch) and Laura are actors who agree to stay married in order to star in a television programme about their lives, but the programme is also meant, in the words of the producer, 'to mirror the lives of an ordinary, happily married couple.' The film contrasts the sentimentalised and saccharine version of marriage that Simon and Laura act out in their television programme with the behind-the-scenes reality of quarrels, upsets and misunderstandings. The irony is that when the rows spill over into the programme ratings soar and the newspapers praise the 'guts and gore in *Simon and Laura*'.

However, our introduction to Simon and Laura suggests that this is a marriage in which balance has not yet been achieved. Simon is both patriarchal and immature, bossing Laura about, getting caught out in golf club affairs and threatening to leave and go to his mother's. Laura, on the other hand, is smart and cruel, reminding him of his age, his recent lack of parts and his previous attempts to leave. The balance in the marriage is joked about – Laura reminds him that the furniture in the house is hers, while the mortgage is his – and the pair assert that they are staying in partnership only to pick up the offer of the TV series: 'it would have to be a purely business arrangement,' says Laura. The plot proceeds through a series of misunderstandings about affairs and professional rivalry and is resolved when the two come to realise, through overheard conversations and backstage revelations, that they do still love each other. In the classic mode of romantic comedy, initial antagonism is transformed into romantic love.

Two points that contrast with the earlier films are worth noting. First, the narrative resolution depends mainly on Simon admitting that he loves Laura as she is. In a touching moment, Finch shows Simon letting down his guard and confessing to the TV producer: 'she's down-to-earth and honest and practical. She's good fun, highly decorative. She's good to have around the house. She's, well, she's my sort.' There is here something of an acknowledgement of Laura as a whole woman and it is this that permits the revelation to be made that Laura had rejected the proposal from the producer that Simon be killed off in the show (and, by implication, in the marriage). The final embrace, then, is achieved through the movement of both characters, a move that involves not so much change as acknowledgement as to what has always been there. Second, and following on from this, although the companionate marriage is only narratively achieved at the end of the film, it has actually been present throughout in the play of comedy between the two protagonists. Unlike *Genevieve*, when Kendall's most significant moment is in the solitary trumpet playing, or *The Constant Husband*, where the by-play between Harrison and Kendall hardly has time to be established, the exchanges between Finch and Kendall are central to the film's pleasures and continually demonstrate that the relationship between them is one of equality. They need each other for the witty exchanges, the flying insults, the double takes and the physical comedy, and the film continually draws parallels between them in different comic scenarios – both get advice, for example, from famous TV personalities, and both get drunk in the catastrophic filming of the Christmas party. Schatz suggests that in classic screwball comedy, the 'relationship is expressed in style and attitude rather than in kisses and declarations of love' (162), and in *Simon and Laura* performance provides the means by which this marriage is defined, through style and attitude, as equal and complementary. It is perhaps not an accident that *Simon and Laura* was directed by a woman, Muriel Box.

Kendall offers a test case of how far the new woman can be represented in the comedies of marriage that were characteristic of the period.[5] I would argue that the approach is successful insofar as the new woman can be accommodated into discourses of stardom that emphasise looks, style and performance but starts to crack when jokes and narrative organisation come into play. The comedies hint, particularly in *Simon and Laura*, at a narrative approach and a performance style based on equality between the male and female protagonists but, in general, the films' jokes and narrative resolution depend on the audience adopting the male viewpoint, a viewpoint that reduces the smart and sophisticated Kay Kendall to looking childish, temperamental and immature.

Virginia McKenna and the mature woman

Virginia McKenna was exceptional in British cinema of the period in a number of ways. She was, according to Brian McFarlane, 'one of the very few British film actresses who became a star in the 1950s' (163). Her *oeuvre* was markedly different from actresses like Kendall, who worked mainly in comedy, and it is significant that McKenna, in her own recollection, felt that she had benefited from the domination of the war film: 'I was lucky because, at the beginning of the 50s, they started to make these wonderful war stories' (163). Like Kendall, she had relatively few large parts in the 1950s and there was press sympathy for her 'quiet revolt' in turning down parts that were not worthwhile (*Daily Sketch*, 23 July 1956).[6]

McKenna's strong stereotype as the English rose gave her star image a national dimension that took her out of the competition with Hollywood's glamour and, as we shall see, underpinned much of her work in the war film. Most significantly in this context, there is in her films an attempt to represent her as the new woman. She is presented as a caring and devoted mother but one who also has responsibilities outside the home. This leads her into positions in which she takes responsibility for others and she is a natural leader who knows what should be done. She does have a sexual life, and with men she is direct and passionate, but she also has moments of frivolity and fun, which are particularly associated with the pleasures of femininity and consumption. But it is a sign of how difficult it is to get the modern woman on to the screen that McKenna's mature femininity is permitted in war films only when it is disguised, sometimes literally, in a masculine garb. It is significant that McKenna achieves her biggest parts and most distinctive successes in *A Town like Alice* (1956) and *Carve Her Name with Pride* (1958), war films in which she adopts the qualities associated with male stars of the period: resolution, toughness and a stiff upper lip.

In the mid-1950s, McKenna's English rose image was built on two cameo roles, in *The Cruel Sea* (1953) and *The Ship that Died of Shame* (1955). These roles are subservient to the male characters and tend to be read as plot functions by later critics; Barr (1977: 149) refers to her as the 'respectable' end of the 'dull polarity' provided by the women in *The Cruel Sea*, while for Kirkham and Thumim (1997: 102) she is a 'guarantor of moral probity' in *The Ship that Died of Shame*. But if these roles are read within the discourses of the new woman, a potentially more interesting figure emerges. In *The Cruel Sea*, she plays Julie Hallam, a young Wren whom we first meet at work. She is highly competent (in a film in which professional competence is highly valued) and in a position that gives her knowledge and some power. When she first meets Lockhart, she initially refuses him entry into the security areas and, later on, when he is about to leave on another sea trip, she knows more about the expedition than he does. 'Take care,' she warns him, 'I know where you're going.' At the same time, her sexuality is heavily marked (she is described as the 'glamour pants from ops ... a smasher'), but she does not tease or prevaricate in her relationship with Lockhart; she offers a love that is clearly passionate but also mature and understanding. This duality between professional competence and sexual commitment is made more complex in her role in *The Ship that Died of Shame*. Although, as Helen Randall, she features only in a brief scene set during the war, she is very much a young version of the modern woman of the 1950s. She is dressed in clothes that smack of fifties fashion rather than wartime restrictions: underneath her wide-cut duster coat, she wears a smart, well-fitted suit and a neat, round-necked sweater and later, in bed, she wears a towelling robe. Her face is lit strongly to emphasise her blonde hair, fair skin and dazzling smile. She is sexually passionate and direct in the way she looks and speaks to her new husband, Bill. In confessing that she has bought no food, she tells him 'when I saw you again, I forgot. You put it out of my head, everything, except that I was seeing you again.' When they are in bed together, she longs for the sun to halt, to stay in the sky, and thus preserve Bill, who serves in the navy, from his next night-time mission. But Helen knows that domesticity is important, not just in the sense of cooking and cleaning but also because the house is going to be her realm. She expresses unease at walking into the borrowed cottage – 'I feel as if we're doing something wrong' – but the 'something wrong' is not sex but settling down domestically in someone else's house. But she recognises the importance of this step. 'This is a home,' she tells Bill, 'it sounds sentimental but it means more that it sounds ... a lot more. And it's a problem.' The problem is that she does not yet have the skills to run the home, but she knows that she will learn, and she is committed to growing into the female role.

Helen's premonitions are fulfilled narratively when the brief holiday is ended by her death in a bombing raid but two later war films confirmed McKenna's ability to represent the mature woman, although they do so in complex ways. *A Town like Alice* is the story, told in flashback, of a group of European women in Malaysia who are trapped by the Japanese invasion and are forced to trek for hundreds of miles because they can find nowhere to stay. McKenna plays Jean, one of the women in the group, who meets and falls in love with the Australian, Joe, with whom she is reunited at the end. The bulk of the film deals with the sufferings of the women and the ways in which they deal with the tensions and difficulties that arise in the group. In that sense, the film is similar in structure and theme to the war films featuring the male group such as *The Cruel Sea* or the male prisoner of war films. *A Town like Alice* was seen as deliberately going against McKenna's image; as one journalist put it: 'the rose wears a dirty sarong, her body slumps with fatigue. The cool beauty of her features is ravaged by violent emotions' (*Picturegoer*, 12 November 1955).

Despite this apparent change of role, the film offers a fuller version of what had already been sketched out in McKenna's earlier cameos. Now she can be seen to be operating across the four strands of femininity that make up the mature woman. The film starts with Jean working as a secretary and throughout the film she is seen to work effectively in the public sphere. She is brave in her dealings with the Japanese, supports and helps those who are made ill by the enforced march through the jungle and is generally calm under pressure. Although Miss Horsfall, the teacher, initially takes the role of the leader, Jean gradually takes over. She seems instinctively to know how to handle the more difficult women and naturally takes charge of a situation without being domineering or bossy. By the end, she is the spokesperson who persuades the Malays to let the group stay in the village.

But unlike Miss Horsfall, who is defined entirely by the values of her public role, Jean also carries domestic burdens, particularly in relation to motherhood. The importance of motherhood as a defining characteristic of this heroine is demonstrated by the somewhat tortuous plot devices that are needed to turn Jean into a mother before she has had a sexual relationship. At the beginning of the film, Jean is contrasted with Mrs Hammond, who is presented as an untidy and disorganised mother. Although she loves her three children, she seems incapable of looking after them properly. Her hysteria when she is forcibly parted from her husband is in marked contrast to the dignity shown by Jean and the others and potentially puts lives at risk by upsetting the Japanese captors. In her dying words, Mrs Hammond tells Jean that she is leaving her children 'in God's hands and yours'. This act of transfer foregrounds, in a contradictory way, both the notion that motherhood is a role that can be consciously adopted and the instinctive and natural desire to look after children that makes Jean such a good mother. Throughout the film, she is pictured with the baby, Robin, in her arms, and other children frequently surround her, holding on to her skirt. The deaths of the two older children cause her profound grief, the more marked because of the control she generally shows. In her reflections towards the end of the film, she puts into words what the images have shown already as she addresses Robin in her mind: 'when the war ended and I gave you back to your father, it was like losing my own child.'

Jean becomes a mother almost overnight, but the film handles the development of her sexual relationship with Joe rather more gradually. Their intimacy is

Figure 9.1 Virginia McKenna in *A Town Like Alice* (J. Arthur Rank, 1956).
Courtesy of the Kobal Collection.

developed through a number of meetings, and the emphasis is on the balance of
the relationship between them. In particular, the two conversations in which
they get to know each other are structurally matched. In the first, Joe tells Jean
about himself, about Alice Springs, the landscape, the red earth, the heat and
the loneliness; in the second, Jean tells Joe about England, 'cool and green',
and confirms that she has no husband. On both occasions, they share cigarettes,
an important action that Jean recalls when she looks back on those moments,
thinking that Joe is dead. Their first kiss occurs only at the end of the film,
when they find each other again, well after the war's end. However, the relative
restraint of this romance needs to be set against the physical expression of sexual
desire in McKenna's acting. Thus after the first conversation, Jean returns to the
hut and tells Mrs Frith: 'He talked about a town called Alice. He made it sound
… all right.' This verbal restraint is typical of the war film, but the words are
accompanied by an almost extravagant gesture as McKenna falls on to the
bedding, as if giving herself up to her lover, presses her head to the pillow and
then raises it to reveal a half smile as she says 'all right'. Similarly, at the end of

the film, when Jean learns that Joe may be still alive, McKenna half turns her head, breathes heavily so that her throat moves, shuts her eyes, raises her chin and smiles. Relief is signified, but so too is sexual fulfilment. Thus, although the romance is relatively low-key, sexual desire is strongly indicated and given an orgasmic intensity at key points.

Finally, although the jungles of Burma offer little scope for consumption, the film does offer limited examples of feminine concern with appearance and luxury. One key moment occurs when the women are able to spend the night in an abandoned villa, which they discover still has running water. That pleasure in washing is a gendered one is marked by the refusal of the small boys to join in the luxury of bathing, soaping and showering. Jean joins in with the other women. For the first time, we see her long hair down in a loose plait and the sequence ends with a shot of her legs in the shower.

A Town like Alice does therefore offer a representation of a mature woman who learns to be competent, feminine, sexual and motherly. However, it is important to note that it does so in a context that takes this mature figure out of the modern world and sets it back into the barbarism of the jungle and, later on, the gentle rhythms of a Malay village. Indeed, the film suggests that in order to become mature, Jean and the women in the group must drop the trappings of European femininity, the arrogance that the Japanese accuse them of. This is marked at two key points in the film. First, immediately after Mrs Hammond's death, Jean tries to barter with a Malay shopkeeper for food for the children. She offers her European shoes, but the man will not agree to the exchange. His wife intervenes, however, and Jean emerges from the little shop not only with tins of food but also dressed in Malay clothes. This abandonment of European dress is commented on disapprovingly by one of the other women – 'There's such a thing as keeping up appearances' – but as the two women walk away from the camera, it is clear that Jean is comfortable because she has adapted to the conditions, while the woman in Western dress is mocked by the children as she teeters in her strappy sandals, weighed down by the suitcases she is still carrying around. The second important moment occurs towards the end of the film, when Jean is pleading with the Malay elders to let the women stay in the village. She couches her plea in their terms, recognising that they would not normally 'talk business with a woman', quoting from their sacred books and assuring them that the women will work. When they question this ('White women have never worked in the rice field'), Jean responds by pointing to the extremity of their position – 'White women have never marched until they died' – and making clear their absolute surrender of status and control. As the camera circles on the strained faces of the watching women, she tells the elders: 'If you say we must go, we must go. We are in your hands.' The subsequent harmonious scenes of the women's life in the village confirms that happiness can be found in the hard circumstances of this abnegation of white femininity.

In a different way, *Carve Her Name with Pride* also situates McKenna as the mature woman, but again with considerable difficulty. Like *A Town like Alice*, *Carve Her Name with Pride* is set in the wartime past and both addresses and backs away from a representation of the mature woman. McKenna plays Violette Szabo, who, following the death of her French husband in the war in North Africa, agrees to undertake resistance work in France. Although she is initially successfully, she is in the end captured, tortured and shot. Vi is a wife, a mother and a professional woman, and one sequence in the middle of the film shows how McKenna in this role can combine the competing demands made of the modern woman. Vi, who has been on a mission to Rouen, meets up with her control, Tony, in Paris. Here, for a few moments, all the elements of her life are brought together. Vi reports on the difficulties of her mission professionally, without fuss, and its success is emphasised when Tony tells her that its aim – the destruction of the viaduct – was achieved. But this is not just a professional meeting. Through his protective attitude, Tony makes his love for her clear, Vi's reaction is warm, and this is one of the few moments in the film when they touch. Female consumption is also referenced here as Vi takes the opportunity to buy the 'most marvellous dress' at Molyneux; although Tony teases her about her extravagance, this criticism is softened by its connection with other discourses of femininity. Window shopping, Vi sees a child's dress, which she wants for her daughter; at the same moment, she looks lovingly at a small girl also looking in the window and hears the voice of her dead husband talking about how he would take their daughter to Paris to buy her a dress. The rhetoric of femininity brings together professional work, motherhood, sexual love and consumption, so that Tony's comments on her extravagance are countered by the positive way the film weaves together these different aspects of the whole woman.

The narrative of *Carve Her Name with Pride* is structured around a trajectory of development and growth, and this moment of balance is achieved at the point at which Vi has matured but before the sacrifices demanded of her begin to take their toll. The early part of the film has a double movement as it concentrates on Vi's shift from girl to mother and shop assistant to resistance fighter. In the early scenes, we are introduced to her chatting to her girl friends, flirting in the park, fighting with her brother and serving on a jewellery counter. The move from girl to mother is effected through her relationship with Etienne, which begins as a piece of fun in the park initiated by her French mother's patriotic wish to entertain a compatriot soldier on Bastille Day. The sexual fulfilment of this relationship is emphasised less than the new seriousness it brings to Vi and her longing to share in Etienne's experience of the wider world: 'if I'd been a man, I'd like to have been a professional soldier,' she tells him, 'all those wonderful places you've seen.' On the honeymoon, the tomboy Vi is still climbing trees, but she also looks forward to her future as mother and worries over Etienne going into danger. It is this new understanding of the private sphere as wife and mother that leads her into her public work. The film makes these links by cutting from the honeymoon to the arrival of the news of Etienne's death on Tanya's second birthday to the proposal that she take on resistance work, compressing the years and months that separate them. The link is then expressed by Vi when she confirms her willingness to agree to the proposal. Dressed in her apron and surrounded by family photographs, she talks of her dead husband and the child he never saw: 'I suppose in his way he was fighting for her and now it's my turn.'

But although the personal offers a motivation for public work, it is also clear that successful work in the public world of work demands the sacrifice of excessive femininity. Thus the second trajectory is from mother to fighter, and the film marks this rite of passage by taking us through the training that enables this transformation. This war film with a heroine at the centre spends more time on the detail of training than those featuring, for instance, Jack Hawkins (*The Cruel Sea*) or Richard Todd (*The Dam Busters*), where the hero is already mature and capable of holding a powerful position. By contrast, Vi does not volunteer for service but has to be sought out by the government. She then has to be trained, put through a rite of passage in which she has to learn to fight and think like a man. It is illuminating to compare these scenes with the struggle that Douglas Bader goes through in *Reach for the Sky*. Both Bader and Vi are preparing for active service. Both are struggling to escape from femininity, since Bader's accident forces him into the feminine world of the hospital, where nurses look after and mother him, and Vi naturally occupies this feminine world in her roles as mother and daughter. But the disabilities that they are struggling against in their efforts to get out are different. Bader is battling for the restoration of the masculine independence and strength that have been lost with his legs, while Vi is battling with her own femininity in order to achieve masculine standards of excellence. *Carve Her Name with Pride* handles this quite delicately. Vi is less frightened of the parachute jump than Tony, who is both male and her superior officer; she is a crack shot before she joins up; the sergeant's humorous despair about his female trainees is not endorsed by the film, since it is clear from the flashback structure that Vi is going to succeed. But structurally, the training scenes make it clear that, while Bader as a male wartime hero struggles to fulfil the ideals of his gender, Vi as a wartime heroine struggles to escape from hers.

Thus the scene in Paris marks the moment when Vi fulfils her wartime masculine role without losing her identity as a wife and mother. But as the narrative progresses, that balance of roles is lost. The second mission is more dangerous, and in order to accomplish it Violette has to reject her own femininity and become more clearly masculine. She makes a will before she goes, passing on jewellery from Etienne and her engagement and wedding rings, and the farewell to her family is solemn, signifying a more dangerous leaving of the private sphere. This time on the mission there is to be no shopping and it is clear that Violette has learned to behave like a male hero. She volunteers to go on a dangerous journey to meet another resistance group, rejecting Tony's protective attitude towards her; she has learned the oblique mode of communicating with friends and lovers so common to the war film, telling Tony as she leaves: 'You might look after yourself too.' For the first time, she is involved in armed combat and behaves with resolute courage. The Frenchman who told her 'You are too young and too pretty for this kind of work' has her to thank for his escape when she holds the German troops back with a machine gun. Offered a cigarette after she is captured, she spits it back in the German commander's face.

But there is a further move for Violette to make and, in the end, the drive to mythologise Violette can be achieved only when distinctive gender traits have fallen away. The film achieves a remarkable physical transformation of McKenna that emphasises the spiritual maturity that Violette is aspiring towards. In the torture scenes, her femininity becomes not just something that has to be temporarily put aside but also a source of temptation. The German interrogator reminds her and the audience of the femininity that the film has valued when he tries to tempt her to speak: 'what will become of your child if you die?' he asks, before offering her new clothes and fun, 'you're young, you're attractive and you're in Paris.' Violette slaps him. After physical torture, memories of Etienne prove an even greater temptation. Her eyes closed and with a half smile, Violette hears Etienne's voice reciting the poem that carries her code: 'it's my turn, I want to say it,' she says in the words she used on honeymoon, but she suddenly realises that she is in a different space and that the poem is now 'a poem of death'. The final scenes of the film, in which Violette is tortured, taken to a prison camp and killed are punctuated by close-ups of McKenna in which her skin is translucent, her cheekbones sharp and her fair hair pushed away from her drawn features. Christian imagery surrounds her – the crosses scratched on to the prison walls, the water she gives to the other prisoners – and at her death an extreme close-up emphasises the way her head and eyes turn upwards to meet the light.

The film's coda, set in 1947, restores order. Tanya, dressed in the dress bought for her in Paris, goes to collect the George Cross that the state has bestowed on her dead mother. The repetition of the poem and the final image of children playing in the street give a hopeful resonance to Violette's sacrifice. But the two separate photographs on each side of the mantelpiece – one of Violette in a glamorous dress and the other of her in uniform – indicate the difficulty of keeping the different aspects of femininity together, and the emphasis on the absence of the mother ends the film on a sombre note.

It is clear, I hope, that the new woman was herself a contradictory construction, which was the subject of fierce reaction and rejection by feminists in the 1960s. Nevertheless, in the context of the 1950s, she was a figure through whom women could be translated into a modern idiom and through whom many of the discourses associated with modernity – psychology, consumption, expertise, the nuclear family – could be appropriated in official and popular forms. Perhaps it is not surprising that this figure proved difficult to translate into cine-matic terms. Kendall and McKenna stand out because their star images flirt with the notion of a mature, modern woman and, in their very different perfor-mances, we catch a rare glimpse of the complex construction of femininity in the 1950s.

10 The fifties war film

Creating space for the triumph of masculinity

If the 1950s is characterised by the failure of female stars to fulfil their potential, the same cannot be said of the men. Male stars such as Jack Hawkins, Kenneth More, Dirk Bogarde and John Mills dominated British productions and, despite Hollywood's counter-attractions, held their own in polls and fan surveys, backed up by a host of character actors like Alastair Sim and comedy stars such as Norman Wisdom. While the women were being tested against standards of glamour defined elsewhere, in Hollywood or Europe, the male star image made Britishness a virtue. Their distinctiveness was confirmed by their nationality, and they were praised for their difference from Hollywood's models.

In this chapter, I want to explore the particular ways in which what Thumim (1992: 63) refers to as 'a variety of models of masculinity' are presented in the fifties war film. It will be clear from other chapters in this book that the theme of masculine behaviour is persistent in the 1950s and could be studied in a wide range of genres and stars. We have seen, for instance, in Chapter 4 how the (largely) masculine professions of science, education and crime are mocked in the comedies of the period; in Chapter 8, we examined how the changing discourses about fatherhood are reflected in films about the family. Elsewhere, there has been analysis of how the British crime film provided a home for tough guys and criminals and gave Stanley Baker his best parts,[1] while famously the end of the 1950s saw the upsurge of a new masculine figure, the 'angry young man', who swept through British film as he had done the theatre and the novel. But even given all these possibilities, it seems essential to examine the British war film both because it was a hugely popular genre that was aimed specifically at the male audience (Harper and Porter: 77) and because its narratives overtly take masculinity as a theme and specifically examine how challenges to male strength, endurance and courage might be worked through and resolved.

Masculinity in the fifties

The importance of the war film to British cinema at the time is not surprising given the way in which military experience had been and continued to be a dominant feature of men's lives. Demobilisation posed difficulties not just because of the problems of readjusting to family life but also because it meant leaving particular forms of companionship and hierarchy. Typical was an ex-serviceman who found that after six years in the army, 'I was a mass of conditioned reflexes'; he was unused to an environment in which 'people got on with their own business and left me to mine. It wasn't so much the attention that I wanted but a structure in which to function ... The army was a big, noisy, energetic and purposeful crowd; civvies seemed listless, preoccupied and aimless' (Turner and Rennell: 185). National Service at 18 was not abolished until 1958, so for much of the 1950s, many young men continued to experience an all-male culture in which their lives were organised by an all-male hierarchy and their work and much of their leisure time would be spent with male companions. As Durgnat pointed out, experience of two wars and post-war conscription meant that 'the armed forces became one of the few social experiences which the adult male half of the nation had in common' (89) and that for many men, 'intensified male friendship and comradeship' (Segal: 86) were a way of getting though the tedium of National Service. Life in the services, both during and after the war, provided a consistent experience of a masculine world operating in a clearly defined and separate space.

Positive memories of the war could also be reinforced when difficulties were experienced in returning to civilian life. Wartime service had given many men skills, responsibilities and experiences that they would not otherwise have had. It was possible to have had a 'good war' in the sense not only that you were still alive at the end of it but also that your position in terms of a post-war career had actually improved. Such men could feel, rather guiltily, that the war had opened up opportunities for them. But for many, there was disillusion as they found that new skills were not needed, that their old jobs were not available on their return or that, if they were, the work was tedious and undemanding. 'He had been "someone" in the army,' a daughter recalls about her father's return home, 'and now he had returned to his dull clerical job' (Turner and Rennell: 174). For those who had won promotion in the services, civilian life could mean starting all over again at the bottom; Turner and Rennell comment that 'some of the saddest cases of failed expectations were to be found among commissioned officers, young men who had succeeded on merit ... and who were now brought to realise that the qualities for which they were justly praised were no guarantee of preference in civilian employment' (182). Such men might seek out new opportunities but universities could not satisfy the demand for entry from mature entrants and training courses from business management to taxi driving were over-subscribed (chapter 7). Thus the memories of comradeship in the services might be combined with the feeling that, despite the hierarchical structure and petty regulations, wartime service in the armed forces offered more responsibility and education than was available in civilian life.

In the civilian world outside, sociological work of the period argued that the masculine role was developing to complement that of the new woman. The husband of the family continued to be thought of as the main breadwinner, and part of the anxiety about working mothers and affluent teenagers was connected with the fear that they would undermine this male role. At a time of

high employment, a man was expected to work, and the ideal domestic arrangement was one in which men were away at work for much of the day while the
woman stayed at home.[2] The emphasis on the male breadwinner tended to
draw attention to traditional modes of male behaviour but as we saw in Chapter
2, sociologists like Willmott and Young identified changes in the behaviour of
men in the home and the emergence of a new role as father and husband in the
companionate marriage. Set against this ideal of marriages based on complementary partnership was the growing debate about homosexuality, fuelled in
the early 1950s by the Home Office decision to tighten up on the enforcement
of the laws criminalising homosexual behaviour. This led to a series of high-
profile prosecutions in the early 1950s, accompanied by lurid press coverage,
although the policy backfired by drawing attention to the dubious procedures
used by the police to get the cases to court. The Wolfenden Committee set up
in 1954 used its report, published in 1957, to propose that homosexuality be
explained through psychology as 'a state of arrested development' (Wilson
1980: 104) and argued not only that the law should distinguish between private
and public acts but that there was 'a realm of private morality and immorality
which is, in brief and crude terms, not the law's business' (quoted in Haste:
171). Although the report failed to lead to a reform in the law in the period
under discussion, its representation of homosexuality was typical of the growing
'psychologisation' of sexuality in the 1950s (Weeks: 244), and it presented a
rather different version of male sexual possibilities than the uxorious husband of
the marriage guidance pamphlets. The report heightened rather than quelled
debate, Dearden's and Relph's 1961 film *Victim* being cinema's most explicit
contribution to discussion.[3]

Underpinning this work is the assumption that there are separate male and
female roles, which, although they are equal and balanced, are clearly defined in
different ways. Femininity and masculinity in the 1950s are defined as complementary opposites, and the debate about homosexuality takes on a particular
intensity precisely because, in the terms in which it is conducted, homosexuality
challenges or undermines the polarity that marks the way in which gender was
explained. Segal concludes that there was 'considerable conflict and ambiguity
about male identity in the 50s' (89), but the sociologists of the period tended
to be more confident that men were undertaking their new roles with some
pleasure and confidence and that masculine difference was being maintained in
the clearly marked divisions of labour and attitude that they recorded. What
emerges here is a concept of masculinity that can be clearly defined through
separate male roles and responsibilities but that has to be worked through in the
context of social discourses that emphasise domesticity and the family as the
source of stability.

There has been a tendency in recent work on British cinema to interpret the
1950s as a period of crisis for masculinity. Thus, Street suggests that the *Doctor*
series can 'at a subtextual level' be understood as a response to the way in which
'the welfare state and a reduction in family size threatened traditional male
responsibilities' (70). At various points in her wide-ranging study of British

genres, Landy suggests that post-war British cinema is preoccupied with an unease and ambivalence around male identity. Thus the 'tragic melodramas' (1991: 240) explore 'varied, shifting, and troubled notions of male identity' (240) and 'dramatize men in the throes of an identity crisis' (269), while in the family melodrama men 'are portrayed as in need of support as they seek to gain a sense of power and authority' (328). Andrew Clay prefaces his discussion of the crime film from 1946 to 1965 with the argument that the genre in the period was marked by 'a crisis in masculinity' made up of 'a feeling of loss of war-time agency and an anxiety about the status of post-war women' (52). While Street and Clay pursue this sense of crisis mainly through a discussion of narrative and theme, Landy bases her analysis on readings of key moments of trouble and excess, moments that under pressure reveal the male anxiety that the film is trying to disguise.

It will be clear from other chapters in the book that I have sympathy with the approaches of all three writers. In particular, my discussion of fatherhood and the family in Chapter 8 indicates that the films explored there do reveal a heightened anxiety about paternal roles and a real difficulty in presenting the new father of the social sciences discourse. Nevertheless, I think that recent criticism has over-emphasised the themes of general male anxiety and crisis in British films of the period and under-estimated the way that British cinema offers an extreme version of masculinity, based on separation and difference, which works not to express anxiety but to offer reassurance about male roles. In this context, the war films are crucial since, in the 1950s, the genre offered a way of representing male actions and feelings in a military context which would have been much more familiar, for good or ill, to many in the audience. Instead of trying to place the issue of gender difference in the domestic context of home and family, the genre allows for masculinity to be expressed largely without the feminine balance that marks the sociological discourses. It is the way in which this is done that the rest of this chapter explores.

Before turning to the specificities of the British war film, it is worth noting that the popularity of films set in the Second World War was not a uniquely British phenomenon and that a number of themes and narrative tropes that will be explored here have a more broadly generic appeal. Thus Basinger, in her study of Second World War US combat films, identifies a number of generic characteristics that are clearly identifiable in the British films. These include an appeal to truth, often through an opening credit that acknowledges the help of the services in the making of the film; the focus on 'a group of men, led by a hero, [undertaking] a mission which will accomplish an important military objective', the group being 'a mixture of unrelated types'; a narrative that moves forward through a 'series of episodes' in which 'action and repose, safety and danger, combat and noncombat, comedy and tragedy, dialogue and action' are contrasted; the demonstration of military technology; conflict within the group itself; death of group members; and 'a learning or growth process' (74–5). Thus we need to be careful about reading specific meanings from generic conventions, of automatically ascribing the tensions within the group to a crisis in masculinity, for instance, when it may be more appropriately understood as a familiar convention necessary for action. In looking specifically at the British fifties war film, we can see how these generic conventions are reworked to establish recognisable variations that make meaning in a particular social context. In this discussion, I will concentrate on four main areas: the use of spectacle and technology; the composition and function of the male group; the role of the hero leader; and the handling of challenges to authority. As Harper and Porter indicate (77), British war films changed during the 1950s, and this discussion will suggest that the genre in its handling of key themes such as leadership, the male group and rebellion against bureaucracy offered a greater flexibility and scope to its audiences than might have been thought.

Spectacle and technology

Durgnat points to the success of the action film with post-war filmgoers, citing the 'unprecedented popularity' of the western with middle-class audiences. He ascribes the popularity of the war film at least in part to this trend, describing it as 'the European Western' (83). The comparison is an interesting one, invoking both a masculine ease of action and an emphasis on spectacle and landscape. Certainly, the war film provides the opportunity for the spectacle of action. Long shots, generally accompanied by music, show action taking place in a natural setting, whether it be naval vessels heading out to sea, aeroplanes wheeling in the sky or tanks sweeping across the desert. In *The Cruel Sea*, for instance, the convoys on the Gibraltar run and the North Russian route move through contrasting seascapes, while *The Dam Busters* features extensive sequences of night flying which emphasise the dramatic beauty of the huge Lancasters flying low against the sunset or over the moonlit sea. In addition, the films feature spectacular military action. *The Dam Busters* offers a long bombing sequence marked by music, flares of light and explosions, while the final sequences of *The Gift Horse*, in which an old battleship is sacrificed to blow up a German harbour, make dramatic use of sweeping shafts of light and fierce explosions in a naval battle. As the genre develops, more arcane spectacle is offered, such as the diving sequences and underwater skirmishes of *Silent Enemy*. Like the western, then, the pleasures of the war film involves watching men taking action in a spectacular setting but the British war films lack the sense of rapport between man and landscape, the physical ease of action characteristic of the western. Two elements contribute to this difference.

First, the emphasis on technology in the war film goes well beyond the western's iconographic use of horses, guns and ranching techniques. The spectacle features machines rather than men in the landscape. The war film goes to considerable lengths to explain its technology to its audiences (radar in *The Cruel Sea*, the bouncing bomb in *The Dam Busters*, the midget submarine in *Above Us the Waves*) and for many in its audience the films' emphasis on the details of the technology of modern war must have contributed to the genre's claim to realism. Extensive use is made of stock footage of wartime action and sequences like the final bombing raid in *Appointment in London* pay attention to the detailed procedures of such an operation as well as to its spectacle. But the effect is to render the technology beyond the control of any one man and to emphasise the lack of a physical connection between action and consequence. The operations room, a key location in the British war film, demonstrates how activity is being planned and monitored on the ground. The heroes of *The Dam Busters* have to carry out precisely the instructions of Barnes Wallis; the rescue activities in *The Sea Shall Not Have Them* are carried out on the orders of the air commodore at base; The *Bismark* is sunk because of the careful planning of Captain Shephard in the Admiralty in London. Even in the height of battle, no one man takes action alone. Ericson in *The Cruel Sea* has to rely on his radar experts to find the U-boat before he can give the command to fire; the raids in *The Dam Busters* and *Appointment in London* show that the leader has to rely on others in his crew to hit the target. Thus the active behaviour of the male heroes of these films is put at one remove and effective action is dependent as much on technology and teamwork as on individual activity.

The second restraint on the spectacle of action in the British war film is the emphasis on confined spaces. This is perhaps to be expected in films that are often set in windowless ops rooms, the cabins of small aeroplanes or submarines, the confined living quarters of large boats or the cramped huts of prisoner of war films. Even so, the emphasis on constriction is striking in, for instance, the RAF films, where the speed and sweep of flying is contrasted with the tightness of the shots of the pilots in the cockpit. Even Douglas Bader's expansive enthusiasms are confined in the tight framing of the shots of him in battle.[4] In the POW films, not only does the narrative action of the films involve repeated attempts to escape from confinement but some of the key moments take place in the restricted spaces of the tunnels that are the most popular form of escape. In the naval films, this physical constraint is also a key factor in the plot. Thus, in *Morning Departure*, the action of the film takes place in a submarine that is damaged in an accident and is unable to return to the surface. Much of the activity of the film takes place in the officers ward-room, which becomes, in the end, the tomb of those who cannot escape. In *The Sea Shall Not Have Them*, the confined spaces of the rescue boat's quarters are the setting for some of the action, but the boat is spacious compared with the dinghy in which four air men, buffeted by gales in the English Channel, wait for rescue. The very title of *Above Us the Waves* emphasises the weight of the water pressing down on the small submarine torpedoes in which the four-man crew works. As in *Morning Departure*, the plot works to emphasise this sense of confinement; during the attack on the German warship, one midget sub loses all navigational aides ('we're blind – no periscope, no compass'), while another is trapped under the keel of the German ship and the crew narrowly escapes being pressed down by the enemy vessel into the sea bed.

Unlike the western, then, the action of the war film emphasises movement that is cramped and restricted by the physical environment. Indeed, far from being a place of freedom of action, the environment becomes something that has to be fought against. This is an explicit theme in *The Cruel Sea*, in which 'the only villain is the sea, the cruel sea'. The theme is reiterated in numerous films. In *The Sea Shall Not Have Them*, the battle against the weather is made a running joke in the seasickness of the new medical orderly but becomes more serious when the lives of those in the dinghy are put at risk. Back at base, the air commodore reflects bitterly that 'every time anyone ditches, the weather immediately starts to make things as difficult as possible,' while McKay, one of the men in the dinghy, cries out against their predicament, 'I hate the bloody sea.' In *Sea of Sand* and *Ice Cold in Alex*, the desert becomes as much of an enemy as the Germans whom the British are trying to escape from; 'he never had a chance out there,' says one soldier of his dead comrade at the end of *Sea of Sand*, while in *Ice Cold in Alex* the desert is described by one of the characters as 'the greater enemy'. It is a cliché of the POW films but, in this context, a significant one that the very earth becomes the enemy that has to be dug through, resisted, shored up and secretly disposed of. 'Why did God make sand so heavy?' one of the tunnellers asks in *Danger Within*. Rattigan has noted that the difference between forties and fifties British war films is that in the latter what is shown is 'the British *winning* the war as opposed to *not losing it*' (148). Even so, what the fifties films emphasise is not just the difficulties and achievements of winning (as any war film might be expected to do) but that winning is achieved by waiting and endurance, by small technical actions in cramped spaces, by dogged persistence in harsh landscapes and hostile waters. The contest is transformed into a generally successful struggle to control nature as well as to defeat the enemy.

The male group

If the notion of endurance is a common theme in forties and fifties films, the fifties war film is different from its predecessors in its representation of who is doing the enduring. In films of the 1940s, the war was fought by whole communities, including the working class, women and civilians, but the fifties war film tends to place an emphasis on a small male group, largely made up of officers and 'boffins' (Geraghty 1984). Rattigan cogently argues that this change can be understood as an attempt to put 'the "people" back into their place' after the post-war settlement by providing 'a revisionist history of the war' (148) in which 'the middle class … are shown to be taking a leading role in *supporting* and *promoting* the cause of Britain' (151). It is perhaps worth noting that in the context of this genre it is the forties films, with their civilian emphasis, which constitute the exception, the concentration on a small, male, military group being a key feature of the war film. Nevertheless, the shift in the British war film is worth exploring further and may be more nuanced than previous accounts have recognised.

The popularity of war films waned towards the end of the war, and it was not until the early 1950s that the genre began to re-establish itself. *Morning Departure* (1950) can be seen as significant here. Although technically not a war film, since it deals with a submarine incident after the war, *Morning Departure* shares many of the war film's generic characteristics, dealing with a small male group that faces disaster when the submarine is involved in an accident and is unable to return to the surface. This group, although it does not extend to civilians, goes wider than the officers to include a number of working-class characters. Richard Attenborough, for instance, reprises his role as a neurotic seaman from the 1942 *In Which We Serve* and as Stoker Snipe learns courage and turns out to be 'a real good 'un'. In the crisis, hierarchies are broken down and the narrative is resolved in death, which takes not only the officers but also Stoker Snipe and Able Seaman Higgens.

Morning Departure indicates that the wartime conventions have not been entirely lost. The naval setting seems to have been particularly conducive to attempts to maintain a representative male group in war drama. Both *Above Us the Waves* and *The Sea Shall Not Have Them* from the mid-1950s sketch out a social group that goes beyond the officers. In *Above Us the Waves* (1955), those volunteering for the dangerous mission of being a 'human torpedo' are a mixed group that includes a steward and a leading seaman as well as Commander Fraser and his officers. The men are organised into three smaller groups, each led by an officer, and the film emphasises the comradeship and sympathy that has developed between the men through involvement in this dangerous mission. In *The Sea Shall Not Have Them* (1954), the attempt to represent the nation through the male group on the rescue ship is handled through comedy. The mix of the crew is sketched in and includes a new and inept middle-class recruit, Milliken; Skinner, the young engineer whose slack work puts their lives in danger; and the working-class Tebbit, whose anxieties about his flighty wife are played for comedy but used to make a misogynist, moral point. The film also gives some attention to two working-class figures in the crew, the flight sergeant and Corporal Robb, whose ranks as non-commissioned officers place them in an intermediary role between captain and crew.

The group waiting to be rescued on the dinghy in *The Sea Shall Not Have Them* is even more clearly marked by an attempt to represent different class experiences brought together by extreme hardship. The four initially seem to be divided by class, the skipper and Air Commodore Wardley being upper middle-class officers who are accompanied by the working-class Sergeant McKay, with his Cockney accent and unstable temperament, and the resilient Canadian, Kirby. While Kirby remains cheerfully outside the complications of the British class system, the narrative works to reorder and complicate the relationships between the other three. The skipper is confirmed as upper class ('his dad's got a big estate,' McKay tells the others), but his injuries cause him to pass out and he can therefore no longer take command. Although McKay is represented as working-class,[5] it is revealed that he has inherited his father's greengrocer's shop in Luton and that much of his anxiety stems from his difficulties in running a small business while he is away in the air force. Wardley, similarly, is not what he seems, revealing himself to be the son of a railway porter, also from Luton; he won a scholarship and thus worked his way up to be a skilled engineer, one of the 'boffins' whose skills will help to win the war. To survive, this mixed group has to support each other. McKay tenderly looks after the skipper and learns to trust Wardley, while Wardley recognises McKay's worth beneath the fear and resentment. The references to scholarships and Luton have a flavour of the 1950s but in the breaching of formal hierarchies of class and rank and in its emphasis on disparate individuals coming together, *The Sea Shall Not Have Them* illustrates how some of the conventions of the forties war film were still a staple of fifties war films.

The prisoner of war films that emerge in the 1950s present a rather different emphasis. Here there is a break with the wartime conventions exemplified in the 1946 POW film *The Captive Heart*, which included the experiences of working-class characters in its narrative and focused on the prisoners' emotional relationships with their wives and families at home. The fifties POW films present a much more homogeneous group, based on the officer class, and the emphasis is on the drive to escape from the claustrophobic captivity of the camp. References to other relationships are limited, and flashbacks to or parallel stories about life at home disappear.[6] Following the success of *The Wooden Horse* in 1950, firm generic conventions were established that allow for an episodic plot structure, based on a number of potential escapes, which is resolved by the group accepting that escape will only be possible through discipline and solidarity. The POW film remained a staple of the British war film throughout the period, moving from the personal histories of *The Wooden Horse* and *The Colditz Story* (1955) to the less tightly focused *Danger Within* (1959) and the MGM British production, *The Password is Courage* (1962). As the genre develops there is less emphasis on what happens after the escape on the journey back to Britain, which occupies almost the last half of *The Wooden Horse*, and more on camp life and the ingenious mechanics of the escapes from the camp.

The British male group in the POW films is made up of prisoners with officer status. Distinctions within the camp are not based on individual characteristics or background but on nationality and attitudes to escape, and it is these factors that define the group. The hero is normally committed to escape from the start, but others have to be won over and drawn into the task. In *The Wooden Horse*, the atmosphere in the group is slack and lackadaisical until the idea of using the vaulting box as a cover for digging the tunnel is taken up. Even those who will not take part in the escape participate in the activity that surrounds it, and those who do escape act for the group as a whole. The criticism that escape activity generates is made more explicit in the later films, and winning over doubters can be more difficult. In *Danger Within*, the first failed escape is greeted with complaints from other prisoners – 'We'll pay for it'; 'Comic-strip hero' – while the theatrical Callander divides the camp into 'the rugger hearties' and 'the cloak and dagger types', complaining that if the latter 'weren't such a nuisance, [they'd] be a joke'. In *The Password is Courage*, similar complaints are made about the proposal to dig a tunnel: 'Is there really any use in trying again?'; 'They'll take it out on any of us left.' In all cases, those complaining are won back into the group in the final escape. In *The Wooden Horse*, the most persistent critic gives the escapees money for their journey; Callender's performance of *Hamlet* provides cover for a mass outbreak from the camp; and in *The Password is Courage*, a vociferous critic of the tunnel acts as chief engineer and volunteers for the escape.

The narratives of the POW films thus work to reinforce the homogeneity of the group by pulling everyone into the story of the escape. Any heterogeneity is provided by contrasting national characteristics which are heavily underlined and normally work to endorse the British position. The films are organised around a basic contrast between the (British) captives and the (German or Italian) captors, and the escape narrative is premised on the latter ultimately looking foolish. This is particularly the case because, in the confined spaces of the prison, what is emphasised in the escapes is not so much physical courage as mental ingenuity and resilience, so that the foreign enemy, although powerful, is always mocked and outwitted. Within this basic division, however, there are some differences in how other nations are represented. The British male group may contain, for instance, a specifically Scottish representative, as it does in *The Colditz Story* and *Danger Within*, thus maintaining some semblance of the wartime notion of pulling the British nation together. *The Wooden Horse*, partly because it takes the escape beyond the prison walls, gives a sympathetic portrayal of the French and Danish resistance who help the British pair. In *The Colditz Story*, the first disorganised attempts at escape fail because there is no co-ordination between the different national groups; at the level of narrative, the film shows some respect for individual acts of bravery by foreigners and underlines the importance of different national groups working together. Nevertheless, the film's broad brushstrokes of national stereotyping (the French are excitable and suspicious, the Poles courageous and extreme, the British persistent and disciplined) serve to emphasise not so much the superiority of the British as the crucial role of national difference in defining the identity of the male group.

The naval films and the POW films have the male group at the heart of their narrative. The films dealing with the air force develop rather differently. Two early examples, *Angels One Five* (1952) and *Appointment in London* (1953), continue to emphasise the importance of the support and comradeship that the male group can give to the pilots who are the heroes. This is expressed through the high jinks that are deemed a mark of the group coming together (the ritual of painting the ceiling with footprints is engineered by the leader in *Appointment in London* as a way of cementing the new men into the squadron) but in addition some attention is paid, as in the naval films, to the individual men in the group, to the stories of Baird, Greeno and Mac, which reveal something of their lives outside the air force. In the mid-1950s, however, two popular films, which came to typify the British war film of the period, reworked the conventions to position the male group rather differently, not only from these British films but also from the US combat films analysed by Basinger. *The Dam Busters* and *Reach for the Sky* both deal with exclusive groups of the officer class, which, backed up by technical and scientific expertise, effectively win the war, but in their handling of this theme they largely dispense with a number of generic conventions about the male group. *The Dam Busters* (1955) does begin to establish the group that will carry out the dangerous mission, but its depiction of the process is very different from the somewhat random way in which the men come to the ship or the prison camp. Gibson and his senior officer choose the other members of the squadron from photographs and files: 'I'd go for these two Australians'; 'I met him when he was collecting a DFC'; 'I know this New Zealander'; 'I taught him to fly in the Oxford University Air Squadron, a rowing blue'; 'a darn good athlete, a miler.' These are men who are deemed to be exceptionally brave and talented, and it is clear that the group is being chosen as members of an elite rather than to be a representative cross-section of the nation. Instead of fighting with the working class, the English, Oxbridge heroes are joined by their equivalents from the white Commonwealth, with only an American beach guard from Coney Island to add a dash of difference.

Once the group is chosen, the film confirms this homogeneity by making little attempt to establish individuals within it. The conversation between the men is largely limited to what is needed for effective operations. Little information is given about their home or family life outside the station or before the war. There is no room here for the conventional story of the nervous or

Figure 10.1 The Dam Busters (ABPC, 1954).
Courtesy of the Ronald Grant Archive.

neurotic participant who wins through to courage, or even for much of the off-duty joshing that marks the earlier flying films. The group welds together on a professional basis rather then through the establishment of relationships based on comradeship. At the outset, they are told that 'discipline is going to be essential and so is security' and it is the secrecy and the technical nature of the operation that defines their identity as a group rather than personal comradeship. Moreover, the narrative does not invite the audience to share the feelings or experiences of the group through opening up the lives of key individuals in it and this restraint in narration is matched by the camera work, which makes little use of close-ups on individual faces but holds back with long and medium shots. The effect of this can be seen, for instance, in the scenes that preface the take-off for the final raid. A camera pans across a large group of men who are shown lounging on the grass, playing cards and chess or engaged in a desultory game of cricket. In long shot, Gibson and Barnes Wallis can just be seen talking to the men. The theme tune plays quietly, so conversations are not heard until, unexpressively and still in long shot, Gibson says 'Well, chaps, my watch says it's time to go.' The huge planes dominate the image as the men climb into them, to reappear as tiny figures in the cockpit as the planes move along the runway. Individuals have disappeared into this efficient and professional working together of men and machine. Only at the end of the sequence do we get close-ups of Gibson's face and then of two hands as his co-pilot takes the controls from him. The emotion of the event is thus briefly given visual expression, but the group on which Gibson depends has become anonymous.

In *Reach for the Sky* (1956), this process is carried further. Here there is not one male group but a series of friends and supporters whom Bader looks to for friendship. But these figures are lightly sketched, generally providing a chorus that urges Bader on and laughs at his jokes. Even his best friend Johnny Sandford, who provides the voice-over, plays only a minor part in the narrative action. The shift of the group into the background of the story is clearly shown in the scenes during the war in which Bader takes command of a squadron, a group of Canadians who he is told are 'a bit fed up especially with authority. They want good leadership.' For once, the viewpoint of the film shifts from Bader to these men, who believe that, since Bader has lost his legs, they are being lumbered with 'a passenger'. When Bader arrives they are sullen, rude and slovenly, clearly a group that is disaffected and using its sense of solidarity in the wrong way. Bader wins them over by his flying skills, by listening to them and forcing the authorities to treat them better. He builds them into 'a good bunch' who dress smartly, welcome newcomers and appreciate his tactical innovations. But the audience watches this from the outside. Focus has shifted back to Bader and his ability to inspire 'young pilots' with his 'breezy confidence'. The film has no time or interest in the stories of the other men in the group.

The leader and male authority

The British war film thus tends to narrow the membership of the male group and take it out of the context of civilian life and transform it from a representative group of individuals with whom the audience can identify to an elite group whom the audience is invited to admire. This also involves a change in the representation of the leader and an increased emphasis on his distance from his men. Again, this change is unevenly developed and is influenced both by the setting of the film and the star. John Mill's naval films offer good examples of the way in which it was still possible to present a relationship between leader and group that depended on a sense of common humanity. Mills, who had a strong line in working-class characters, plays Lieutenant Commander Armstrong in *Morning Departure* and Commander Fraser in *Above Us the Waves*. In both roles he demands discipline but his command is based on establishing a shared bond with his men. This is done from the start in the latter film when Fraser, meeting the group for the first time, greets each man personally, showing that he knows something of their skills and background and gently teasing one about his age, another about his girlfriends. The intimate, personal tone of this first roll call is maintained later, when Fraser shares his enthusiasms and ideas with the rest of the group, even reading to them a dismissive letter he has received from the Admiralty. In *Morning Departure*, this relationship is won with more difficulty. Armstrong has to learn to appreciate his men, a point made when he recognises that it is not enough, in the crisis, just to break down the formal barriers by opening up the officers' wardroom to the men. As his 'number one' points out, there has to be an acceptance of different attitudes and behaviour, since 'there doesn't seem much point in declaring open house in the wardroom if you're going to swear at the chaps every time they speak.' In these films, although the leader is clearly in command, the narrative works to emphasise what he shares with his men.

However, elsewhere in the early 1950s there is a tendency to mark the leader as being separate from the group because he is more sensitive and carries a greater moral burden than his men. The most famous example of this is *The Cruel Sea*, in which the troubled, angry tone of the best-selling novel is expressed through Jack Hawkins' performance as Ericson. *The Cruel Sea* precisely explores the removal of the leader not only from the support of the group but from the comradeship of individual friendships. In the middle of the film, Ericson, anguished by the thought that he may have killed allied sailors in the pursuit of a phantom U-boat, is accused of murder by one of the crew and is reduced to drunken tears. His feelings are at least acknowledged by Lockhart, his 'number one', and the trio of his peers, foreign captains who salute him as 'a brave man'. In the final sequences of the film, however, Ericson withdraws entirely into himself, his emotions as frozen as the seas through which the convoy sails. *The Cruel Sea*'s anti-war leanings are bound up with the notion of the human cost of this emotional denial demanded by the war, and the tears have more impact because of the expectation of control.

Other films offer a less emotional account than *The Cruel Sea* but the theme of the isolated and morally troubled leader is strongly established in the early 1950s. Dirk Bogarde, perhaps not surprisingly given his star image as a rather unstable and neurotic figure, starred in two early examples, the internationally oriented *They Who Dare* and Leacock's reflective *Appointment in London*. In the latter, Mason has to face not only his personal exhaustion as he heads towards his ninetieth mission but also a challenge to his authority as wing commander. As the man in charge of the flying operations, Mason is known for his disapproval of his men involving themselves with wives and girlfriends when they should be 'thinking about nothing but flying'. Following the death of one of his pilots, Mason has to meet his wife, who very quietly confronts him with the fact of her existence: 'I know you don't like married men in bombers ... I hated you.' Mason later admits to his girlfriend Eve that the squadron's losses 'might have been my fault' and asks himself 'did I go wrong? How much of it was due to me?' Both Eve and Mrs Greeno join in the rebuilding of the group that Mason undertakes before the final raid by attending the party that welcomes the new recruits. *Appointment in London* is unusual in giving strong roles to women in a film that reflects on male authority, but both it and *The Cruel Sea* allow for the possibility that the leader could be at fault, even though the resolution of both films celebrates his heroic endurance.

This theme of the isolated leader is carried through into films of the mid-1950s but now this isolation is reworked into a more comfortable scenario in which the leader is alone because that is the state his natural superiority demands; isolation helps him to reach the right decisions. *The Colditz Story*, *The Dam Busters* and *Reach for the Sky* all address the issue of the role of the leader and reaffirm his natural authority and moral position. *The Colditz Story* quite clearly sets up tension between Colonel Richmond, who is the senior British officer in the camp, and the men beneath him, particularly Reid and Mac, who accuse him of not wanting to escape and call him all the worst insults they can think of: 'an old woman'; 'a bloody foreigner'; ' a wash out.' Initially, there seems to be some truth in the accusation since, in Eric Portman's controlled and sardonic performance, the urbane colonel does seem to be indifferent to plans for escape. However, it emerges that Richmond is as passionate about escaping as Reid but determined that it should be planned in an organised manner. Richmond gradually seizes control of the process, initially by setting up the necessary escape committees and finally by taking over the organisation himself. The film ends not with Reid and Jimmy on the successful 'home run' to Switzerland but with Richmond, who, having given the good news of their escape to the remaining prisoners, walks off alone into the gloom of Colditz.

Although Richmond's concerns seem to be organisational, he is faced with the same kind of moral dilemma as Ericson and Mason. Taking charge of the final escape, he asks its instigator, Mac, to pull out because he is too tall to get away with the disguise of a German officer, and the escape will be ruined not just for those who are going with him but also for others who might use the same ploy. Mac is angry and will not agree but the next day climbs over the fence and gets himself shot. Richmond advises Reid that Mac was going to stand down at his suggestion; Reid effectively accuses Richmond of murder – 'That sentry didn't kill him' – but Reid assures him that Mac had agreed to the proposal: 'You have my word for it.' If his word is to be believed, it can be only be on the basis that Richmond could read what was in Mac's mind as he made his hopeless attempt at escape. Richmond is faced with the classic dilemma of the leader – the sacrifice of one for the good of the greater number – and he retains his moral authority only if the audience accepts his godlike power to understand Mac's action as acquiescence rather than anger. What is significant about this episode, however, is that there is no attempt to represent to the audience the conflict or unease that Richmond might be assumed to feel or the emotional guilt that accompanied similar decisions by Ericson and Mason. Richmond maintains his impervious public persona and his leadership is untroubled by doubts.

The Dam Busters also demonstrates that a leader's intelligence, courage and moral integrity set him apart from the group. Gibson is not only able to understand the ideas of the scientist, Barnes Wallis, but can also contribute, through his suggestion about the use of lights for low-flying purposes, to the science that will make the raids possible.[7] Like Ericson, Gibson has a single-minded sense of mission, but this determination is shown as a necessary commitment, taken on for the nation, rather than an obsession that will have a cost in his personal life. Gibson is continually shown apart from the other men, studying the maps while they socialise, thoughtful in the theatre while they enjoy the show, joining in for a brief moment of horseplay but moving on to meet the group captain to get orders for the raid. Gibson's suppression of feelings is presented as appropriate rather than problematic, and the use of the dog as his most explicit emotional attachment is in keeping with the way in which class and masculinity are brought together in this isolated but self-sufficient figure. Gibson is saddened by the loss of men on the raid but is able to reassure Barnes Wallis about its necessity. Gibson's lone walk into the future at the end of the film underlines that, while the film's title refers to the male group, its focus has been on the way in which one man took the responsibility for the group without wavering.

Reach for the Sky is a bio-pic as well as a war film, and as the concluding voice-over reminds us, for Douglas Bader 'the war was only an episode in a greater victory.' Its concentration on its main hero can be explained by this, but it is no accident that such a biographical film could be made successfully at this point. *Reach for the Sky* has a rather different central character. While in Richard Todd's playing of Gibson, actor and character are fused, Kenneth More gives a performance in *Reach for the Sky* that is marked by his own star qualities of broad humour and a boisterous physical presence as well as the feats of acting required to play a man with 'tin legs'. This combines with the film's narrative to present a larger-than-life character who apparently reaches too far and too fast. Bader is thus less conventional and restrained than Richmond or Gibson, but the film proposes a similar model of a leader who supports but stands apart from his men and whose natural qualities find their best expression at moments when action and intelligence are brought together. Bader's frustrations in a civilian job and in his home life are lifted once the crisis of the war permits him to rejoin the RAF. The war finds a use not only for his reckless bravery but also for his strategic and tactical understanding of aerial warfare. Since Bader's story would have been well known to the audience, there can be no question about the film's outcome. The tale of Bader's life – the story of his early life, the flying accident, the amputation of his legs and the struggle to walk and fly again – is given meaning by the audience's knowledge of his status as a war hero. Although the film hints at the obsessive nature of Bader's reckless determination not to be constrained, it ends up celebrating the way in which the war provided him with the means to express himself as a hero. The film ends with Bader incorporated into the national celebrations of the Battle of Britain as he leads a fly-past above London, but it reminds us of his uniqueness as a character. 'Don't get into any fights this time,' his wife reminds him patiently as he takes off.

The heroic and impervious figure of the mid-fifties war film helped to define the British war film genre and it continued to mark the genre. Huxley, the senior officer in *Danger Within* (1960), is, like Richmond, criticised by some of the men but is proved to be right and successful in the final escape. In the hugely popular *Sink the Bismark* of the same year, Shephard runs the complex operation against the German ship unchallenged. But the repression and obsession that such a figure requires is criticised in a number of later films. David Lean famously used the genre for such a portrayal in *The Bridge over the River Kwai* (1957), but perhaps more typical than this massive co-production was the highly successful *Ice Cold in Alex* (1958). Picked out in the 1980s by lager advertisers as a typical piece of repressed British myth making, *Ice Cold in Alex* is, in Medhurst's phraseology, much less a repressed film than a film about repression (1984b: 37) as it self-consciously challenges the untroubled model of male leadership that Gibson and Bader represented. Set in North Africa when the British are retreating, *Ice Cold in Alex* is a war film that has a number of elements of Basinger's combat film, including the focus on a small group, an episodic structure, the demonstration of technology in the feats required to get the ambulance up hills and across salt marshes, and the resolution of conflict through a learning process. In addition, it has a number of the characteristics of the British war film, including the confined setting of the ambulance which contrasts with the dangerous expanses of the desert, the emphasis on endurance, and the winning of a small but significant victory through patience and care. Captain Anson leads a small group escaping across the desert to Alexandria in a battered ambulance, but this group breaks the generic rules since, as well as Sergeant Major Pugh, it includes two women, nurses fleeing the German advance, and a German spy, Van der Poel, who is pretending to be an Afrikaner fighting with the British. Although one of the nurses is killed, the group wins through to its destination and, in their final drink at the bar in Alexandra, recognise the bonds that the terrible journey has made between them.

The film makes some attempt to establish Anson as the same kind of isolated but morally troubled leader as *The Cruel Sea*. He is played by John Mills, whose star qualities embodied a 'sincerity and believability' (Spicer 1997: 148) that, as we have seen, he brought to a number of leadership roles in earlier war films. Unlike Ericson, though, Anson is from the beginning of the film presented as a man who has ceased to be a good leader: he is drinking heavily; he has allowed his love affairs to interfere with his relationship with a fellow captain; he lies to his men ('Tell them everything's going to be all right'); and he is clearly unnerved by gunfire and explosions. The audience expects both an explanation for this and that the film will work to restore Anson as a leader who is at ease with command. The explanation is duly given by the loyal Pugh, who tells Diana that Anson has 'never spared himself' and has been badly affected by the experience of being captured by the Germans and spending two nights alone in the desert when he escaped. But the task of restoring this flawed leader is difficult and made the more so because the generic framework of the male group has been destabilised.

Although by the end of the film the group has forged a unity through the experiences of their journey, it is quite clear that it can only be a fragile one, since it is not sustained by either army hierarchies or male friendship. The presence of Diana as a central member of the military group means that male/female relationships become a central rather a peripheral issue. Diana falls in love with Anson and, although the love scenes between them were cut, what is left of them exposes Anson's inadequacy as a lover. Diana participates in the actions of the group and, unlike the wives and girlfriends in the war film, she cannot be relegated to the margins nor are her questions adequately answered. In addition, Sylvia Syms' performance as Diana is marked by an emotional frankness not usually associated with the genre. She gently accuses Anson of not understanding women, a characteristic trait of war heroes but not one that is usually articulated so clearly, and warns him: 'You certainly don't understand me.' The effect is not only to distract attention from the group's story by setting up the possibility of a romantic narrative but also to raise questions about sexual and emotional relationships, which the war film normally blocks off, and to underline Anson's inability to deal with personal relationships.

The presence of Van Poel, the German spy, is even more disruptive, since he provides a challenge to Anson in terms of the genre's representation of masculinity. In general, the British war hero, although courageous, does not engage in demonstrations of physical strength, and his body is covered by a formal uniform or a duffel coat, polo-necked sweater and scarf, which help him to endure the cold and damp. Van Poel not only challenges Anson by his allegiance to a different, enemy, authority, but his physical presence draws attention to Anson's frailties. Van Poel, played by Anthony Quayle, has enormous physical strength, which the visual organisation of the film emphasises by putting his body on display. Lee Thompson's somewhat crude use of close-ups and cutting, very different from the restraint of most war films, is here used to emphasise the physical differences between Van Poel and Anson. The first shot of Van Poel is not of his face but of his huge legs, on each side of the screen, which frame Anson as he looks up. It is striking that while Sylvia Syms remains almost entirely covered up, the men in the film are on display; the bare chests, legs and arms of Quayle and Mills are continually shown as they engage in strenuous physical activity in the heat of the desert. In this contest, the British hero, Mills, looks pale, shrunken and stringy when his body is set against the broad shoulders and muscular arms and legs of Quayle. The narrative underlines the point. While Van Poel's natural physical strength is demonstrated by, for instance, the scene in which he takes the full weight of the ambulance on his back, Anson's toughness has a driven, willed dimension, which has a cost. His physical exhaustion is matched at various points in the narrative by a frustrated rage, which he vents on the group. By the end of the film he has regained control but the British hero as a model of masculine authority and courage has been severely and somewhat unusually undermined.

Rebellion and bureaucracy

Ice Cold in Alex demonstrates that anxieties about male authority are expressed in films of the period, and indeed it is possible to argue that it shares with films outside the genre (*Passage Home* and *Hell Drivers*, for example) a sense of anxiety about excessive masculinity that finds expression in the late 1950s. Some commentaries on the war films have tried to read the genre more generally as a means of expressing tensions about masculinity. Thus I argued that 'the devil-may-care attitude of Bader and the stoicism of Ericson both seem in the end strained and uneasy' (Geraghty 1984: 67), while Landy comments that 'these films ... are more concerned with issues of male identity and power, troubled adjustment, underlying sexual conflict, the breakdown of consensus, the failure of performance, and the tenuousness of the male group' (1991: 60).[8] Such readings accord with the notion of the 1950s as a time of masculine crisis and with theoretical readings that focus on moments of excess, such as Ericson's tears, or absence, such as the disappearance of women from the lives of these heroes. But such readings now seem to me to over-emphasise certain elements of the genre and underplay the way in which the war film generally provides a safe place in which problems around masculinity can be resolved effectively. The British heroes lack the physical ease with the landscape that their western counterparts show but they bring nature under control through the careful use of technological resources and their own patient endurance. When the group comes to the fore, as it does in the naval and POW films, the emphasis is on a disciplined acceptance of the hierarchies that maintain the group and that give each of them a secure role. Leaders have a natural authority, and if under the pressure of action they become isolated, that is an understandable outcome of their difference from the rest of us rather than a source of anxiety. The pleasures of these films surely lie in the way in which they take the aspects of masculinity that were beginning to seem problematic, as we saw in Chapter 8, and through the context of the war genre made them seem inevitable, natural and controllable. If they made war seem 'routine, manly and easy' as Durgnat suggests (83), they did so in response to those members of the audience who felt the need expressed by many ex-servicemen and women to 'recreate the spirit of companionship' or perhaps found in the films the experience, once again, of a 'big, noisy, energetic and purposeful crowd' (Turner and Rennell: 61, 185).

It is a sign of the confidence of the genre that alongside the emphasis on the discipline and purposefulness, the war film also overtly offers the pleasures of rebelliousness through the presentation of the hero. This is handled in two ways. First, one of the tasks of the leader is to set himself up against bureaucracy, and a consistent theme in the films is that of the leader who wins through by setting his judgement against those of his superiors. Thus, in *Appointment in London*, Mason disobeys specific orders that he not fly any more; he successfully manages the raid and returns to the cheers of the squadron and a gentle rebuke from his commanding officer, who 'has persuaded Bomber Command to ignore the episode'. Fraser in *Above Us the Waves* is a rebel who attacks the admiral's ship in the British Home Fleet to demonstrate the effectiveness of his human torpedoes, while the captain in *The Gift Horse* has a pre-war history of being court-martialled and adopts unorthodox methods to support his crew. In *Danger Within*, Huxley, as senior officer, specifically ignores the War Office order that bans escapes in the event of a possible armistice. Thus, although Bader in *Reach for the Sky* is presented as highly exceptional, the way in which he breaks the rules, defies regulations and unclogs the bureaucracy of 'the usual channels' is merely an extremely energetic version of the leader's usual role of evading or ignoring bureaucracy.

The second convention that allows for rebellion to be both expressed and managed is the way in which many of the films offer two distinct types of hero. Here the films offer excellent examples of what Durgnat identifies as a persistent trope in the fifties, the pairing of 'the "eternal cadet"' with the 'effective father' (142). In this formulation, the rebellious role is taken by the cadet but his energy and enthusiasm is channelled by the father, who is both older and higher up the hierarchical ladder. In *The Colditz Story*, Reid not only criticises Richmond but is himself offered as an energetic hero who adopts a much more overtly defiant attitude to the Germans. The same structure can be found in *Danger Within*, where Huxley is challenged by the escape officer, Baird, who is impatient with the conventional rules of the camp. Reid and Baird are played by stars who have played senior leaders themselves, John Mills and Richard Todd, so the cadet role has sufficient weight to express rebelliousness, while the narrative organisation makes sure that it is always controlled. *Silent Enemy* offers an interesting example of this in the individualistic mines expert, Crabb, who acts in a freelance fashion when he attaches himself to the diving service in Malta. Played by Lawrence Harvey, he could be the epitome of the angry young man in his disregard for rules and his loud contempt for hierarchies. But the admiral knows how much leeway to give the diving expert and Crabb's final mission, which breaches the rules of engagement, takes place with the tacit permission of his leader.

Linked to this streak of managed rebelliousness is the use of humour. The films under discussion share a strong steak of comedy, which opens up their appeal beyond the military setting. This goes further than the episodes of horse-play that are a feature of some of the RAF films and becomes a running commentary on the rules and regulations of service life. Even as austere a film as *The Dam Busters* offers semi-comic caricatures in its representation of the bureaucrats who block Barnes Wallis, while lower down the hierarchy officers are liable to be mocked. 'He's an officer and knows nothing and therefore he's entitled to be called "sir",' says the flight sergeant of his captain in *The Sea Shall Not Have Them*, while when Crabb joins the diving team in *Silent Enemy*, he is greeted with the comment: 'Be nice to have an officer around the place, make us look respectable.' In *The Gift Horse*, the crew keeps up a comic grumbling at the pretensions of the officers and the pervasiveness of regulations and in *Silent Enemy* Sid James as the chief petty officer drills the diving team with routines straight out of his future *Carry On* roles. While Rattigan is right that working-class characters are associated with humour, the popularity of comedy as a fifties genre that offered scope for the criticism of bureaucracy gives these moments more weight than they might otherwise have had. The comedy both widens the war film's range and, in many cases, provides the common-sense moments of relaxation that underpin the drama.

In the POW films, the comedy is an essential element based on the national stereotyping and the pleasure taken in comic put-downs of the enemy. This emphasis on comedy has an interesting effect in other ways. The POW films raise more directly than others in the genre the question of how men live together and thus perhaps edge closer to the dangerous question of how far homosexuality is implied by comradeship. The films generally deal with this through a form of humour that ranges from some self-conscious flirting with possibilities in *The Wooden Horse* to the positively camp overtones of *Danger Within*. Such humour is often connected with dressing up or disguise. In *The Wooden Horse*, the hero, Peter, teases John with 'You're beautiful' as they blacken their faces for a night-time excursion to get wood to shore up the tunnel. Theatrical shows such as 'The Colditz Capers' are a convention of the POW films and provide the opportunity for a provocative display of legs in music hall parodies. Inside and outside the shows, suggestive sexual undertones are often expressed in an upper-class drawl, exemplified by Richard Wattis and Ian Carmichael in *The Colditz Story*, and since both class and sexuality are being used to puzzle and confuse the Germans, characters of this type can be as much part of the resistance as the more conventional Reid. *Danger Within* suggests that more conscious use is being made of this material than a modern viewer might suspect. Among its potential escapees are an inseparable couple, Marquand and Piker, the former played by Michael Wilding with flamboyant arm waves and expressive shrugs. Their sexuality is suggested in a series of camp jokes: when asked why he needs a ladder to go over the barbed wire, Marquand responds 'Do you want me to prick myself on the wire?' and when the pair steal the rugby posts to make the ladder, they defer to each other with 'After you Claude,' 'After you Cecil.' It is worth noting that the two are not presented as being outside the male group or indeed as ineffective; the failure of their efficiently planned escape confirms to the others that an informer is giving away their plans. This undertone of the POW films suggests that the relationship between Charlie (Dirk Bogarde) and Billy (Alfred Lynch) in *The Password is Courage*, expressed through significant glances and mutual support, could be understood as something more than comradeship.

In stressing the role of rebellion and comedy in the war film, I am not arguing that the films have a hidden agenda that can be read against the more dominant emphasis on masculine discipline discussed earlier. Rather, I am suggesting that this element is overt in the genre and, indeed, that the war film can be understood as running parallel with the other popular genre of the period, the comedy. On the one hand, they share common ground, even when they work in opposition to each other. While the comedies defy the claims of scientific expertise, the war films celebrate the success of technology but stress its alienating effects. While the comedies mock the pretensions of the nationalist state, the war films use comedy as well as drama to offer a reassuring view of British superiority. While the comedies refuse to take the 'new man' seriously by emphasising male incompetence in the domestic sphere, the war films reassert male competence and authority by representing a confined and ordered public world. While the comedies satirise women and their modern ways, the war films marginalise them. But, at the same time, the two genres share many of the same attitudes and concerns. The war film, like the comedies, attacks bureaucracy but offers the security of hierarchies in which male relationships are the norm. It provides opportunity for rebellion against the restrictions of a state organisation, particularly through its successful rebels, but makes sure that they are contained within the establishment. The war films assert the possibility of a British national identity but root it in the past and have difficulty translating it into support for a modern Britain. Like the comedies, the war films take class as the basis of their organisation and turn away from the notion of a classless society. In this sense, it is no accident that the two genres produced the most popular British films of the 1950s; they both provide a safe space in which the demands of modern citizenship can be resiliently shrugged off, an opportunity for relaxation in the old-fashioned spaces of the cinema. It could not last. In 1963, Billy's daydream, at the beginning of *Billy Liar*, mocks both genres. 'We had won the war in Ambrosia,' he muses, imagining himself as both soldier and leader. 'Democracy was back in our beloved country.' The hierarchies, the class patterns and the gender separations that had marked the rearguard action of British cinema in the 1950s were by this point under inexorable attack.

Notes

Chapter 1

1   Stacey (1994) offers a valuable account of the problems of using reminiscences and memories as a source. Here I am less concerned with the accuracy of the accounts than with what they tell us about how cinema was thought about and associated with certain kinds of people and behaviour.

2   See Corrigan (1983) and Doherty *et al.* (1987) for statistical material on cinemagoing in the late 1940s and a discussion of the subsequent decline. See also Harper and Porter (1999) for their analysis of cinemagoing on the 1950s, which discusses audiences in terms of indiscriminate, regular and occasional cinemagoers.

3   See Barr (1986) for a more extended discussion of cinema's representation of television in this period.

Chapter 2

1   Finch and Summerfield note that although this term was used in the 1920s and 1930s:

> it is in the post-war period that it appears more widely, being used to summarise a set of ideas about marriage which ranged from the notion that there should be greater companionship between partners whose roles essentially were different, through the idea of marriage as teamwork, to the concept of marriages based on 'sharing' implying the breakdown of clearly demarcated roles.
>
> (6)

Chapter 3

1   Raymond's hero expresses his feelings in poetry celebrating England's 'long green pastures', 'quiet hamlets' and 'ploughland, park and wood' (261), while in the opening scenes of *Pastoral*, the pilot hero takes pleasure in fishing in 'the broad, gravelly pool' by the old mill, 'in pasture fields, very sunny and bright' (10).

2   The story is thus similar to that of *Tawny Pipit*, but whereas in the wartime film modern aviation and bird life can live in harmony, the post-war film sets them in opposition. The rural identity represented by the birds is in the past.

3   See Chapter 6 for a discussion of how Davidson is redeemed. *Hunted*, which is discussed in Chapter 8, is another thriller that makes use of the rural landscape in this way.

Chapter 4

1   In choosing the films to discuss as examples from a huge genre I have tended to avoid the films of the Boulting brothers, which have received attention in a specialist study (Burton *et al.* 2000), although they would fit the pattern presented in this chapter.

2   It is significant that James Robertson Justice's combination of malice, wit and traditional values, so effectively used here, was carried into numerous roles in films dealing with the law, education and the services.

3   Another criminal comedy, *Too Many Crooks* (1959), takes as its central joke the disastrous consequences for the gang of an incompetent leader.

Chapter 5

1   This doubling is repeated frequently in *It Always Rains on Sunday.* Quite apart from the contrasts between the younger and older Rose and Vi and Doris, we have Lou and Morrie Hyams as the successful and unsuccessful brothers, the dubious activities of the two brothers set against the good works of their sister, Bessie, and the contrast between the naive Vi and Sadie, Morrie's dark-haired and sardonic wife.

2   See Perkins (1996) for a discussion of attitudes to housework in four other post-war forties films.

Chapter 6

1   The wartime diaries of Nella Last and the correspondence of Kay and Richard Titmuss in Oakley give an indication of civilian attitudes to Germany as the war drew to an end.

2   Following the chronology of the novel, Susan, aged 19 in 1946, would have been born in 1927. In her first appearance in the film, she looks much more like a contemporary (1958) teenager, who would have been a child during the war, thus making the choice between her and Alice much more clearly a choice between past and future in the late 1950s rather than the late 1940s. Although this is an arcane point, having Susan and Joe look and behave like fifties teenagers is important in making Joe's rebellion speak to the youthful audience who responded to it.

Chapter 7

1   It is interesting to note that many scenes were still shot in the studio. Virginia McKenna remembers that she and Bogarde did their filming at Pinewood, with doubles being used on location (McFarlane: 164), while the Eastern village built at Pinewood for *Windom's Way* was praised by *Picturegoer* for its realism (16 November 1957).

2   Similar responses are used in *Sapphire* (1959) as examples of prejudice in a British context.

3   For an indication of the sensationalist reporting of Mau Mau initiation and oath-taking ceremonies, see Lapping: 421–3.

4   See Chapter 9 for further discussion of the romance genre.

5   Although the actors were not English, since John Cairney was Scottish and Natasha Parry partly Russian, an exotic fact that was used for publicity purposes for *Windom's Way.*

6   *The Wind Cannot Read* (1958) did feature an inter-racial love affair comparable to the one thwarted here but it ended unhappily with the death of the Japanese woman.

Chapter 8

1   See Wicks (129–31) for stories of evacuees making long official and unofficial journeys as a consequence of evacuation. One penniless twelve-year-old managed to get back home from Newcastle to Croydon, helped by Canadian soldiers and various transport officials.

2   Landy (1991), for instance, discusses *Hunted* as a 'tragic melodrama' and *The Yellow Balloon* as a social problem film.

3   Note though that Medhurst's important essay on *The Spanish Gardener* discusses the 'forbidden desire' (1993: 95) that, he suggests, permeates the film.

4   In this, I would disagree with Landy's emphasis in her discussion of *The Yellow Balloon*, which sees the film as a study of the 'determinants of juvenile delinquency' (1991: 450). Although there are strong elements of this, I see it much more as a film that expresses parental anxiety about childhood.

5   The director, Philip Leacock, had previously made *The Kidnappers* (1953), which mounted a similar critique of a patriarchal figure in a historical context.

6   It is rather pleasing that after this impeccably liberal approach, Rilla went on to present a more demonic view of children in *Village of the Damned*.

7   See Hill (1986) and Chibnall (1997) for accounts of the film from this angle.

Chapter 9

1   I am grateful to Justine Ashby at the University of East Anglia for showing me this example of the lengths to which the image of the ideal woman could be pushed.

2   See Philips and Haywood's *Brave New Causes* (1998) for a discussion of the way in which the professional new woman was treated in post-war popular fiction.

3   The success of Muriel and Betty Box as screen writers, directors and producers is relatively unmarked in this discussion, which tends to centre on stars.

4   The cocktail bar, often incorporated into a sideboard, was a distinctively modern piece of furniture at the time. Attfield cites a furniture dealer in Harlow, commenting in puzzlement: 'The strange thing was that people couldn't afford cocktails or any of the other drinks that went with it … so how the fashion caught on I don't know' (225–6).

5   Others that are of interest are *Young Wives' Tale*, *It's Never Too Late*, *True as a Turtle* and *Upstairs and Downstairs*.

6   McKenna cut back on her career at the end of the 1950s in order to look after her family. According to Lewis Gilbert, who directed her in *Carve Her Name with Pride*, it was at this point that she turned down an offer from Hitchcock to film with him in Hollywood. Gilbert told a National Film Theatre audience of Hitchcock's interest at a screening of the film in 1998.

Chapter 10

1   See essays by A. Clay, A. Spicer and S. Chibnall in S. Chibnall and R. Murphy (eds) for an examination of this phenomenon.

2   See Willmott and Young (1976) for a classic example of this 'split between the lives of husband and wife' in the diaries of Mr and Mrs Matthews (25–7).

3   See Medhurst (1984a) for a discussion of *Victim*.

4   By comparison, the aircraft in US combat films are filmed in ways that emphasise their spaciousness.

5   In a period when the conventional acting voice was trained into upper middle-class tones, Bogarde's strong accent here marks him as working-class despite his rather bourgeois inheritance of his father's shop.

6   In some ways, though, one of the attractions of the POW films may have been that, despite their specific setting, they offer an account of wartime experiences that were not confined to those who had been captured. POW films, for instance, reproduce the waiting, the boredom, the hanging about, which were a recognised feature of army life and of National Service in particular. In addition, although the POW films have a military setting, they offer a version of the civilian experience of a wartime economy. The prison camp is heavily bureaucratised, and the factory-style production of clothing and fake documents replicates the wartime economy in which the whole population works to provide equipment for 'the few' taking action. And, despite the emphasis on active escape, the prisoners, like British civilians during the Blitz, spend much of the time reacting to the activity of the enemy and always feel vulnerable to enemy attack. But this experience of permanent fear combined with a communal acceptance of disciplined working for the greater good is now represented through a male group that is largely confined to the upper middle classes.

7   In the book, the connection made between lights in the theatre and the use of lights to check height is a joke; in the film, the insight is given to Gibson as a sign that he is never off-duty.

8   Landy is referring specifically to *The Cruel Sea*, *The Colditz Story* and *The Dam Busters* here. Later, she describes these post-war war dramas as using the war 'as an occasion for an examination of male malaise' (1991: 181).

Bibliography

Abrams, P. (1964) 'Radio and television', in D. Thompson (ed.) *Discrimination and Popular Culture*, Harmondsworth: Penguin.

Addison, P. (1985) *Now the War is Over: A Social History of Britain 1945–51*, London: British Broadcasting Corporation and Jonathan Cape.

Adorno, T. and Horkheimer, M. (1997) 'The culture industry: enlightenment as mass deception' in *Dialectic of Enlightenment*, trans. by J. Cumming, London: Verso.

Aspinall, S. (1983) 'Woman, realism and reality in British films 1943–53', in J. Curran and V. Porter (eds) *British Cinema History*, London: Weidenfeld & Nicolson.

Aspinall, S. and Murphy, R. (1983) *Gainsborough Melodrama*, London: British Film Institute.

Attfield, J. (1989) 'Inside Pram Town: a case study of Harlow house interiors, 1951–61', in J. Attfield and P. Kirkham (eds) *A View from the Interior: Feminism, Women and Design*, London: The Women's Press.

Attfield, J. and P. Kirkham (eds) (1989) *A View from the Interior: Feminism, Women and Design*, London: The Women's Press.

Barr, C. (1977) *Ealing Studios*, London: Cameron and Tayleur (Books).

—— (ed.) (1986) *All Our Yesterdays: 90 Years of British Cinema*, London: British Film Institute. [includes his own essay 'Broadcasting and cinema 2: screens within screens']

Basinger, J. (1986) *The World War II Combat Film: Anatomy of a Genre*, New York: Columbia University Press.

Benjamin, W. (1992) 'The work of art in the age of mechanical reproduction', in H. Zohn (ed.) *Illuminations*, trans. by H. Arendt, London: Fontana Press.

Bennett, T. (1981) *Popular Culture and Hegemony in Post-war Britain* (Block 5, Unit 18 of popular culture course), Milton Keynes: Open University Press.

Berman, M. (1982) *All that is Solid Melts into Air: The Experience of Modernity*, London: Verso.

Beveridge, W. (1942) *Social Insurance and Allied Services*, London: HMSO.

Bordwell, D. and Thompson, K. (1979) *Film Art: An Introduction* New York: Knopf.

Bourke, J. (1994) *Working-Class Cultures in Britain 1890–1960: Gender, Class and Ethnicity*, London: Routledge.

Bowlby, J. (1965) *Child Care and the Growth of Love*, Harmondsworth: Penguin.

Boxer, A. (1996) *The Conservative Governments 1951–1964*, London: Longman.

Breakwell, I. and Hammond, P. (1990) *Seeing in the Dark: A Compendium of Cinemagoing*, London: Serpent's Tail.

Brown, G. (1997) 'Paradise found and lost: the course of British realism', in R. Murphy (ed.) *The British Cinema Book*, London: British Film Institute.

Brunsdon, C. and Moseley, R. (1997) 'She's a foreigner who's become a British subject: *Frieda*', in A. Burton, T. O'Sullivan and P. Wells (eds) *Liberal Directions: Basil Dearden and Post-war British Film Culture*, Trowbridge: Flicks Books.

Burton, A., O'Sullivan, T. and Wells, P. (eds) (1997) *Liberal Directions: Basil Dearden and Post-war British Film Culture*, Trowbridge: Flicks Books.

—— (2000) *The Family Way: The Boulting Brothers and British Film Culture*, Trowbridge: Flicks Books.

Calder, A. (1969) *The People's War*, London: Jonathan Cape.

Cameron, K.A. (1994) *Africa on Film: Beyond Black and White*, New York: Continuum.

Chapman, J. (1997) 'Films and Flea-pits: *The Smallest Show on Earth*', in A. Burton, T. O'Sullivan and P. Wells (eds) *Liberal Directions: Basil Dearden and Post-war British Film Culture*, Trowbridge: Flicks Books.

Chibnall, S. (1997) 'The teenage trilogy: *The Blue Lamp*, *I Believe in You* and *Violent Playground*', in A. Burton, T. O'Sullivan and P. Wells (eds) *Liberal Directions: Basil Dearden and Post-war British Film Culture*, Trowbridge: Flicks Books.

—— (1999) 'Ordinary people: "New Wave" realism and the British crime film 1959–63', in S. Chibnall and R. Murphy (eds) *British Crime Cinema*, London: Routledge.

Chibnall, S. and Murphy, R. (eds) (1999) *British Crime Cinema*, London: Routledge.

Clarke, D.B. (1997) 'Introduction: Previewing the cinematic city', in D.B. Clarke (ed.) *The Cinematic City*, London: Routledge.

Clay, A. (1999) 'Men, women and money: masculinity in crisis in the British professional crime film 1946–65' in S. Chibnall and R. Murphy (eds) *British Crime Cinema*, London: Routledge.

Commoli, J. and Narboni, J (1976) 'Cinema/ideology/criticism', in B. Nicholls (ed.) *Movies and Methods*, Vol. 1, California: University of California Press.

Cook, P. (1983) 'Melodrama and the women's picture', in S. Aspinall and R. Murphy (eds) *Gainsborough Melodrama*, London: British Film Institute.

—— (1996) *Fashioning the Nation: Costume and Identity in British Cinema*, London: British Film Institute.

Coronation of Her Majesty Queen Elizabeth II: Approved Souvenir Programme, London: Odhams Press.

Corrigan, P. (1983) 'Film entertainment as ideology and pleasure: a preliminary approach to a history of audiences', in J. Curran and V. Porter (eds) *British Cinema History*, London: Weidenfeld & Nicolson.

Curran, J. and Porter, V. (eds) (1983) *British Cinema History*, London: Weidenfeld & Nicolson.

Deighton, A. (1993) *The Impossible Peace: Britain, the Division of Germany and the Origins of the Cold War*, Oxford: Clarendon Press.

Dimbleby, R. (1953): *Elizabeth Our Queen*, London: University of London Press.

Docherty, D., Morrison, D. and Tracey, M. (1987) *The Last Picture Show? Britain's Changing Film Audiences*, London: British Film Institute.

Durgnat, R. (1970) *A Mirror for England*, London: Faber.

Dyer, R. (1988) 'White', *Screen* 29(4): 44–64.

—— (1997) *White*, London: Routledge.

Finch, J. and Summerfield, P. (1991) 'Social reconstruction and the emergence of the companionate marriage, 1945–59', in D. Clark (ed.) *Marriage, Domestic Life and Social Change: Writings for Jacqueline Burgoyne*, London: Routledge.

Fyvel, T.R. (1961) *The Insecure Offender*, London: Chatto & Windus.

Giddens, A. (1990) *The Consequences of Modernity*, Cambridge: Polity Press.

Geraghty, C. (1984) 'Masculinity', in G. Hurd (ed.) *National Fictions: World War Two in British Films and Television*, London: British Film Institute.

—— (1986) 'Diana Dors', in C. Barr (ed.) *All Our Yesterdays: 90 Years of British Cinema*, London: British Film Institute, 341–5.

Gledhill, C. (1996) '"An abundance of understatement": documentary, melodrama and romance', in C. Gledhill and G. Swanson (eds) *Nationalising Femininity: Culture, Sexuality and British Cinema in the Second World War*, Manchester: Manchester University Press.

Gledhill, C. and Swanson, G. (1996) *Nationalising Femininity: Culture, Sexuality and British Cinema in the Second World War*, Manchester: Manchester University Press.

Gorer, G. (1955) *Exploring the English Character*, London: The Cresset Press.

Gosling, R. (1980) *Personal Copy*, London: Faber and Faber.

Harper, S. (1996) 'From *Holiday Camp* to high camp: women in British feature films 1945–51', in A. Higson (ed.) *Dissolving Views: Key Writings on British Cinema*, London: Cassell.

Harper, S. and Porter, V. (1999) 'Cinema audience tastes in 1950s Britain', *Journal of Popular British Cinema* 2: 66–82.

Haste, C. (1992) *Rules of Desire: Sex in Britain: World War I to the present*, London: Chatto & Windus.

Hemming, J. (1960) *Problems of Adolescent Girls*, London: Heinemann.

Hennessy, P. (1993) *Never Again: Britain 1945–1951*, London: Vintage.

Higson, A. (ed.) (1996) *Dissolving Views: Key Writings on British Cinema*, London: Cassell.

—— (1997) *Waving the Flag: Constructing a National Cinema in Britain*, Oxford: Oxford University Press.

Hill, J. (1986) *Sex, Class and Realism: British Cinema 1956–63*, London: British Film Institute.

HM Government (1960) *Report of the Committee on the Youth Services in England and Wales* (the Albermarle Report), London: HMSO.

Hobsbawm, E. (1994) *The Age of Extremes: The Short Twentieth Century 1914–1991*, London: Michael Joseph.

Hoggart, R. (1958) *The Uses of Literacy*, Harmondsworth: Penguin.

Hopkins, H. (1964) *The New Look: A Social History of the Forties and Fifties in Britain*, London: Readers Union and Secker & Warburg.

Howarth, T.E.B. (1985) *Prospect and Reality: Great Britain 1945–55*, London: Collins.

Hunt, A. (1964) 'The Film', in D. Thompson (ed.) *Discrimination and Popular Culture*, Harmondsworth: Penguin.

Hutchings, P. (1993) *Hammer and Beyond: The British Horror Film*, Manchester: Manchester University Press.

Jackson, B. and Marsden, D. (1966) *Education and the Working Class*, Harmondsworth: Penguin.

Jervis, J. (1998) *Exploring the Modern*, Oxford: Blackwell.

Judd, D. (1996) *Empire: The British Imperial Experience from 1765 to the Present*, London: HarperCollins.

Kerr, M. (1958) *The People of Ship Street*, London: Routledge & Kegan Paul.

Kirkham, P. (1995) 'Dress, dance, dreams and desire: fashion and fantasy in *Dance Hall*', *Journal of Design History* 8(3): 195–214.

—— (1996) 'Fashioning the feminine: dress appearance and femininity in wartime Britain' in C. Gledhill and G. Swanson (eds) *Nationalising Femininity: Culture,*

Sexuality and British Cinema in the Second World War, Manchester: Manchester University Press.

Kirkham, P. and Thumim, J. (1997) 'Men at work: Dearden and gender', in A. Burton, T. O'Sullivan and P. Wells (eds) *Liberal Directions: Basil Dearden and Post-war British Film Culture*, Trowbridge: Flicks Books.

Klein, J. (1965) *Samples from English Culture*, Vols I and II, London: Routledge & Kegan Paul.

Klein, V. (1965) *Britain's Married Women Workers*, London: Routledge & Kegan Paul.

Laing, S. (1986) *Representations of Working Class Life 1957–64*, London: Macmillan.

Landy, M. (1991) *British Genres: Cinema and Society 1930–1960*, Princeton: Princeton University Press.

—— (1994) '*They Were Sisters*: common sense, World War II, and the woman's film', in *Film, Politics and Gramsci*, Minneapolis: University of Minnesota Press.

Lane, P. (1985) *Europe since 1945: an introduction* London: England.

Lapping, B. (1985) *End of Empire*, London: Granada.

Last, N. (1981) *Nella Last's War: A Mother's Diary 1939–45*, R. Broad and S. Fleming (eds), Frome: Falling Wall Press.

Lewis, J. (1992) *Women in Britain since 1945*, Oxford: Blackwell.

Light, A. (1991) *Forever England: Femininity, Literature and Conservatism Between the Wars*, London: Routledge.

Lovell, A. (1997) 'The British cinema: the known cinema?' in R. Murphy (ed.) *The British Cinema Book*, London: British Film Institute.

Low, R. (1948) 'The implications behind the social survey', *Penguin Film Review 7*, September: 107–12.

McArthur, C. (1982) *Scotch Reels: Scotland in Cinema and Television*, London: British Film Institute.

McCabe, C. (1974) 'Realism and the cinema: notes on some Brechtian theses', *Screen* 15(2): 7–27.

McFarlane, B. (1992) *Sixty Voices*, London: British Film Institute.

Manvell, R. (1953) 'Britain's self-portraiture in feature films', *Geographical Magazine*, August: 222–34.

—— (1961) *The Living Screen*, London: Harrap and Co.

Mash, M. (1996) 'Stepping out or out of step? Austerity, affluence and femininity in two post-war films', in C. Gledhill and G. Swanson (eds) *Nationalising Femininity: Culture, Sexuality and British Cinema in the Second World War*, Manchester: Manchester University Press.

Medhurst, A. (1984a) 'Victim: text as context', *Screen* 25(4–5), July–October: 22–35.

—— (1984b) '1950s war films', in G. Hurd (ed.) *National Fictions: World War Two in British Films and Television*, London: British Film Institute.

—— (1986) 'Dirk Bogarde', in C. Barr (ed.) *All Our Yesterdays: 90 Years of British Cinema*, London: British Film Institute.

—— (1993) '"It's as a man that you've failed": masculinity and forbidden desire in *The Spanish Gardener*', in P. Kirkham and J. Thumim (eds) *You Tarzan: Masculinity, Movies and Men*, London: Lawrence & Wishart.

Miles, R. and Phizacklea, A. *White Man's Country*, London: Pluto Press.

Murphy, R. (1989) *Realism and Tinsel: Cinema and Society in Britain 1939–49*, London: British Film Institute.

—— (1992) *Sixties British Cinema*, London: British Film Institute.

—— (ed.) (1997) *The British Cinema Book*, London: British Film Institute.

Newsom, J. (1963) *Half Our Future: A Report of the Central Advisory Council for Education (England)*, London: HMSO.

Newson, J. and Newson, E. (1965) *Patterns of Infant Care in an Urban Community*, Harmondsworth: Penguin.

Oakley, A. (1997) *Man and Wife*, London: Flamingo.

O'Brien, M. and Eyles, A. (eds) (1993) *Enter the Dream-House: Memories of Cinemas in South London from the Twenties to the Sixties*, London: British Film Institute and Museum of the Moving Image.

Osgerby, B. (1993) 'From the roaring twenties to the swinging sixties: continuity and change in British youth culture 1929–65', in B. Brivati and H. Jones (eds) *What Difference Did the War Make?* Leicester: Leicester University Press.

O'Shea, A. (1996) 'English subjects of modernity', in M. Nava and A. O'Shea (eds) *Modern Times: Reflections on a Century of English Modernity*, London: Routledge.

Partington, A. (1989) 'The designer housewife in the 1950s', in J. Attfield and P. Kirkham (eds) *A View from the Interior: Feminism, Women and Design*, London: The Women's Press.

Patterson, S. (1965) *Dark Strangers: A Study of West Indians in London*, Harmondsworth: Penguin.

Perkins, T. (1996) 'Two weddings and two funerals: the problem of the post-war woman', in C. Gledhill and G. Swanson (eds) *Nationalising Femininity: Culture, Sexuality and British Cinema in the Second World War*, Manchester: Manchester University Press.

Petley, J. (1986) 'The Lost Continent', in C. Barr (ed.) *All Our Yesterdays: 90 Years of British Cinema*, London: British Film Institute.

Philips, D. and Haywood, D. (1998) *Brave New Causes: Women in British Post-war Fictions*, London: Leicester University Press.

Phillips, M. and Phillips, T. (1998) *Windrush: The Irresistible Rise of Multi-racial Britain*, London: HarperCollins.

Pimlott, B. (1996) *The Queen: A Biography of Elizabeth II*, London: HarperCollins.

Porter, V. (1997) 'Methodism versus the market-place: the Rank organisation and British cinema', in Murphy, R. (ed.) *The British Cinema Book*, London: British Film Institute.

Priestley, J.B. (1948) 'Foreword', *The Neglected Child and his Family*, Sub-Committee of the Women's Group on Public Welfare, London: Geoffrey Cumberlege, Oxford University Press.

Radway, J.A. (1984) *Reading the Romance: Women, Patriarchy and Popular Literature*, Chapel Hill: University of North Carolina Press.

Rank, J.A. (1948) 'A speech to the General Council of the Cinematographic Exhibitors' Association', London: British Film Institute library.

Rattigan, N. (1994) 'The last gasp of the middle class: British war films of the 1950s', in W.W. Dixon (ed.) *Re-Viewing British Cinema 1900–1992*, New York: State University of New York Press.

Raymond, E. (1941) *The Last to Rest*, London: Cassell.

Richards, J. (1984) *The Age of the Dream Palace*, London: Routledge & Kegan Paul.

—— (1997) *Films and British National Identity From Dickens to 'Dad's Army'*, Manchester: Manchester University Press.

Richards, J. and Sheridan, D. (eds) (1987) *Mass Observation at the Movies*, London: Routledge & Kegan Paul.

Roberts, E. (1995) *Women and their Families: An Oral History 1940–70*, Oxford: Blackwell.

Schatz, T. (1981) *Hollywood Genres: Formulas, Filmmaking and the Studio System*, McGraw-Hill.

Schofield, M. (1968) *The Sexual Behaviour of Young People*, Harmondsworth: Penguin.

Segal, L. (1988) 'Look back in anger: men in the 50s', in R. Chapman and J. Rutherford (eds) *Male Order: Unwrapping Masculinity*, London: Lawrence & Wishart.

Shute, N. (1944) *Pastoral*, London: Heinemann.

Smart, C. (1996) 'Good wives and moral lives: marriage and divorce 1937–51', in C. Gledhill and G. Swanson (eds) *Nationalising Femininity: Culture, Sexuality and British Cinema in the Second World War*, Manchester: Manchester University Press.

Smith, H.L. (1996) *Britain in the Second World War: A Social History*, Manchester: Manchester University Press.

Spicer, A. (1997) 'Male stars, masculinity and British cinema 1945–1960', in R. Murphy, (ed.) *The British Cinema Book*, London: British Film Institute.

—— (1999) 'The emergence of the British tough guy: Stanley Baker, masculinity and the crime thriller', in S. Chibnall and R. Murphy (eds) *British Crime Cinema*, London: Routledge.

Stacey, J. (1994) *Star Gazing: Hollywood Cinema and Female Spectatorship*, London: Routledge.

Street, S. (1997) *British National Cinema*, London: Routledge.

Summerfield, P. (1993) 'Approaches to women and social change in the Second World War', in B. Britavi and H. Jones (eds) *What Difference Did the War Make*, Leicester: Leicester University Press.

—— (1994) 'Women in Britain since 1945: companionate marriage and the double burden', in J. Obelkevich and P. Catterall (eds) *Understanding Post-war British Society*, London: Routledge.

—— (1996) '"The girl that makes the thing that drills the hole that holds the spring…" discourses of women and work in the Second World War', in C. Gledhill and G. Swanson (eds) *Nationalising Femininity: Culture, Sexuality and British Cinema in the Second World War*, Manchester: Manchester University Press.

Thompson, D. (ed.) (1964) *Discrimination and Popular Culture*, Harmondsworth: Penguin.

Thumim, J. (1992) *Celluloid Sisters*, London: Macmillan.

—— (1996) 'The female audience: mobile women and married ladies', in C. Gledhill and G. Swanson (eds) *Nationalising Femininity: Culture, Sexuality and British Cinema in the Second World War*, Manchester: Manchester University Press, 35–52.

Timmins, N. (1996) *The Five Giants: A Biography of the Welfare State*, London: Fontana.

Titmuss, R.M. (1958) 'War and social policy', in *Essays on 'the Welfare State'*, London: George Allen & Unwin.

Tomlinson, J. (1997) 'Reconstructing Britain: Labour in power 1945–51', in N. Tiratsoo (ed.) *From Blitz to Blair*, London: Weidenfeld & Nicolson.

Turner, B. and Rennell, T. (1995) *When Daddy Came Home: How Family Life Changed Forever in 1945*, London: Hutchinson.

Vaughn, J. (1959) 'The dark continent in the wrong light', *Films and Filming*, January.

Weeks J. (1989) *Sex, Politics and Society*, London: Longman.

Whitehead, F. (1964) 'Advertising', in D. Thompson (ed.) *Discrimination and Popular Culture*, Harmondsworth: Penguin.

Whittaker, S. (1978/9) '*It Always Rains on Sunday* Part II', *Framework* 9: 21–6.

Wicks, B. (1988) *No Time to Say Goodbye: True Stories of Britain's 3,500,000 Evacuees*, London: Bloomsbury.

Williams, R. (1977) 'A lecture on realism', *Screen* 18(1): 61–74.

Willmott, P. and Young, M. (1976) *Family and Class in a London Suburb*, London: New English Library.

Wilson, E. (1977) *Women and the Welfare State*, London: Tavistock.

—— (1980) *Only Halfway to Paradise: Women in Postwar Britain 1945–68*, London: Tavistock.

——(1991) *The Sphinx in the City*, London: Virago.

Winnicott, D.W. (1964) *The Child, the Family and the Outside World*, Harmondsworth: Penguin.

Worpole, K. (1983) *Dockers and Detectives*, London: Verso.

Wright, P. (1985) *On Living in an Old Country*, London: Verso.

Young, L. (1996) *Fear of the Dark: Race, Gender and Sexuality in the Cinema*, London: Routledge.

Young, M. (1961) *The Rise of Meritocracy 1870–2033*, Harmondsworth: Penguin.

Young, M. and Willmott, P. (1962) *Family and Kinship in East London*, Harmondsworth: Penguin.

Yudkin, S. and Holme, A. (1963) *Working Mothers and their Children*, London: Michael Joseph.

Filmography

D: Director(s); S: Starring.

29 Acacia Avenue (1945) D: Henry Cass. S: Gordon Harker, Jimmy Hanley, Dinah Sheridan.

80,000 Suspects (1963) D: Val Guest. S: Claire Bloom, Cyril Cusack.

Above Us the Waves (1955) D: Ralph Thomas. S: John Mills, John Gregson.

Against the Wind (1948) D: Charles Crichton. S: Jack Warner, Simone Signoret.

Angels One Five (1952) D: George M. O'Ferrall. S: Jack Hawkins, Michael Denison, Dulcie Gray.

Appointment in London (1953) D: Philip Leacock. S: Dirk Bogarde, Dinah Sheridan.

Bachelor of Hearts (1958) D: Wolf Rilla. S: Hardy Kruger, Sylvia Syms.

Beachcomber, The (1954) D: Muriel Box. S: Robert Newton, Glynis Johns.

Beat Girl (1959) D: Edmond T. Greville. S: David Farrar, Noelle Adam.

Belles of St Trinians (1954) D: Frank Launder. S: Alistair Sim, Joyce Grenfell.

Bells Go Down, The (1943) D: Basil Dearden. S: Tommy Trinder, James Mason.

Bicycle Thieves ((Ladri di Biciclette) 1948 (Italy)) D: Vittorio de Sica.

Billy Liar (1963) D: John Schlesinger. S: Tom Courtenay, Julie Christie.

Black Narcissus (1947) D: Michael Powell, Emeric Pressburger. S: Deborah Kerr, Sabu, Flora Robson.

Blackboard Jungle, The (1955 (US)) D: Richard Brooks. S: Glenn Ford, Anne Francis.

Blue Lamp, The (1950) D: Basil Dearden. S: Jack Warner, Jimmy Hanley, Dirk Bogarde.

Blue Peter, The (1954) D: Don Sharp, Wolf Rilla. S: Kieron Moore, Greta Gynt.

Bridal Path, The (1959) D: Frank Launder. S: Bill Travers, George Cole.

Bridge over the River Kwai, The (1957) D: David Lean. S: Alec Guinness, Jack Hawkins.

Brief Encounter (1945) D: David Lean. S: Celia Johnson, Trevor Howard.

Bulldog Breed (1960) D: Robert Asher. S: Norman Wisdom, Ian Hunter.

Cage of Gold (1950) D: Basil Dearden. S: Jean Simmons, David Farrar.

Campbell's Kingdom (1957) D: Ralph Thomas. S: Dirk Bogarde, Stanley Baker.

Canterbury Tale, A (1944) D: Michael Powell, Emeric Pressburger. S: Sheila Sim, Eric Portman.

Captive Heart, The (1946) D: Basil Dearden. S: Michael Redgrave, Mervyn Johns.

Carlton-Browne of the FO (1958) D: Roy Boulting, Jeffrey Dell. S: Terry-Thomas, Peter Sellars.

Carry On Teacher (1959) D: Gerald Thomas. S: Ted Ray, Kenneth Connor, Joan Sims.

Carve Her Name With Pride (1958) D: Lewis Gilbert. S: Virginia McKenna, Paul Scofield, Jack Warner.

Clouded Yellow, The (1950) D: Ralph Thomas. S: Jean Simmons, Trevor Howard.

Colditz Story, The (1955) D: Guy Hamilton. S: John Mills, Eric Portman.

Comin' Thro' the Rye (1924) D: Cyril Hepworth.

Conflict of Wings (1954) D: John Eldridge. S: John Gregson, Muriel Pavlow.

Constant Husband, The (1955) D: Sidney Gilliat. S: Rex Harrison, Margaret Leighton, Kay Kendall.

Cosh Boy (1952) D: Lewis Gilbert. S: James Kenny, Joan Collins.

Cruel Sea, The (1953) D: Charles Frend. S: Jack Hawkins, Donald Sinden, Denholm Elliott.

Cry From the Streets, A (1958) D: Lewis Gilbert. S: Max Bygraves, Barbara Murray.

Dam Busters, The (1955) D: Michael Anderson. S: Richard Todd, Michael Redgrave.

Dance Hall (1950) D: Charles Crichton. S: Donald Houston, Bonar Calleano, Petula Clark, Natasha Parry.

Danger Within (1959) D: Don Chaffey. S: Richard Todd, Richard Attenborough.

Derby Day (1952) D: Herbert Wilcox. S: Anna Neagle, Michael Wilding.

Doctor at Sea (1955) D: Ralph Thomas. S: Dirk Bogarde, Brigitte Bardot.

Doctor in the House (1954) D: Ralph Thomas. S: Dirk Bogarde, Muriel Pavlow, Kenneth More.

Easy Money (1948) D: Bernard Knowles. S: Greta Gynt, Dennis Price, Jack Warner.

Emergency Call (1952) D: Lewis Gilbert. S: Jack Warner, Anthony Steel, Joy Shelton.

Esther Waters (1948) D: Ian Dalrymple, Peter Proud. S: Kathleen Ryan, Dirk Bogarde.

Four Feathers, The (1939) D: Zoltan Korda. S: John Clements, Ralph Richardson.

French Mistress, A (1960) D: Roy Boulting. S: Cecil Parker, James Robertson Justice, Agnes Laurent.

Frieda (1947) D: Basil Dearden. S: David Farrar, Glynis Johns, Mai Zetterling.

Genevieve (1953) D: Henry Cornelius. S: Dinah Sheridan, John Gregson, Kenneth More, Kay Kendall.

Gentle Trap, The (1960) D: Charles Saunder. S: Spencer Teakle, Felicity Young.

Geordie (1955) D: Frank Launder. S: Alistair Sim, Bill Travers.

Gift Horse, The (1952) D: Compton Bennett. S: Trevor Howard, Richard Attenborough.

Glass Mountain, The (1949) D: Henry Cass, Edoardo Anton. S: Michael Denison, Dulcie Gray.

Go to Blazes (1962) D: Michael Truman. S: Robert Morley, Dennis Price, Maggie Smith.

Golden Disc, The (1958) D: Don Sharp. S: Lee Patterson, Mary Steele, Terry Dene.

Golden Salamander, The (1950) D: Ronald Neame. S: Trevor Howard, Anouk Aimée, Herbert Lom.

Goodbye Mr Chips (1939) D: Sam Wood. S: Robert Donat, Greer Garson.

Green Grow the Rushes (1951) D: Derek Twist. S: Roger Livesey, Honor Blackman, Richard Burton.

Guinea Pig, The (1948) D: Roy Boulting. S: Richard Attenborough, Sheila Sim.

Happy Ever After (1954) D: Mario Zampi. S: David Niven, Yvonne de Carlo, George Cole.

Happy Family, The (1952) D: Muriel Box. S: Stanley Holloway, Kathleen Harrison.

Hard Day's Night, A (1964) D: Richard Lester. S: The Beatles, Wilfrid Brambell.

Heart of the Matter, The (1953) D: George M. O'Ferrall. S: Trevor Howard, Elizabeth Allan.

Hell Drivers (1957) D: Cy Enfield. S: Stanley Baker, Herbert Lom, Peggy Cummins.

Hell is a City (1960) D: Val Guest. S: Stanley Baker, Billie Whitelaw.

Here Come the Huggetts (1948) D: Ken Annakin. S: Jack Warner, Kathleen Harrison.

High Noon (1952 (US)) D: Fred Zinnemann. S: Gary Cooper, Grace Kelly.

Highly Dangerous (1950) D: Roy Ward Baker. S: Margaret Lockwood, Dane Clark.

Hiroshima Mon Amour (1959 (France)) D: Alain Resnais.

Holiday Camp (1947) D: Ken Annakin. S: Flora Robson, Dennis Price, Jack Warner.

Hue and Cry (1947) D: Charles Crichton. S: Alastair Sim, Jack Warner.

Huggetts Abroad, The (1949) D: Ken Annakin. S: Jack Warner, Kathleen Harrison.

Hunted (1952) D: Charles Crichton. S: Dirk Bogarde, Kay Walsh.

I Believe in You (1952) D: Basil Dearden, Michael Relph. S: Celia Johnson, Cecil Parker.

I Know Where I'm Going (1945) D: Michael Powell, Emeric Pressburger. S: Roger Livesey, Wendy Hiller.

Ice Cold in Alex (1958) D: J. Lee Thompson. S: John Mills, Sylvia Syms, Anthony Quayle.

In Which We Serve (1942) D: Noel Coward, David Lean. S: Noel Coward, John Mills, Celia Johnson.

It Always Rains on Sunday (1947) D: Robert Hamer. S: Googie Withers, Jack Warner.

It's All Happening (1963) D: Don Sharp. S: Tommy Steele, Michael Medwin.

It's Never Too Late (1956) D: Michael McCarthy. S: Phyllis Calvert.

Kidnappers, The (1953) D: Philip Leacock. S: Duncan McRae, Jon Whiteley.

King's Rhapsody (1955) D: Herbert Wilcox. S: Anna Neagle, Errol Flynn.

Lady Godiva Rides Again (1951) D: Frank Launder. S: Dennis Price, John McCallum.

Ladykillers, The (1955) D: Alexander MacKendrick. S: Alec Guinness, Cecil Parker, Katy Johnson.

Lavender Hill Mob, The (1951) D: Charles Crichton. S: Alec Guinness, Stanley Holloway, Sidney James.

Laxdale Hall (1952) D: John Eldridge. S: Ronald Squire, Kathleen Ryan, Fulton Mackay.

Lease of Life (1954) D: Charles Frend. S: Robert Donat, Kay Walsh, Denholm Elliott.

Listen to Britain (1941) D: Humphrey Jennings, Stewart McAllister (documentary).

London Belongs to Me (1948) D: Sidney Gilliat. S: Richard Attenborough, Alistair Sim, Fay Compton.

Loneliness of the Long Distance Runner, The (1962) D: Tony Richardson. S: Tom Courtenay.

Long Memory, The (1953) D: Robert Hamer. S: John Mills, John McCallum, Elizabeth Sellars.

Love Story (1944) D: Leslie Arliss. S: Margaret Lockwood, Stewart Granger.

Loves of Joanna Godden, The (1947) D: Charles Frend, Robert Hamer. S: Googie Withers, Jean Kent, John McCallum.

L-Shaped Room, The (1962) D: Bryan Forbes. S: Leslie Caron, Tom Bell.

Madonna of the Seven Moons (1944) D: Arthur Crabtree. S: Phyllis Calvert, Stewart Granger.

Maggie, The (1953) D: Alexander MacKendrick. S: Paul Douglas, Alex MacKenzie.

Magnet, The (1950) D: Charles Frend. S: Kay Walsh, William Fox.

Make Mine a Million (1959) D: Lance Comfort. S: Arthur Askey, Sidney James.

Man Between, The (1953) D: Carol Reed. S: James Mason, Claire Bloom.

Man From Tangier (1957) D: Lance Comfort.

Man in the Moon, The (1960) D: Basil Dearden. S: Kenneth More, Michael Hordern, Charles Gray.

Mandy (1952) D: Alexander MacKendrick. S: Phyllis Calvert, Jack Hawkins.

Meet Mr Lucifer (1953) D: Anthony Pelissier. S: Stanley Holloway, Kay Kendall.

Morning Departure (1949) D: Roy Ward Baker. S: John Mills, Richard Attenborough.

Mouse on the Moon, The (1963) D: Richard Lester. S: Margaret Rutherford, David Kossoff.

Mouse that Roared, The (1959) D: Jack Arnold. S: Peter Sellars, David Kossoff,.

Murder in Reverse (1945) D: Montgomery Tully. S: William Hartnell, Jimmy Hanley.

Next to No Time (1958) D: Henry Cornelius. S: Kenneth More.

No Time for Tears (1957) D: Cyril Frankel. S: Anna Neagle, George Baker.

Noose (1948) D: Edmond T. Greville. S: Carole Landis, Derek Farr.

Operation Amsterdam (1959) D: Michael McCarthy. S: Peter Finch, Eva Bartok.

Oracle, The (1953) D: C. M. Pennington-Richards. S: Robert Beatty, Joseph Tomelty, Virginia McKenna.

Overlanders, The (1946) D: Harry Watt. S: Chips Rafferty, John Nugent Haywood.

Passage Home (1955) D: Roy Ward Baker. S: Anthony Steel, Peter Finch.

Passionate Summer (1958) D: Rudolph Cartier. S: Virginia McKenna, Bill Travers.

Passport to Pimlico (1949) D: Henry Cornelius. S: Stanley Holloway, Margaret Rutherford.

Passport to Shame (1959) D: Alvin Rakoff. S: Diana Dors, Herbert Lom.

Password is Courage, The (1962) D: Andrew L. Stone. S: Dirk Bogarde, Maria Perschy.

Penny Princess (1952) D: Val Guest. S: Yolande Donlan, Dirk Bogarde.

Pit of Darkness (1961) D: Lance Comfort. S: William Franklyn, Moira Redmond.

Planter's Wife, The (1952) Ken Annakin. S: Claudette Colbert, Jack Hawkins.

Rake's Progress, The (1945) D: Sidney Gilliat. S: Rex Harrison.

Reach for the Sky (1956) D: Lewis Gilbert. S: Kenneth More, Muriel Pavlow.

Rebel Without a Cause (1955 (US)) D: Nicholas Ray. S: James Dean, Natalie Wood.

Red Shoes, The (1948) D: Michael Powell, Emeric Pressburger. S: Moira Shearer.

Rififi ((Du Rififi Chez Les Hommes) 1955 (France)) D: Jules Dassin.

Ring of Spies (1963) D: Robert Tronson. S: Bernard Lee, William Sylvester.

Room at the Top (1959) D: Jack Clayton. S: Simone Signoret, Laurence Harvey.

Sapphire (1959) D: Basil Dearden. S: Nigel Patrick, Yvonne Mitchell.

Saturday Night and Sunday Morning (1960) D: Karel Reisz. S: Albert Finney, Shirley Anne Field.

Scamp, The (1957) D: Wolf Rilla. S: Richard Attenborough, Colin Petersen.

Sea of Sand (1958) D: Guy Green. S: Richard Attenborough, John Gregson.

Sea Shall Not Have Them, The (1954) D: Lewis Gilbert. S: Michael Redgrave, Dirk Bogarde.

Serena (1962) D: Peter Maxwell. S: Patrick Holt, Honor Blackman.

Seven Thunders (1957) D: Hugo Fregonese. S: Stephen Boyd, James Robertson Justice, Anna Gaylor.

Seventh Veil, The (1945) D: Compton Bennett.. S: James Mason, Ann Todd.

Ship that Died of Shame, The (1955) D: Basil Dearden, Michael Relph. S: Richard Attenborough, George Baker, Virginia McKenna.

Silent Enemy, The (1958) D: William Fairchild. S: Laurence Harvey.

Simba (1955) D: Brian Desmond Hurst. S: Dirk Bogarde, Donald Sinden, Virginia McKenna.

Simon and Laura (1955) D: Muriel Box. S: Peter Finch, Kay Kendall.

Sink the Bismarck (1960) D: Lewis Gilbert. S: Kenneth More.

Smallest Show on Earth, The (1957) D: Basil Dearden. S: Virginia McKenna, Bill Travers.

Snowbound (1948) D: David MacDonald. S: Robert Newton, Dennis Price.

Spanish Gardener, The (1955) D: Philip Leacock. S: Dirk Bogarde, Jon Whiteley, Michael Hordern.

Square Ring, The (1953) D: Basil Dearden, Michael Relph. S: Jack Warner, Robert Beatty, Kay Kendall.

State Secret (1950) D: Sidney Gilliat. S: Douglas Fairbanks Jr., Glynis Johns.

Street Corner (1953) D: Muriel Box. S: Anne Crawford, Peggy Cummins.

Subway in the Sky (1959) D: Muriel Box. S: Hildegarde Knef.

Svengali (1954) D: Noel Langley. S: Hildegarde Knef, Donald Wolfit.

Tawny Pipit (1944) D: Bernard Miles, Charles Saunders. S: Bernard Miles, Rosamund John.

They Were Sisters (1945) D: Arthur Crabtree. S: Phyllis Calvert, James Mason.

They Who Dare (1954) D: Lewis Milestone. S: Dirk Bogarde, Denholm Elliott.

Third Man, The (1949) D: Carol Reed. S: Joseph Cotton, Alida Valli, Orson Welles.

Third Secret, The (1964) D: Charles Crichton. S: Stephen Boyd, Jack Hawkins, Richard Attenborough.

Time, Gentlemen, Please (1952) D: Lewis Gilbert. S: Eddie Byrne, Thora Hird, Dora Bryan, Ian Carmichael.

Titfield Thunderbolt, The (1953) D: Charles Crichton. S: Stanley Holloway, George Relph.

Too Many Crooks (1959) D: Mario Zampi. S: Terry-Thomas, George Cole.

Town Like Alice, A (1956) D: Jack Lee. S: Virginia McKenna, Peter Finch.

Trottie True (1948) D: Brian Desmond Hurst. S: Jean Kent, James Donald.

True as a Turtle (1957) D: Wendy Toye. S: John Gregson, June Thorburn.

Two Way Stretch (1960) D: Robert Day. S: Peter Sellars, Wilfred Hyde-White.

Upstairs and Downstairs (1959) D: Ralph Thomas. S: Michael Craig, Anne Heywood.

Venetian Bird, The (1952) D: Ralph Thomas. S: Richard Todd, Eva Bartok.

Vessel of Wrath (1938) D: Erich Pommer. S: Charles Laughton, Elsa Lanchester.

Victim (1961) D: Basil Dearden. S: Dirk Bogarde, Sylvia Syms, Dennis Price.

Village of the Damned (1960) D: Wolf Rilla. S: George Sanders.

Violent Playground (1958) D: Basil Dearden. S: Stanley Baker, Peter Cushing, Anne Heywood.

Wall of Death, The (1950) D: Lewis Gilbert. S: Laurence Harvey, Earl Cameron, Susan Shaw.

Watch Your Stern (1960) D: Gerald Thomas. S: Kenneth Connor, Eric Barker, Leslie Phillips.

Went the Day Well (1942) D: Alberto Cavalcanti. S: Leslie Banks, D. Farrar, V. Taylor.

Where No Vultures Fly (1951) D: Harry Watt. S: Anthony Steel, Dinah Sheridan.

Whisky Galore! (1948) D: Alexander MacKendrick. S: Basil Radford, Joan Greenwood, James Robertson Justice, Gordon Jackson.

Wicked Lady, The (1945) D: Leslie Arliss. S: Margaret Lockwood, James Mason.

Wind Cannot Read, The (1958) D: Ralph Thomas. S: Dirk Bogarde.

Windom's Way (1957) D: Ronald Neame. S: Peter Finch, Mary Ure.

Woman for Joe, The (1955) D: George M. O'Ferrall. S: Diane Cilento, George Baker.

Woman in Question, The (1950) D: Anthony Asquith. S: Jean Kent, Dirk Bogarde.

Wooden Horse, The (1950) D: Jack Lee. S: David Tomlinson, Anthony Steel.

Wrong Arm of the Law, The (1962) D: Cliff Owen. S: Peter Sellars, Lionel Jeffries.

Yellow Balloon, The (1952) D: J. Lee Thompson. S: Kenneth More, Kathleen Ryan.

Yield to the Night (1956) D: J. Lee Thompson. S: Diana Dors, Yvonne Mitchell.

You Know What Sailors Are (1954) D: Ken Annakin. S: Donald Sinden, Naunton Wayne.

Young Lovers, The (1954) D: Anthony Asquith. S: Odile Versois, David Knight.
Young Wives' Tale (1951) D: Henry Cass. S: Joan Greenwood, Nigel Patrick, Audrey Hepburn.

Sources

Goble, Alan (ed.) (1991) *International Film Index, 1895–1990*, London: Bowker Saur.
Goble, Alan (ed.) (1999) *Complete Index to British Sound Film Since 1928*, London: Bowker Saur.
Halliwell, Leslie (1999) *Halliwell's Film & Video Guide 2000*, London: HarperCollins.

Index